P9-AOK-744

Man's Best Friend

NATIONAL GEOGRAPHIC BOOK OF DOGS

A volume in the
NATURAL SCIENCE LIBRARY
edited and prepared by the
NATIONAL GEOGRAPHIC BOOK SERVICE

Editorial Consultants: ARTHUR FREDERICK JONES
American Kennel Club
JOHN W. CROSS, JR.
Westminster Kennel Club

Foreword by MELVILLE BELL GROSVENOR
Editor-in-Chief and Chairman of the Board, National Geographic Society

Chapters by
JOHN W. CROSS, JR.
ARTHUR FREDERICK JONES
ROLAND KILBON
EDWARD J. LINEHAN
FREEMAN LLOYD
HOWARD E. PAINE
GEORGE PICKOW
MERLE SEVERY
FREDERICK G. VOSBURGH

364 illustrations, 225 in full color

Paintings by
WALTER A. WEBER
ROBERT LOUGHEED
EDWIN MEGARGEE
EDWARD HERBERT MINER
WILLIAM H. BOND
and other artists

Photographs by
WALTER CHANDOHA,
KATHLEEN REVIS, J. BAYLOR ROBERTS,
ROBERT F. SISSON, B. ANTHONY STEWART,
and others

Man's

REVISED EDITION

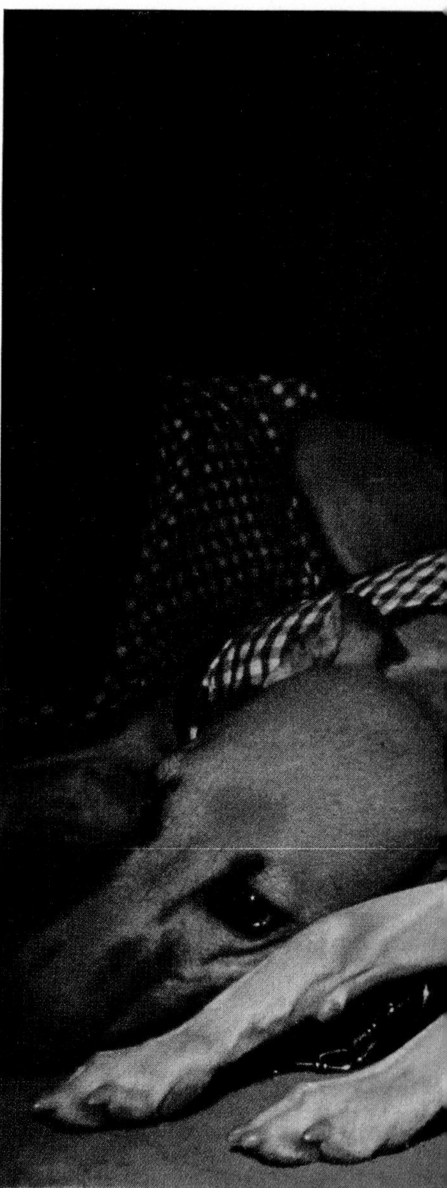

WHIPPETS BY KATHLEEN REVIS

WASHINGTON, D.C.

Best Friend

NATIONAL GEOGRAPHIC BOOK OF DOGS

THE NATIONAL GEOGRAPHIC SOCIETY

Staff For This Book

MELVILLE BELL GROSVENOR
Editor-in-chief

HOWARD E. PAINE
Designer

ROSS BENNETT, SEYMOUR L. FISHBEIN, EDWARD LANOUETTE,
EDWARD J. LINEHAN, DAVID F. ROBINSON, MERLE SEVERY
Editorial staff

JOHN R. HOOPES, JOCELYN C. WHITE
Assistants

ANNE DIRKES KOBOR, ANDREW POGGENPOHL, LINDA C. BRUMBACH
Illustrations

JAMES P. KELLY, FRANCES H. PORCHER,
WILHELM R. SAAKE
Production

KAREN F. EDWARDS, PAULA C. SIMMONS, WERNER L. WEBER
Assistants

DEE J. ANDELLA, JOE M. BARLETT,
WILLIAM W. SMITH
Engravings and printing

First edition: 125,000 copies
Revised edition (1966), 1st printing: 75,000 copies;
2nd printing: 50,000 copies; 3rd printing: 75,000 copies
Printed and bound by R. R. Donnelley
and Sons Company, Chicago.

LIBRARY OF CONGRESS CIP DATA
National Geographic Society, Washington, D. C. Book
Service.
Man's best friend: National Geographic book of dogs.

(Natural science library)
First published in 1958 under title: The National
Geographic book of dogs.
1. Dog breeds. 2. Dogs. I. Cross, John W.
II. Title.
SF426.N37 1974 636.7'1 74-7147
STANDARD BOOK NUMBER 87044-014-4

Basset takes a bashful bow in introducing the parade of dogs.

WALTER CHANDOHA

FOREWORD

How well we come to know our dog, his every mood and action from the comic clumsiness of puppyhood to the dignity of age! How eloquent his pleading when we leave him, and how warm his welcome home! The feel of his ears between our fingers, his hangdog look when scolded, the tentative little wag that melts our sternest displeasure—these little things we know so well.

Yet I find few days go by that my German Shepherd, Paula, does not reveal some fresh and unexpected side of her personality. Like everyone else, I am convinced that of all 33 million dogs in the United States, *my* dog is unique.

Paula is, of course. And so is your dog, whether he is a veteran friend dozing on your hearth or a new puppy. But all are blessed with the well-known virtues—devotion, loyalty, eagerness to please—that make dogs such fine companions, especially for children. Every youngster—like my son Edwin, whose warm relationship with Paula will provide him lasting memories—gains in responsibility and the appreciation of animals through growing up with a dog for a friend.

Though I choose Shepherds, I can readily see why the Poodle has become America's favorite dog. It's so companionable. I came to know this lively, intelligent breed through my sister's Poodles, and then through Beau, my son Gilbert's black Miniature. Each weekday when Gil left for work Beau retired to his corner for a nap. On Saturday, however, he fretted if his master did not stay to

play with him. It's uncanny, but somehow he knew when the weekend arrived.

Shepherds and Poodles, of course, are only two of many splendid breeds, each with its own distinct personality. Here in this book you will find a biography of your dog, practical counsel on his care, and reasons for his quirks. The story of his kind brims with heroism and humor, delightful anecdote, and high adventure.

Since dog first sidled from the forest toward caveman's fire—long before the horse or the cat joined man's inner circle—he has reflected his master's life. In these pages the story of that companionship unfolds.

The creation of the original *Book of Dogs* (1958) and this revised edition, *Man's Best Friend,* makes a story in itself. It all began as a labor of love with Franklin L. Fisher, for many years Illustrations Editor of *National Geographic* when my father, Gilbert Grosvenor, was President and Editor. Under their guidance the Society's outstanding series of dog paintings began. Gradually there grew a reservoir of quality color plates from the magazine.

Then, in long months of preparation, our Book Service staff evolved a work ambitious in scope. New paintings were commissioned, new color photographs taken, existing plates remade in double size. Illustrations in museums, archives, and private collections were tracked down the world over. The quest for a single painting—the Egyptian hunting scene on page 38—led from Washington to London to an archeological expedition on the Nile. With Arthur Frederick Jones, editor of the American Kennel Club's official publication, serving as consultant, more than 100,000 words of text were written, edited, and checked.

The result? A treasury of canine lore that won the "Distinctive Quality Award" of the Dog Writers' Association of America and brought a flood of praise: "The most wonderful and informative book on the subject I have ever read...." "A most valuable source ... skillfully authenticated...." "Truly a book to treasure." Though our print order was the largest for any National Geographic book to that time, the entire first edition sold out.

Demand continued to mount for the book. But instead of a simple reprint, we decided to bring out a new edition, even more exciting than the first. We commissioned new paintings, added color plates, prepared biographies of newly registered breeds. Project editor Ross Bennett worked closely with John W. Cross, Jr., show committee chairman of the Westminster Kennel Club, to bring text and pictures up to date.

Quality paper, inks, and binding fit your copy of *Man's Best Friend* for an enduring, busy life on your bookshelf. What better work, indeed, to grow "dog-eared" through frequent use!

All those whose hands, minds, and hearts went into fashioning this book join me now in dedicating it to our dogs everywhere.

Melville Bell Grosvenor

Might meets mite at a dog show: Irish Wolfhound and Yorkshire Terrier.

KATHLEEN REVIS AND ROBERT F. SISSON, NATIONAL GEOGRAPHIC PHOTOGRAPHER

WALTER CHANDOHA

Pert, perky Miniature beguiles fanciers; many believe their Poodles are people.

CONTENTS

The

Wonderful World of Dogs

THE PATH TROD BY MAN AND DOG winds from beyond the range of history. They have traveled far, these two, hunting and working together, comforting each other. Little wonder that dog regards master with jealous affection, and that every man considers his dog the best. Today this pride finds its most dramatic expression at the annual Westminster Kennel Club show. Here, while dogdom's elite are on display, John W. Cross, Jr., the show committee chairman, takes us for a stroll past ring and bench to meet Great Dane and Chihuahua, exotic Afghan, bluff Bulldog, and Collie. Where did they come from, these varied members of *Canis familiaris?* National Geographic editor Merle Severy assembles the clues and in the second chapter traces the dog through the ages. Here now is the fact and folklore, history and humor, of the wonderful world of dogs.

KATHLEEN REVIS

CHAPTER ONE

Westminster,

THE EXCITED MURMUR of milling crowds in New York's Madison Square Garden; choruses of soprano- to bass-voiced barking; bursts of applause from rings where dogs, handlers, and judges enact a stylized ritual—how chaotic all this must seem to the first-time viewer of America's number one dog event!

But order and pattern begin to emerge for him. And on the second night of the Westminster Kennel Club Dog Show he sees the February spectacle draw to a dramatic and memorable conclusion. One proudly poised contestant stands alone, acclaimed Best in Show—the highest honor any of the 33,000,000 dogs in the United States can achieve.

Westminster has been held every year since 1877. England instituted dog shows at Newcastle 18 years earlier; and the famed Cruft's Show in London, started in 1886, draws more

JOHN W. CROSS, JR.

World Series of Dogdom

entries than any other in the world. But wartime interruptions to these English events give Westminster an unchallenged record of consecutive shows.

In the United States, only the Kentucky Derby and two other Churchill Downs races first run in 1875 have a sporting record as long and unbroken. But even the Derby has not always had its present prominence, while Westminster has always been queen of American dog shows, with a win there prized above all others.

Although many people imagine that dogs don't like dog shows, the fact is that the great majority enjoy nothing more. To them the traveling crate and station wagon that bring them to the Garden are what the clanging bell was to the fire horse in days gone by. They act as if the whole affair is being put on in their honor and for their personal delight.

When their showing days are over and they are left behind as the younger dogs go off to shows, veterans of bench and ring are as disconsolate as politicians put out to pasture by the electorate. Many a kindhearted owner has taken an old dog to a show, entering him "For Exhibition Only," just so that he could once again savor the life he has learned to love.

The average spectator, looking at and listening to a row of yapping terriers on a bench, decides that they must be expressing distaste for the proceedings. This is because he attributes to dogs his own reactions. Mr. and Mrs. Public

ROBERT F. SISSON, NATIONAL GEOGRAPHIC PHOTOGRAPHER

"Stay and show," the handlers command. Sealyham Terriers await the judge at the Westminste

would not like to be chained to a bench with all that noise around them; therefore the dogs can't possibly like it! The fact that human beings willingly go to noisy parties, conventions, and political rallies is conveniently forgotten.

Another popular misconception is that show dogs can't be house dogs and vice versa. Actually many show dogs—some of the very best—are house dogs all their lives. The house dog's intimate association with people seems to help bring to full flower the responsiveness so important in the ring. An alert dog,

og show in New York's Madison Square Garden.

eager to please, will show to advantage in front of the judge.

The popularity of breeds changes, as do clothing fashions, and sometimes for equally inexplicable reasons. One known factor in the rise of the smaller breeds, however, has been the tremendous increase in the dog population in cities. Great Danes and St. Bernards may live with their owners in small apartments, but this is exceptional. Certainly one reason for the enormous registration of five of the ten most popular registered breeds in the United States (Beagles, Dachshunds, Toy Poodles, Cocker Spaniels, and Miniature Schnauzers) is that they are "apartment-size" dogs that don't require much room.

Among the most popular of city dogs are the terriers. These little dynamos seem to enjoy the fast pace of modern city life, and they relish the company of human beings as much as their encounters with other dogs when being walked. While many terriers enjoy the canine counterpart of a fist fight, there is little doubt that the leash and collar which restrain the city dog add to his apparent belligerence. Should the owners let their dogs loose, it is quite possible that a joyful romp rather than a dog-fight would result.

There is a widespread tendency to make sweeping statements about a certain breed, based upon experience with a single dog. Experts have learned, the hard way, to protect their statements with such words as "most," "many," and so on. One may say, for instance, that in most terrier breeds the majority of dogs are highstrung and that they like to be heard as well as seen. But if you recommend a Fox Terrier to your non-doggy friend as a peppy animal, the puppy he acquires inevitably turns out to be a lazy bones, rousing himself only for the pleasant task of eating and then returning to sleep.

Dogs as individuals differ as greatly as do human beings. Thousands of dogs have the same unreasoning and uncontrollable fear of thunder that your Aunt Matilda or your cousin Jim has. More than one owner afflicted with this animal reaction rides out each thunderstorm in a dark closet, clutching his dog, both of them trembling as if upon the edge of doom.

Some dogs plainly prefer the company of men to women and vice versa. This is simply because they have been raised entirely by one or the other sex, but it is often a blow to the person who cheerfully says, "All dogs like me."

Dogs' reactions varied widely when the National Geographic Society sent a team of four staff photographers—Kathleen Revis, Willard R. Culver, Robert F. Sisson, and David S. Boyer—to make the color pictures that illustrate this chapter. Bulldogs never dropped their masks of monumental dignity. St. Bernards exemplified their breed's placidity, Keeshonden were sweetly obedient to their small mistress's commands, while Samoyeds were as gentle as they looked. But some of the others proved to be a problem.

Said Miss Revis afterward: "As we walked along in front of the benches, we spotted dogs just begging for their pictures to be taken. By the time we set up the lights and focused the camera, the pose was gone. We had to re-create it."

"That's when we started clowning," said Mr. Sisson. "We mewed like cats, chirped like birds, banged tin pans—anything to get the dog's attention."

At the end of the two-day event all four were dog-tired, but they had a notable gallery of canine character studies.

Day by day a dog's life is not very different from that of his owner; most days are routine and uneventful. There are a few gold-starred ones—the day the steak is dropped on the kitchen floor and he is quick enough to grab it and run; or the first day of hunting season. But always there is the matter of an education; dogs have to go through it just as humans do.

A show dog learns two basic lessons: to stand and hold a position so that he may be displayed to best advantage in front of the judge, and to trot in a straight line beside his handler so the quality of his gait and movement may be observed. This is part of what we mean when we say that a dog "shows well," and the keener the competition the more important this becomes.

In training dogs the two dominant factors are the desire to please the master and the love of food. Fear used as a means of training is neither successful nor intelligent and is used only by those who lack patience and understanding of a

Chihuahua and Lhasa Apso boast a regal ancestry. The Aztecs believed Chihuahuas (top left and below) piloted the human soul through the underworld. After the fall of Montezuma's empire the tiny, vivacious Mexican breed was lost, to be found again only about 100 years ago. The hardy Lhasa Apso (top right) earned the name "Bark Lion Sentinel Dog" as house guard to Tibetan aristocracy for nearly 800 years.

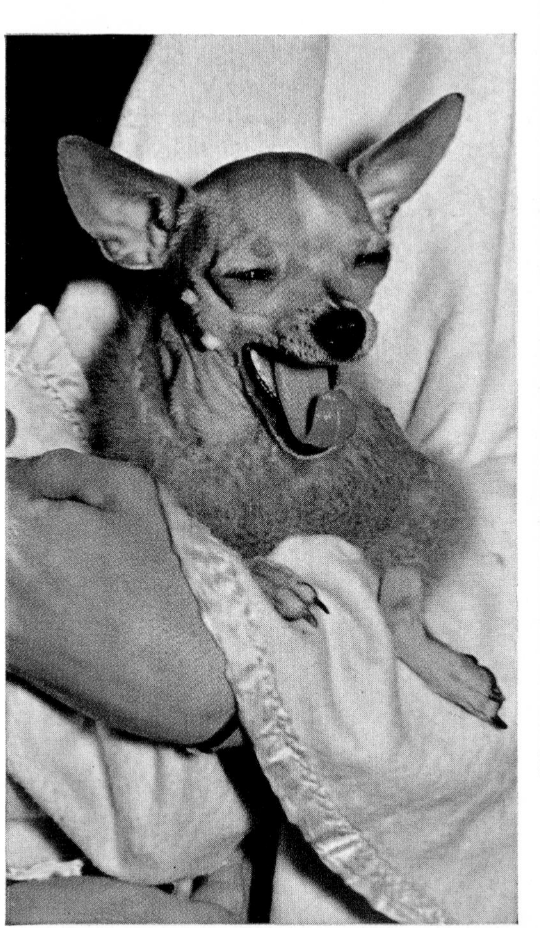

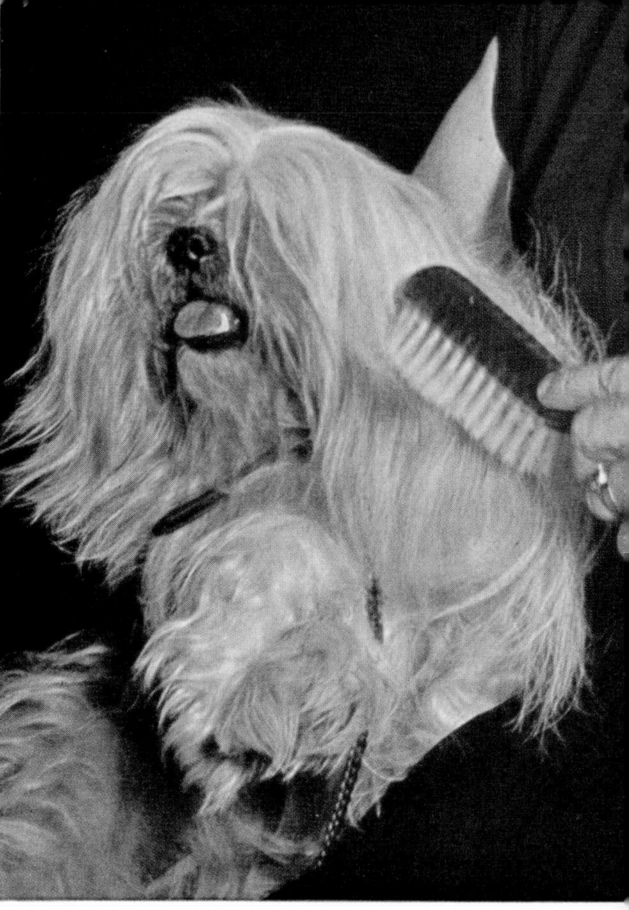

KATHLEEN REVIS (TOP LEFT), ROBERT F. SISSON, AND WILLARD R. CULVER

Spectacled Keeshonden snuggle close to their mistress. The thin black line from eye to ear is a characteristic of this Dutch cousin of the Pomeranian. The Keeshond first won fame in the late 18th century as a popular symbol of revolt against the House of Orange. But long before, this "dog of the people" had become a familiar sight guarding Dutch barges. The less his bushy coat is brushed, the better it looks.

Primping is a must for an aristocratic little Yorkshire Terrier. For the show, his silky coat is dressed with water from an atomizer; at home, wax paper curlers keep his tresses from matting. The ribbons were won by his mistress's four Yorkshires. Although called terriers, they are classed as toy dogs.

KATHLEEN REVIS (TOP) AND WILLARD R. CULVER

dog's basic make-up. He will appreciate a tidbit now and then, but he will never perform as consistently and as joyfully for a tidbit as he will for a pat on the head or a word of praise.

Many well-trained animals have apparently been taught to understand words. Actually, of course, the word itself is totally unimportant. If the dog is taught to bring your slippers, he will always bring your slippers even if you say, "Bring in the kitchen stove," provided you have always said "kitchen stove" when referring to slippers. He brings them because he has learned that it pleases you, and pleasing you is his dominating desire in life.

While much of a dog's behavior and many of his reactions are similar to a child's, he has certain habits that people cannot understand. We forget what the life of a dog was like in the wild state, and he has become so closely attached to man that we interpret a dog's behavior in the light of our own.

Have you ever taken your dog for a walk on the beach and had him walk up to a well-decayed fish tossed up by the waves? He will sniff it delightedly and then hurl himself upon it with glee, rubbing himself into the smelly remains. We are appalled by such behavior. People don't do it, so why should dogs? Countless generations of dogs have done it and for a very good reason, although that reason no longer exists. The theory is that their forebears did it to acquire

The Poodle's powder-puff haircut was designed during his career as a retriever. The cut protected joints from cold water while lightening the weight of hair. If this Curly Poodle's coat were allowed to grow, it would become a ropy mass, and the dog a Corded Poodle.

WILLARD R. CULVER

DAVID S. BOYER (LEFT) AND ROBERT F. SISSON, NATIONAL GEOGRAPHIC PHOTOGRAPHERS

Time hangs heavy for waiting contestants. The eyes of the Old English Sheepdog (left) stare into a shaggy curtain, but keen hearing and smell compensate for the visual handicap. Dozing at right is the gentle St. Bernard. His breed has saved some 2,500 lives in Alpine rescues.

a strong smell that would overpower their own scent and enable them to hunt without having prey warned of their approach by a shift in the wind.

A far less unpleasant habit, but one that also stems from days gone by, is burying bones. In his wild state the dog often killed more than he could consume at one time and buried the leftovers so that he might return to finish them. Another peculiar habit of many dogs—circling three or four times before lying down—is believed to be carried over from the wild animal's habit of trampling down the grass to make his bed.

A frightened dog, we all know, tucks his tail between his legs. Why? The wild dog was a hunter, but he was also hunted—and the explanation may be that if his tail were between his legs it could not be grabbed in a pursuer's mouth. Thus, many of the dog's actions today can be easily understood if we recall what his life in the wild state was like. Far less easy to understand are some of the remarkable and well-authenticated cases in which dogs have exhibited supernormal perception.

We know that dogs have powers of hearing far superior to our own; they can pick out the sound of a beloved footstep from among a hundred strange ones. Many of us have known dogs that could tell the sound of the family car from that of others of the same make. These are striking but understandable demonstrations of their powers of hearing. But how do we explain the ability of a dog in a city apartment to tell that an approaching elevator will stop at his floor and, beyond that, to know whether the passenger is someone he likes and goes to greet silently with wagging tail or someone at whom he barks before the elevator has even stopped? Yet I knew such a dog and saw him demonstrate these remarkable powers dozens of times.

We accept the fact that homing pigeons return from wherever they may be released, although we do not understand how they do it. We have all heard of dogs that have returned from great distances, but did you know that there

The Bulldog's sour look veils a sunny disposition. To equip him for bullbaiting in the 17th century, English breeders pulled his lower jaw out, pushed his nose back, and bred for ferocity.

ROBERT F. SISSON, NATIONAL GEOGRAPHIC PHOTOGRAPHER

WILLARD R. CULVER, NATIONAL GEOGRAPHIC PHOTOGRAPHER

Champion Boxer sits for his portrait. Named perhaps for his fighting stance, the Boxer, like his cousin the Bulldog, was long used in bullbaiting and dog-fighting. Police-trained, he also served in two world wars.

is a completely authenticated case of a dog, left behind in Idaho when his master moved away, that set out and found his master at a place near Oakland, California? Could you do as much?

How can a dog have foreknowledge of a human death? I knew a dog that did. At the instant his master, who was upstairs, suffered a heart attack this dog bolted through the screen door onto the lawn. There he howled for three-quarters of an hour—he stopped the moment of his master's death. In another case, fully authenticated, a strange dog appeared in front of a house in which the owner lay dying. The dog wailed dismally. Driven away, he kept returning. After the man's death he was never seen there again.

So when an owner tells you strange stories about what his dog has done, hesitate before you lay it all to a too-lively imagination.

EVERY YEAR Westminster is visited by ladies and gentlemen of the press who never go to any other dog show. Their reporting has a strong tendency toward the humorous approach. The perennial favorite of the cartoonist is the lady of the dreadnought class with a leash on the microscopic Chihuahua to which she belongs. Each year at least one columnist can be counted on to dig into the dogs' names listed in the catalogue and come up with a word picture of a fond owner calling to his dog: "Here, Ch. Hailstone Golden Enchantment! Here, Ch. Hailstone Golden Enchantment!" That the picture drawn is good for a hearty laugh, no one would deny. That it is far from reality could also hardly be denied, even by the ladies and gentlemen who suggest the picture for our entertainment.

At first glance, the only information to be gleaned from the purely imaginary name Ch. Hailstone Golden Enchantment would probably be that the dog is a champion (a title retained for life) and that its color is somewhat akin to gold, although this is not certain. The dog might be a Great Dane, a Boxer, a Golden Retriever, or a dog of any other breed that produces varying shades of yellow, fawn, or red. To the fancier, however, the name would mean that the dog was bred at the Hailstone Kennels in Erewhon, New Jersey. Hailstone is known to breed only Golden Retrievers, so that is the dog's breed. It was probably sired by Ch. Hailstone Golden King and its dam was probably Ch. Hailstone Enchanting Girl.

In this case the name gives no clue to the sex of the animal, and this is not unusual in naming animals other than dogs. Thousands of people thought the famous race horse Native Dancer was a mare because to them the name sounded feminine. This name, incidentally, illustrates the turf's method of paying tribute to ancestry—his sire was Polynesian and his dam, Geisha Girl.

People often ask why dogs cannot be given a single name, such as Polynesian. The answer lies in simple mathematics. Nearly 27,000 Thoroughbred horses are registered in one year in the Jockey Club Stud Book, while more than one million purebred dogs are registered annually in the Stud Book of the American Kennel Club. Add to this the fact that thousands of dogs live to be more than ten years of age and that there are many authenticated cases of dogs living more than twenty years, and the reason for kennel names becomes clear. There are simply not enough single names to go around.

Kennel names are owned, for a fee, and no one may use them but the proper owner. You may register your dog as Hailstone Rover and there will be no other dog with that name—although there may be a Rainstorm Rover and a Snowflake Rover. For breeding purposes each dog must have a name which prevents the possibility of confusion with another.

How does the owner call his dog with the fancy name? He probably says, "Here, Spike!" or "Here, Molly!" Show dogs are usually given a "call name" wholly different from their registered name. This is done for the dog's protection

Shetland Sheepdogs and Chow Chows came from opposite ends of the earth. The warm-eyed miniature Collies (above), affectionately called Shelties, developed in the Shetland Islands. The squinting Chow Chow (below), with blue-black tongue and lionlike mane and paws, calls China home. There he has been a hunter, guard, pet, even a substitute for mutton.

WILLARD R. CULVER (TOP) AND DAVID S. BOYER, NATIONAL GEOGRAPHIC PHOTOGRAPHER

The Collie for centuries herded sheep in the Scottish Highlands. To traverse narrow sheep paths, he became agile and strong; to brave cutting winds, he grew an abundant coat.

When Queen Victoria visited Balmoral Castle in the mid-19th century, she fell in love with this intelligent friend of her people and spread his praises.

These Westminster contenders display the show Collie's aristocratic nose and elegant ruff.

at shows, where spectators walk down the aisles of benching, catalogue in hand. If a dog responded to every reading of his name from the catalogue he would soon be exhausted trying to find a friend among all the strangers addressing him.

A search through old Westminster catalogues will show, not too surprisingly, that things were quite different three-quarters of a century ago. In one class for English Setters there were four Rovers and three Toms, all with unknown ancestry. In those days, animal breeding was haphazard, but a stud book—like anything else—has to have a beginning.

Once there existed a variety of classes which would be a nightmare in today's swiftly paced competition. In 1880, for instance, there was a class for "Red

English Setter points live quail caged amid corn for an indoor field trial. Sportsmen say pointing dogs have a hypnotic effect on birds, which stay in covert until a dog breaks point.

ROBERT F. SISSON, NATIONAL GEOGRAPHIC PHOTOGRAPHER

Setters" of either sex, to be exhibited by ladies only, and the prize, which the judge placed upon the winning lady right in the ring, was a gold necklace.

Today a sterling silver medal is given for Best of Breed and sterling silver bowls for group winners and Best in Show. Cash prizes reward owners of winning contestants. Contrast these simple trophies with two of the prizes at Westminster's first show: a "Gold and Silver Mounted Pearl Handled Revolver" and a "Russian Leather Silver Mounted Fly Book and One Gross Assorted Flies."

In the early days it was quite common to take a dog to a show with the idea of selling it, and the asking price was listed in the catalogue right after the dog's name, something no longer permitted.

At the very first Westminster, in 1877, its benches were graced not only by royal dogs but by dogs of royalty. A Londoner, T. Medley, Esq., exhibited two Deerhounds, Oscar and Dagmar, bred by "Her Majesty the Queen of England from the late Prince Consort's famous breed," and you could purchase either of them for $50,000. The royal touch appeared again in 1889 when a Mr. Edward Kelly of New York entered a Siberian Wolfhound named Ivan Romanoff. The fact that the breeder of this hound was the Czar of Russia probably accounted for the $10,000 price tag, but a prospective purchaser might have had reservations about the Czar's breeding operations when he read in the catalogue that Ivan was listed as "Pedigree Unknown."

The following year Ivan was back, but he had a rival, most appropriately named Rival, bred by the Emperor of Germany and duly possessed of a pedigree. The price for royal Wolfhounds held steady, for Rival also could be yours for a mere $10,000. Apparently, however, the most valuable of all dogs entered in those days was a "white and lemon, two-and-a-half-year-old imported Maltese Terrier" named Mozart. He was owned by Miss Eva P. Russell of New York City. In the place in the catalogue where the sale price of a dog was usually listed, Miss Russell put just one word—"Priceless."

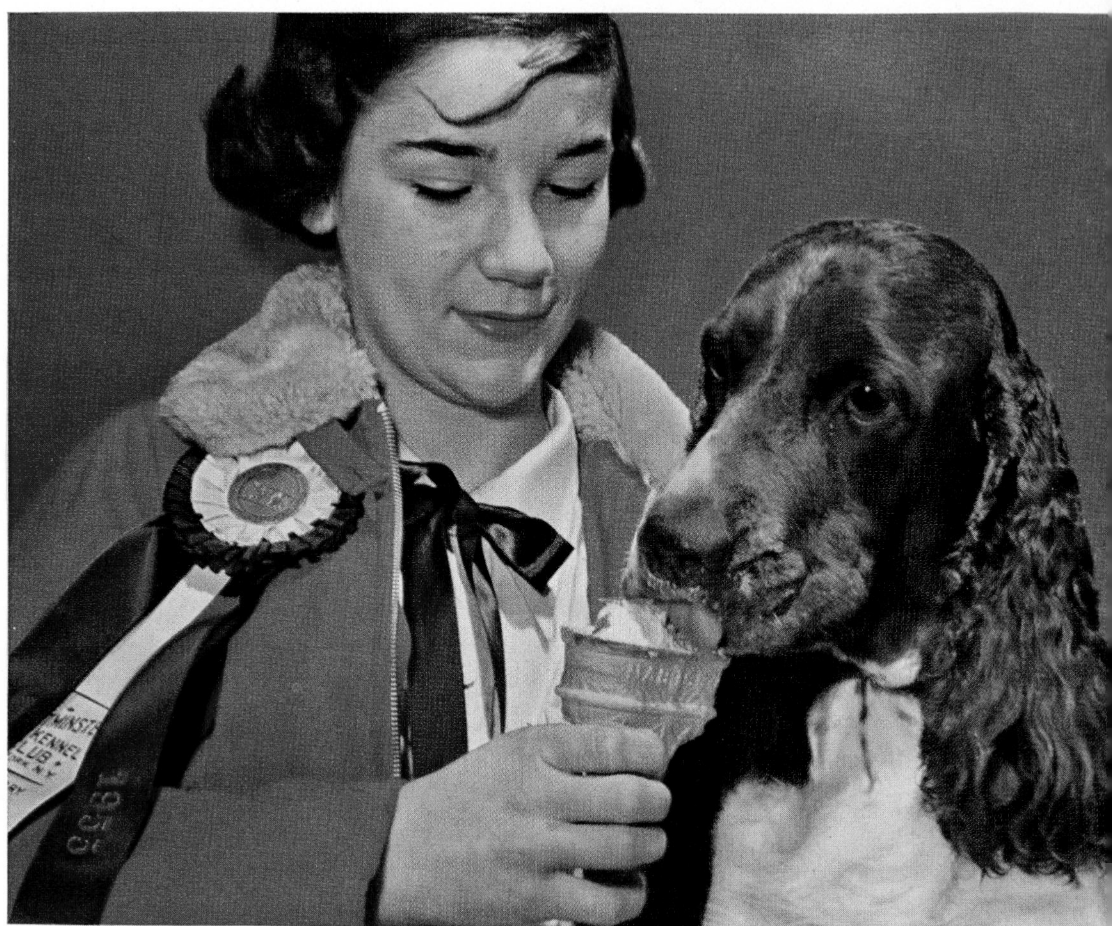

DAVID S. BOYER, NATIONAL GEOGRAPHIC PHOTOGRAPHER

For more than 80 years Westminster had a "Miscellaneous" class which was always of great interest to spectators. For many years entries were confined to dogs of breeds recognized in foreign countries but not sufficiently represented in this country to be given official recognition. In the early shows, however, you could enter anything that resembled a dog. Not even the normal complement of four legs was a requisite, for in the very first show, Nellie, "a brown two-year-old bitch," was entered in this class although she had been born with only two legs.

In 1880 a two-year-old Australian wild dog, or dingo, was entered, pre-

ROBERT F. SISSON, NATIONAL GEOGRAPHIC PHOTOGRAPHER

Huge Irish Wolfhound, one of the world's tallest dogs, fails to impress a beribboned Yorkshire Terrier, safe in her mistress's lap. The Wolfhound's ancestors hunted wolves and giant elk and fought in Irish clan wars.

English Springer Spaniel laps up his winner's reward. This bench champion watches over children at home and serves his master as a gun dog. To this girl, he is a hero for having saved her young brother from drowning.

sumably having received a day off from the zoo, for his owner was listed as Mr. W. A. Conklin, whose address was given as the Central Park Menagerie.

If you had wished to own a dog whose career it would be impossible to duplicate, you could have acquired Nero, a cross between a Siberian Bloodhound and a St. Bernard, who was "in charge of the first baby elephant that was ever exhibited in America." His owner, Mr. James McLaughlin, was willing to part with Nero for $250.

As the years went by, however, fewer and fewer of those crossbreds and freaks appeared. In their places could be found the first representatives of many of the breeds which today are most popular in this country. The Pekingese, the Chow Chow, the Lhasa Apso, the Shih Tzu, and even the Boxer, whose rise to eminence has been almost unbelievably rapid, made their first public appearances at the humble level of "Miscellaneous." Who can tell what breed will next rise from obscurity to rival some of the popular breeds which may today be on their way down?

In the early days of Westminster, field dogs dominated the show. Pointers and setters accounted for more than half the entries. The club had been founded by a group of sportsmen who were primarily interested in bird dogs and their work in the field. For many years the club had kennels at Babylon, Long Island, where members raised and trained their own Pointers, mostly from stock imported from England. One of its first and greatest importations lives on today as the club's symbol—the immortal Sensation, on point with his left forefoot raised.

As time passed and interest in purebred dogs of all breeds increased, this dominance of the field dogs ceased. At the turn of the century, for example, there was tremendous interest in St. Bernards and one class at Westminster had 53 of these huge dogs entered. Then interest in them waned and only recently has revived again to the point that 40 or more are shown each year. Collies, too, became great favorites and rivalry between the kennels of the elder J. Pierpont Morgan and Samuel Untermyer was fierce. Although fashions in dogs change greatly over the years, Collies still rate among the most popular breeds competing at the Westminster show.

Miniature Schnauzers sport the bushy beards for which their German breeders named them. Ancestors of these lively little terriers were the larger Standard Schnauzers, farmers' dogs that helped their masters keep down rats and other vermin. These four serve primarily as pets.

DAVID S. BOYER (LEFT) AND ROBERT F. SISSON, NATIONAL GEOGRAPHIC PHOTOGRAPHERS

Siberia's Samoyeds helped conquer the Arctic. The famed sled dogs pulled explorer Nansen "farthest north" in 1895. Smiling face, snowy coat mark the breed. Samoyeds have no doggy odor.

Boston Terrier prepares dinner with bag-ripping teeth. White collar and shirt make him a proper Bostonian. As American as baked beans, he was bred for city living, wholly free of his ancestor's fighting instincts.

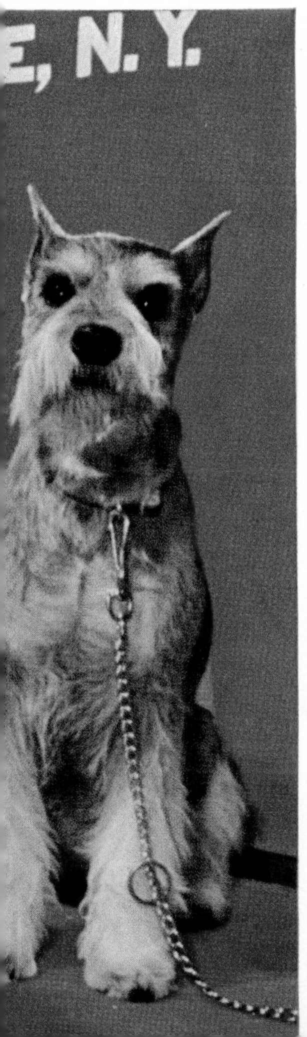

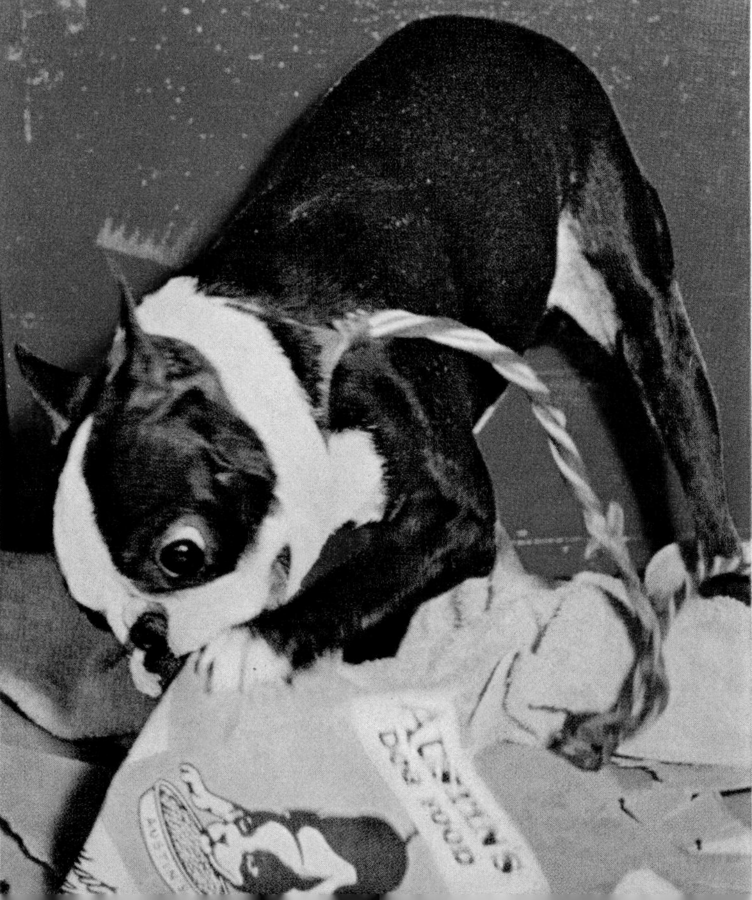

TODAY there are 120 breeds recognized by the American Kennel Club and classes for them are provided at Westminster. These breeds are divided into six groups: Sporting Dogs, Hounds, Working Dogs, Terriers, Toys, and Non-sporting Dogs. You will usually find one hundred or more of these breeds on the bench at the Westminster show, a greater variety than you are likely to see anywhere else in your life at one time.

The judging rings for the dog show are set up on the arena floor of Madison Square Garden, where the circus, the rodeo, and hockey, basketball, boxing, and other athletic events take their turns. Sports writers have referred to a boxing ring as the "squared circle"; at Westminster the judging rings are "rectangular circles" and there are eight of them. Those spectators not fortunate enough to find seats stand in the aisles all around the judging rings.

Competition at a dog show is, to put it simply, an elimination contest. A dog is usually entered in one class in his breed. If he wins in his class he competes with the winners of the other dog (male) classes for his breed. The best of these is known as Winners, Dog, and a reserve is also selected. The winner is next judged against his counterpart, Winners, Bitch, for Best of Winners. Finally, Best of Breed is to be judged, and champions of both sexes, plus the Best of Winners, come into the ring. If Best of Breed is awarded to a dog, then a somewhat anticlimactic award of Best of Opposite Sex is given to the best bitch, or vice versa. This latter award has been described by certain acid exhibitors as Best of Losers.

There are two more steps in the contest. The first is known as group judging, in which the Best of Breed winners in each of the six groups compete. Finally the six group winners compete for that most coveted award, Best in Show.

Few events take place in this world without offering an opportunity for laughter, and a dog show is no exception. Probably Westminster's all-time record for levity was set in 1937 when the Masters of Foxhounds held their show at Madison Square Garden in conjunction with Westminster. On the final night, before a capacity crowd, judging for the best pack of hounds took place. Each pack in turn was brought to the center for judging and then returned to its location at the edge of the ring.

When the pack of American Foxhounds returned, however, one lone dog remained in the center—his leg raised high in a familiar position. He posed motionless for what seemed an eternity as the crowd roared with laughter and encouragement. The gesture was an empty one, if the expression may be used, and at last the hound lowered his leg and returned to the obscurity of the individual in the pack.

Although Westminster runs for only two days, a full year's work goes into the making of the show. The club's Dog Show Committee starts its preparations by selecting judges. Some 35 to 45 experienced men and women are chosen to officiate—probably one or two judges from England, a couple from Canada, several from California (a great state for dogs), and the rest from ten or more states. Most judges have but one or two breeds assigned to them, but usually there are four "all 'rounders" who have a large number of dogs to judge, including most of the rarer breeds. The all 'rounder is usually a man who is approved by the American Kennel Club to judge all breeds and is paid a fee. The vast majority of judges are amateurs licensed for a comparatively few breeds. The judges for the groups and those for Best in Show have no other assignments, so the dog that wins Best in Show must be passed upon by three different judges.

How does a judge get to be a judge? First, he has to have the background, preferably as a breeder and exhibitor. On his application form, which goes to the American Kennel Club, he has to give his background and answer ques-

Afghan Hounds were portrayed on Egyptian tombs 5,000 years ago. Developed on the Sinai Peninsula, the breed became established in Afghanistan, whence it was taken to England. Centuries have little changed the dog's appearance. Powerful hindquarters make Afghans champion hurdlers.

WILLARD R. CULVER

tions which test his knowledge of dogs, of the duties of a judge, of ring procedure, and the like. His name is published in *Pure-Bred Dogs, American Kennel Gazette*, the official organ of this body, and anyone may write to support or oppose his application.

Then comes a period of apprenticeship, in which the applicant serves under an approved judge who is working with the proper breed. The apprentice does this three times, under three different judges. After each show he writes a report which goes to the American Kennel Club. These reports are evaluated along with material already on file. When the apprentice has passed these tests he is qualified to judge—though disappointed exhibitors later may dispute the use of the word "qualified." If exhibitors develop confidence in him, they will show under him, and the judge's reputation will grow.

The theory of judging is based on "standards." Each breed has a written standard of perfection which supposedly describes the ideal specimen. The dog that comes closest to that standard, in the opinion of the judge, is placed first. In practice this is not as simple as it sounds. To begin with, no mere mortal or group of mortals can perfectly describe a perfect dog. Next there is the fact

ROBERT F. SISSON (TOP) AND DAVID S. BOYER, NATIONAL GEOGRAPHIC PHOTOGRAPHERS

Brittany Spaniels share a picnic lunch at Westminster. Called the "vest-pocket hunting dog," this long-legged, naturally tailless or stub-tailed breed hails from France. Unlike most other spaniels, the Brittany points rather than flushes his game.

Great Dane keeps watch over sleeping companions. German nobles used the breed as bodyguards; English squires hunted wild boar with it. American families find the sleek and graceful Dane a loyal guard and gentle pet.

that probably no two people will interpret that standard in exactly the same way. Then there are added factors and complications, such as the physical condition of the dog, the condition of his coat, the way he shows, temperament, and other small but important things that enter into the final judgment.

When it comes to group and Best in Show judging, the goal is the same—to decide which dog comes closest to the standard of perfection for his or her breed. There is an old adage among dog fanciers that judging poor dogs is the hardest job there is, so it is not surprising that group and final judging are not considered especially difficult.

Westminster's pre-eminence is emphasized by the fact that it is quite literally the blue-ribbon show. To be eligible a dog must have won a first prize against a specified number of his own breed in another show held under American Kennel Club rules. This regulation was put into effect when lack of space in Madison Square Garden forced the club to limit entries to 3,000 dogs. The number may run over that figure because all entries in the mail delivery that brings the entry blank for the 3,000th dog must be accepted.

Actually the rule requiring a first prize works little hardship on a dog of quality, for there are dog shows now in every one of the 50 states. Some may have but 200 dogs entered; others as many as 2,000. But all are important parts of the picture. These are the clubs that make up the American Kennel Club, the supervising body that registers dogs in the Stud Book, records show results, enforces regulations, and performs innumerable other thankless tasks.

As much as five or six days before the show goes on, huge trailer trucks start arriving at Madison Square Garden. Benching is unloaded and set up in the exhibition rotunda, in the concourse outside the arena, with signs to show where the various breeds are located. Dogs coming from far away may arrive two or three days before the show opens, and facilities must be available for them.

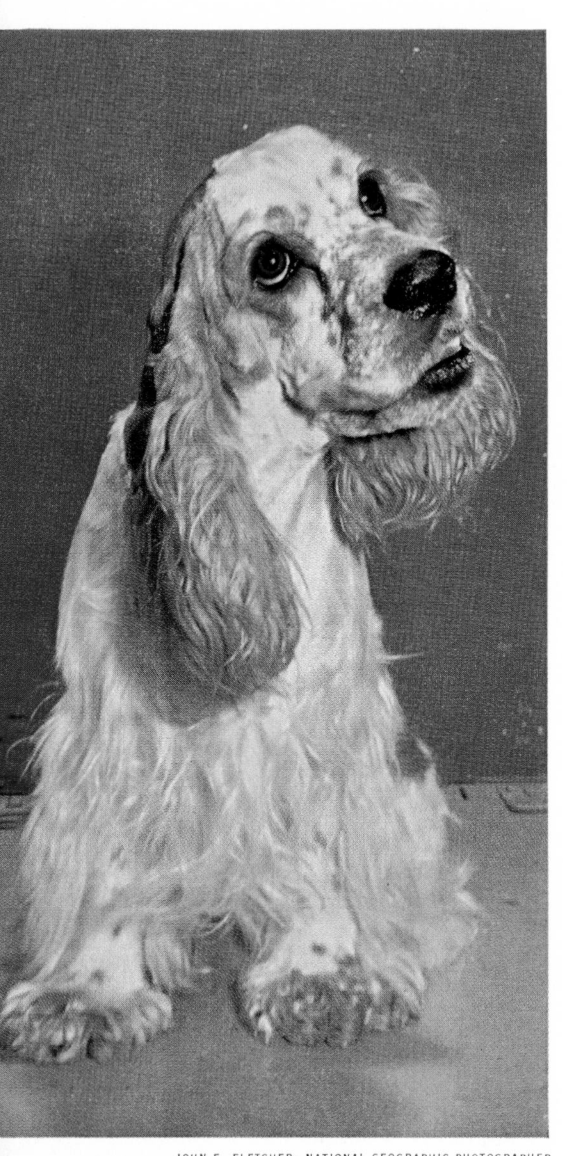

JOHN E. FLETCHER, NATIONAL GEOGRAPHIC PHOTOGRAPHER

Wistful Cocker, one of the smallest of spaniels, is a U.S. favorite. His popularity stems from his being an apartment-size pet as well as a first-class bird dog.

The night before the show opens there is usually a hockey game in the arena. In the concourse the benching is in place and hundreds of dogs are already sleeping in their stalls. The whole organization is waiting for the move inside. As the game ends, hot water is pumped through the pipes to melt the ice. As it breaks up, motor trucks push it into a chute that takes it below. When the floor is dry the all-night task begins. The sideboards for the rings are set up and green canvas mats are laid over the entire floor of each ring, giving the dogs a good footing on which they can move without slipping. Seats for spectators are placed around the rings, telephone lines are run from each ring to the benching areas, and big blackboards are erected for posting the awards.

The whole first day, from 10 a.m. until about 11 p.m., and the entire morning of the second day are devoted to breed judging. Then the rings are dismantled and the whole arena floor is transformed into one emerald-carpeted ring for the group judging. Best hound, best toy, and best non-sporting dog are chosen; also the best brace (two of a breed) in each of the six groups.

By this time it is about 5 o'clock and the nature of the competition changes. People are judged instead of dogs! Teen-age boys and girls walk into the ring with their dogs. For a year these youngsters have competed in Junior Showmanship classes throughout the country. Each has won competitions at five shows to be eligible to come to Westminster and compete for the Leonard Brumby, Sr., Memorial Trophy—highest award in Junior Showmanship. The competition is judged by professional handlers, many of whom started up the ladder of their careers in just such a manner. They judge not the dogs but the skill with which the juniors show their canine charges. These young people will be the stars of tomorrow in the field of professional handling.

In the evening the show builds slowly to its climax: best sporting dog is judged, then best working dog and best terrier. Next there is a break in the tension as a special performance is put on. It may be Border Collies working a band of live sheep, or perhaps a guard-dog demonstration, or selected bird dogs displaying their skill. Next, six pairs of dogs compete for Best Brace in Show. And then comes the finale.

Six dogs are called to the middle of the green expanse. The peak of canine fame looms within the grasp of each. Television cameras swing as the judge moves from dog to dog. A hush descends on the great arena—shattered at intervals by applause from partisans as each contestant is put through his paces. The judge surveys them one final time and, giving no hint of his selection, goes to the judge's table and writes down the winner's name. He turns once more to the ring, walks forward, and motions the winner to the center. Another Westminster has run its course; another dog has reached the pinnacle.

Which dog? What breed? He may be lean or stocky; sleek, wiry, or long-haired. But one thing is certain: he shares his original ancestor with every other dog in the show, regardless of shape or size. Who was this ancestor and what was he like?

Th

FROM AN EGYPTIAN TOMB FRESCO, XVIII DYNASTY

Triumphant hunter, gazelle hound at his side, was painted at Thebes 3,400 years ago.

CHAPTER TWO

Dog Through the Ages

No one recorded, of course, the happy moment when a dog first licked a man's hand instead of biting it. Man and dog had signed their pact countless dim centuries before an unknown Egyptian artist portrayed the fruits of their teamwork on the wall of a tomb at Thebes.

When these partners strode forth into history's light, man had already shaped a civilization along the banks of the Nile, and dog had long since channeled wild instincts to the service of his master.

We read our first clear records of this unique relationship in such paintings as this from Thebes, and in tablets and inscriptions carved in stone as long ago as 5,000 to 6,000 years and preserved under the hot, dry sands of Egypt. Here, captured for eternity, are sleek hounds of the Pharaohs coursing the desert for the swift gazelle; stalwart dogs guarding flocks and fields; others finding favor in the home. In our museums today are toy dogs fashioned in ivory played with by children along the Nile.

To these ancients, however, the dog was more than mere household pet or assistant in the chase. He was the object of reverence as well. Egyptians venerated him as symbolic guide and protector in the realm of the dead. They gave their god Anubis the body of a man and crowned him with a doglike head. They put his image on the walls of burial chambers and temples, held ceremonies, sacrificed black dogs and white ones alternately—even built a city in his honor. Cynopolis—City of Dogs—was the Greek name for it, and when citizens of a neighboring city committed the outrage of killing and eating dogs from Cynopolis, the Cynopolitans settled the matter in bloody civil war.

But this kowtowing to canines was not just a matter of priests and civic pride. It went right into the people's homes. Herodotus, the Greek historian and traveler, tells us that when a dog died in Egypt, the whole household went into deep mourning. Heads were shaved, food went untouched. The body was ceremoniously embalmed, swathed in fine linen, and carried in solemn procession to the special burial place set aside for dogs in every town. Attendants scourged themselves and wailed in loud lament.

MUSEUM OF FINE ARTS, BOSTON

We no longer mummify dogs, nor include them in our religion, but the death of a dog can still plunge a modern family into grief. Man seems always to have had strong feelings about the dog. Strong feelings, yes—but hardly consistent ones. Reactions range all the way from revulsion to mystic adulation. Man has scorned the dog, and worshiped him. He has caressed the dog lovingly, and turned his name into the foulest of epithets. Seldom has he looked at dog with unconditioned eye.

Dog devotees went to extremes, for example, in Ethiopia, where tribesmen once crowned a dog king. He showed approval of his "advisers'" measures by wagging his tail, his disapproval by barking. If he licked your hand, honors were to be conferred upon you. If he growled it could mean your head.

When Pythagoras returned from Egypt he taught his Greek followers to hold a dog to the mouth of a dying man, for what animal was more worthy to receive the departing spirit and perpetuate its virtues? Socrates' favorite pledge was to swear by the dog, and Plato characterizes the dog as philosopher.

Dogs played their part in Greek religion, too. Sacred dogs kept in the sanctuary of Asclepius, god of medicine, at Epidaurus were said to heal the sick by licking them, as did the sacred serpents. The dog of the mighty

Ancient heroes prized hunting as a manly prelude to victory in war.

DAVID S. BOYER, NATIONAL GEOGRAPHIC PHOTOGRAPHER

Twin jackals of Anubis guard a tomb at Thebes. Egypt's doglike god of the underworld conducted the spirits of the dead to the hall of judgment, where he weighed their hearts against the feather of truth. He had counterparts in the religions of ancient Greece, Rome, India, and Mexico.

hunter Orion was transformed into the brightest star in the heavens, and the rise of this Dog Star, Sirius, marked the Athenian New Year.

The Romans as well as the Greeks sacrificed dogs to the gods, and they put three dog heads on Cerberus and posted him as guard at the gates of hell. On the other hand, watching at the gates of paradise—so North Borneo tribesmen believed—was a fiery dog who took possession of all virgins.

These were not the only peoples to put dogs on pedestals. Dog worship preceded sun worship in ancient Peru, and tribes in places as far apart as Alaska and Sumatra once traced their descent from dog ancestors. It's a good thing Rover can't read, because he would feel a terrible burden of responsibility. The Potawatomi Indians believed that when the old woman who sat in the moon finished making a basket the world would come to an end. Luckily, each time she neared completion a big dog saved mankind by chewing up her work, and that is what causes eclipses.

Ever stop to wonder where your dog got his cold nose? From saving Noah and all his passengers on the ark, says one folk tale. The ark sprang a leak and would

his Greek hunter and dog date from the fifth century B.C.

BAS-RELIEF FROM NINEVEH, BRITISH MUSEUM

With nets and straining mastiffs, Ashurbanipal hunted the Assyrian lion 2,500 years ago.

have foundered had not the resourceful dog plugged it with his nose, chilling it forever. Another version has it that Noah's ark was so crowded that the dog, last aboard, had to stand at the door with his nose poked out. It was chilled by exposure to forty days and nights of rain.

Cold nose and all, the dog ranked high with the ancient Persians. Their god Ahura Mazda took pride in having made him "self-clothed and self-shod, watchful, wakeful, and sharp-toothed, born to watch over man's goods."

It was a heinous offense to strike a dog, and safer to kill a man than to give a dog bad food, "for no house could subsist on the earth but for the shepherd's dog and the house dog." And no faithful soul could safely pass over the bridge to the next world if the yellow-eared, four-eyed dog who stood watch there did not bark away the powers of darkness.

THE ISRAELITES, curiously, had little but contempt for the dog. Of some forty references to the dog in the Bible, almost all are derogatory. (This might seem a bit ungrateful, since not one dog in Egypt gave tongue on the night of the Jewish Exodus.) The Old Testament Jews pictured the dog not as pet and companion but as the pariah dog, gaunt and unclean scavenger of the streets that licked the blood of Jezebel. The term "dog" became the vilest of insults.

Today we find this feeling reflected in such expressions as "dog in the manger," "gone to the dogs," "leads a dog's life," and "dog that bites the hand that feeds it."

Although the ancient Jews used dogs to guard their dwellings and herds, their kings were not huntsmen like the Assyrian kings, or the Pharaohs with their hunting parties numbering hundreds of men and dogs. Not for the Israelites were the joys of racing along in chariots behind Egypt's Greyhounds in swift pursuit of antelope and gazelle; nor the excitement of baying the mighty lion or running down the wild ass with Assyria's splendid Mastiffs.

Greeks and Romans also knew "the Greyhound swift, and Mastiff's furious breed." The lean-limbed Greyhound joined Spartan heroes in the chase. The Mastiff types—the fierce Molossian dogs of Epirus and burly dogs from Britain—fought savage beasts in Rome's arena.

More than 2,300 years ago the Athenian general Xenophon wrote the sporting world's first treatise, *Hunting with Dogs*, in which he described netting the hare with hounds that hunt by scent. The Greek historian Arrian later wrote of hounds that hunt by sight, and advised: Always pat your Greyhound's head after he catches a hare and say, "'Well done, Cirrus! Well done, Bonnas! Bravo, my Horme!' . . . for like men of generous spirit they love to be praised."

Romans further distinguished among house dogs, shepherd dogs, hunting dogs, and fighting dogs. However, if a tiny Maltese, Pomeranian, or Pekingese is closest to your heart, fear not that your favorite was ignored—quite the contrary. These little dogs of luxury are among the oldest of breeds, and were found in noble homes and royal palaces from the Mediterranean to the Orient. Some were bathed and perfumed as ceremoniously as a princess; they were petted, fed dainty food, and carried from room to room on silk cushions. In China, sacred little dogs lolled at the Emperor's court, tended by eunuchs; their puppies were nursed by slaves whose own babies had been destroyed at birth. Death by torture was the penalty for raising a hand against a royal dog.

In Rome, lap dogs became so popular that Julius Caesar asked if Roman ladies had ceased to have children and had dogs instead!

Classical literature abounds with tributes to the dog: Ulysses' faithful hound Argus who alone recognized his master when Ulysses returned home after long years of wandering; the royal dog who leaped upon his fallen master's pyre; the dog who recognized his master's murderer in a crowd and attacked him with such fury that the villain confessed.

Corinth, it is recorded, was saved by watchdogs who patrolled the ramparts while their masters slept off drunken revels. The enemy crept in for a surprise attack, but the keen-eared dogs sprang for their throats. The dogs fought until only one remained, but he lived to rouse the garrison and save the city.

"Such fidelity of dogs in protecting what is committed to their charge, such affectionate attachment to their masters, such jealousy of strangers, such incredible acuteness of nose in following a track, such keenness in hunting—what else do they evince but that these animals were created for the use of man." So wrote Cicero 2,000 years ago. Is it any wonder that dogs are still called Fido, the Latin word for faithful?

Bold dogs of Pompeii sink bronze fangs into a sculptured boar. Romans crowded the arenas to see wild beasts die in mock hunts or savage fights with dogs.

NATIONAL MUSEUM, NAPLES

DUNCAN EDWARDS

Trussed boar, en route to please a Roman circus mob, casts a doleful eye on the powerful dog that bayed him. Imperial expeditions shipped whole menageries from Africa and Asia to fight in Rome's Colosseum. Mounted huntsmen stampeded quarry into nets, burned incense to Diana for success in the chase. Mosaics in Maximian's villa in Sicily reveal life 1,600 years ago.

GIACOMO BROGI

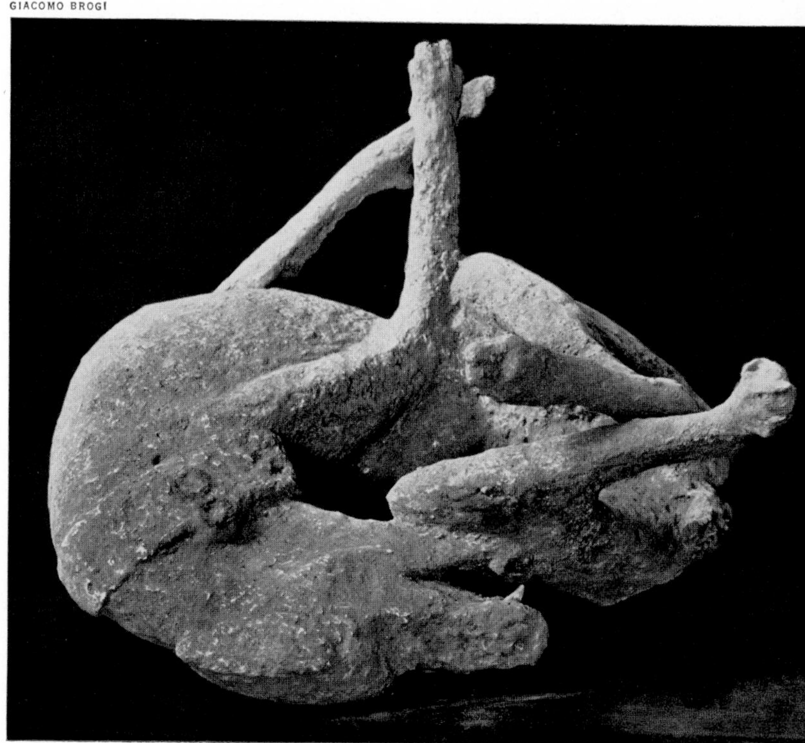

Death agony of a Pompeii pet is revealed in this cast of a dog that perished in the eruption of Vesuvius, A.D. 79. Kenneled behind the home of Vesonius Primas, he climbed as high as his chain would allow before volcanic ash overwhelmed him.

Excavators of the buried city discovered the form of another dog lying across a child, as if in a last attempt to guard his playmate. The engraved silver collar told that Delta, the dog, had once saved his master Severinos from a wolf.

Ancient even in Cicero's time was the scene one sees today when the Australian aborigine is on the hunt. As if from out of the Stone Age he strides across the vast outback, armed with primitive spear, dog at his side. The latter, called the dingo, is said to be the oldest living race of dog. It probably entered Australia with the first men to cross a land bridge that once linked the island continent to Asia.

A 19th century observer reported that tribesmen along the Herbert River in Queensland reared with their children wild dingo puppies they found in hollow trees. The keen-scented dingo was valuable on the hunt, tracking and running down game swiftly and silently. But he was temperamental, sometimes refusing to go any farther and expecting his master to carry him on his shoulders.

The man never struck him, though he sometimes threatened to. Threats gave way to extravagant affection: he "caresses it, eats the fleas off it, and then kisses it on the snout." Responding to this kindly treatment, the dingo became a one-man dog. But sometimes the call of the wild grew too strong and he would join the pack in throat-tearing attacks on cattle and sheep, never to return.

Perhaps you've wondered how the naked aborigines keep warm on cold desert nights. Actually, they don't sleep naked—they "wear" their dogs as cover. A chilly night is known in the Australian outback as a "three-dog night"; a "five-dog night" is really cold. Temperatures plunging to freezing would make it a "six-dog night," but the aborigines seldom have to put on the dog that much.

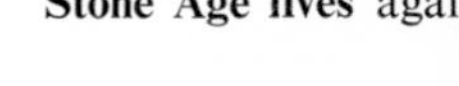

Stone Age lives agai

The 20th century visitor to the back-country camp sees many mongrel hounds, crosses between the white man's dogs and tamed dingoes. But Freeman Lloyd encountered a real canine surprise.

"Upcountry, in Western Australia," Lloyd wrote in the *National Geographic Magazine*, "we came across a black fellow and his three 'gins'—his wives or 'lady friends'—fast asleep near the embers of three fires. Cuddling among their savage companions were a purebred Greyhound and a well-bred smooth-coated Fox Terrier. Men, women, and dogs had evidently been hunting together, and the stomachs of the feasters were distended with food. Against the trees stood four long, slender spears with jagged notched hardwood points. Here was a living picture of primitive savages with their canine allies."

Lloyd mused on how these two fine dogs—one whose regal ancestors ran down the gazelle in Egypt, the other whose forebears dueled the fox in England—came into the hands of these primitives "down under," then continued: "The

/hen this Australian Nimrod stalks kangaroo with spear. His fast dingo-greyhound outruns game.

Greyhound, they knew instinctively, would be especially useful in overtaking and 'sticking up' even the largest of kangaroos. Its speed is equal to that of any marsupial. The dog was not expected to kill the quarry; its jaws and pluck would be of no avail against the ripping and disemboweling claws on the hind feet of an 'old man' kangaroo. The Greyhound was to hold the animal at bay until the hunters could come up and kill it with their crude spears, just as they must have done thousands of years ago in the prehistoric stage of the time-honored man-dog relationship."

How did this partnership begin? And when in the vast wilderness of the prehistoric world did man and dog forge a bond that lasts until this day? Legend provides a ready answer.

Soon after the Creation a chasm split the earth in two. Man was left on one side, animals on the other. The four-footed creatures didn't mind this separation from man—all except the dog. He ran up and down whining, seeking a way across. Man heard him and saw the pleading look in his eyes. "Come," he cried.

The dog sprang, but the chasm was too wide; only his forepaws struck the far edge. He hung there, struggling in vain to clamber up.

Man stooped and pulled the dog up to safety beside him. "You shall be my companion forever," he said.

Scientists take a less rhapsodic view. Man was early associated with doglike animals. But association, they point out, is a long way from domestication, and farther still from friendship. Primitive man no doubt had to fight wild dogs just as he had to fight other wild animals he met. And with their strength and speed and cruel slashing teeth these wild dogs would prove no mean foes. Probably many an early encounter ended with the man torn to pieces.

But man had two arms and prehensile fingers. He could climb a tree, wield a

club, hurl a stone; he won the wild dog's grudging respect. Also they had something in common. Both man and dog were carnivorous and lived mainly by the hunt. When man made his kill, the dogs, lurking at a respectful distance, would move in to finish off parts of the carcass he did not carry off.

Again, the dogs might run down quarry too fast for man, yet too dangerous for them to kill. Man with his crude weapons would dispatch their enemy, take what he needed, and leave them a feast. (The word "quarry" originally meant entrails of game, given to dogs after the chase.) Thus man and dog forged a wary alliance in the hunt.

Cave man's sloppy housekeeping also helped draw wild dog and man together. Attracted by the scraps he tossed outside, the scavengers rid him of unsanitary waste that in time would offend even his rude nostrils. The wary creatures accepted man's leftovers long before they accepted him; and he may have looked on dogs more as a convenient source of meat than of companionship. But with wild dogs prowling near his camp, man doubtless found their dens and carried puppies home—just as Australian aborigines do with the dingo.

The puppies grew up unafraid of man, and their playful, friendly ways won tolerance for their kind in the household. Succeeding generations grew tamer still, ultimately so accustomed to serving their new master and sharing the comfort and protection of his fire that life in the wild held little appeal.

Who was this four-legged creature that dogged man's steps on the hunt, cleaned up his garbage, was successively camp follower, hanger-on, dependent, and finally companion to man? Was he a jackal or was he a coyote, both wild dogs noted for scavenger ways? Or was he a tractable wolf?

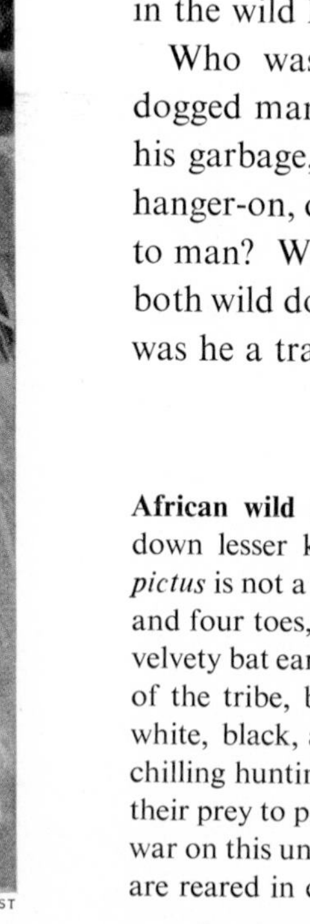

WALTER A. WEBER, NATIONAL GEOGRAPHIC STAFF ARTIST

African wild dogs, pied with hyenalike spots, run down lesser kudu, a 250-pound antelope. *Lycaon pictus* is not a true dog, having slightly different teeth and four toes, not five on his forefeet. Black snout, velvety bat ears, and white brush mark every member of the tribe, but each has his own body pattern of white, black, and yellow. "Hoo! hoo! hoo!" is the chilling hunting call. Attacking in relays, they tear their prey to pieces on the run. Man wages relentless war on this untamable stock and game killer. Young are reared in dens burrowed in the ground.

WALTER A. WEBER, NATIONAL GEOGRAPHIC STAFF ARTIST

Wild dogs of India, pursuing a chital, run in a pack, a hunting co-operative common to most canines. The dhole, Kipling's "Red Dog," growls, whimpers, fawns, follows a scent, and wags his tail in pleasure. But a difference in tooth structure puts him in the genus *Cuon*, apart from *Canis*, the true dog. The dhole's slashing flank attacks harry even the tiger; he is reported untamable.

A sharp-fanged dingo surveys his hunting ground. Australia's coyote-sized wild dog is a fierce predator of the bush, but tribesmen often raise *Canis dingo* to be a pet and a loyal partner on the hunt.

AUSTRALIAN N.T.A.

"Zoologists generally agree that our household pet developed from the Eurasian wolf." So said Stanley P. Young, a senior biologist with the U.S. Fish and Wildlife Service and, until his death, an authority on the wolf. "The domestic dog is a carnivore, a flesh-eater in the same group with wolves, coyotes, foxes, jackals, dingoes, and other wild dogs.

"The dog's story begins in the lush forests of some 50 million years ago with a small, rather brainy tree-climbing creature, *Miacis*. This undoglike patriarch was also the progenitor of both bear and raccoon. From him evolved a carnivore we call *Hesperocyon*. Though Hesperocyon's long weasel-like body and short legs little resembled the dog's, he had developed many doglike characteristics.

'urbing his own appetite, a dingo stands guard as his mate feeds on wallaby.

"Some 25 to 30 million years ago two larger, shorter-tailed, distinctly doglike forms named *Temnocyon* and *Cynodesmus* made their appearance on the open plains. Both derived from Hesperocyon. Temnocyon is considered the ancestor of today's wild dogs of India, Africa, and Brazil. Cynodesmus, through an intermediate wolflike form called *Tomarctus*, became the ancestor of our modern wolves, coyotes, jackals, foxes, and domestic dogs.

"Many offshoots appeared and died off," continues Dr. Young. "We have well-preserved skeletal remains of one—the dire wolf—from the La Brea tar pits in Los Angeles. Carrion-feeding habits led these huge wolves to the oil

pools to attack mired animals, only to become trapped themselves and leave their embalmed bodies for 20th century naturalists to dig out and study.

"In this survival of the fittest, the dog family tended always toward increased length of limb and running speed which enabled it to chase down prey and kill it with snapping jaws. The dog acquired group instincts in the hunt, in sharp contrast to the solitary stalking, clawing cat.

"Though wolves and dogs sprang from a common ancestor, the former maintained their wildness and ferocity; the latter became tractable and domestic."

Still, time has not erased their basic similarities. Both dogs and wolves gestate in about 63 days, can crossbreed and produce fertile offspring, and fall prey to the same parasites and diseases. They "wolf" or gorge food, often to stupefaction; and the whole dog family, from the lean rover of forest and plain to the beribboned blue blood of milady's boudoir, will turn away from its usual fare to eat carrion or roll on it.

Both wag their tails in pleasure, tuck them between their legs in fright, curl lips into a snarl when angered. (The bristling fur which accompanies the growl makes the challenged canine look larger and more formidable.) Both use scent-marked runways. Whether it is your pedigreed Poodle's favorite route from tree to mailbox to hydrant, or a wolf family's elliptical circuit

WALTER A. WEBER, NATIONAL GEOGRAPHIC STAFF ARTIST

Snarling timber wolves slash at the flanks of a grizzly bear caught raiding their cache of caribou meat. Like their European brothers, these nimble, powerful-jawed Alaskans are members of *Canis lupus*. Co-operation in attack shows the gregarious nature typical of canines.

Dog and wolf cross readily. Howl and bark distinguish them, but each can learn to imitate the other. Tooth and bone structure are similar. Modern opinion is that they share a common ancestry.

of 100 miles or more, wild species and domestic dog alike mark their bulletin boards with urine, leaving messages for friend and foe.

Yet one of these close relatives has been hated ever since the howl of ravening wolves and the moonlit gleam of eyes struck terror in the heart of early man. The other—the dog—is held higher in our affection than any other animal.

Man unconsciously shaped the dog he wanted. At first he kept only those most useful in the hunt. When he domesticated sheep and cattle, to guard them he chose the dog best equipped to fight off predators. Everywhere man went, dog went too, thus becoming the most widely distributed of four-footed animals. The dog adapted to every clime and every use. The baffling variety we see in our dogs today once served a practical purpose. The Dachshund's body was bred sausage-shaped so he could wriggle into the badger's den; the tuft of hair on the brow of the vermin-killing Scottie served to keep dirt out of his eyes when he, too, went to earth. The sled dog's fur coat and plumed tail functioned as sleeping bag and muffler. Protective hair between the toes shielded the swift Saluki's feet from rock-strewn desert. The Poodle's dense coat, suited for work in wintry duck marsh, was trimmed to speed his swimming.

Hunting dogs became specialists: long-legged deerhounds "taketh the pray with a jolly quickness"; others "in smelling singular" track like the keen-nosed

WALTER A. WEBER, NATIONAL GEOGRAPHIC STAFF ARTIST

Serenading the setting sun is *Canis latrans* (barking dog). The prairie coyote's unforgettable cry has been described as a "prolonged howl which the animal let out and then ran after and bit into small pieces." The wolf's day is over in much of America but his smaller cousin thrives from Alaska to Costa Rica. Litters as large as 19 and a cunning, resourceful nature make the hardy coyote indestructible.

Often mated with the Indians' dogs, coyotes have been tamed as pets. The wolf has doglike looks and mentality, relatively short ears, heavy muzzle; the coyote is foxlike, with pointed ears, nose, eyes, and disposition. His name comes from the Aztec *coyotl*.

Mates for life, a wolf couple rear their whelps in an Alaskan cave. Litters, born in spring, average seven. Ranging across Eurasia and North America, from Mexico to the Arctic, wolves have been hunted with vengeance through the ages. Weighing 60 to 175 pounds, they attack game, stock, sometimes man. The Romans, however, erected a statue honoring the she-wolf that suckled Romulus and Remus, legendary founders of the Eternal City.

Plains Indians interbred their dog with the wolf to get a large hybrid for pulling loads. Polar explorers often couldn't tell Eskimo sled dogs from wolves. Tamed wolves make one-man pets.

A stag hunt in Renaissance Italy was a scene of clamorous pageantry. Mounted nobles, attende

Bloodhound. Some breeds pursued the hare; others, the otter, fox, or raccoon. Huntsmen deliberately bred melodious voices into hounds and alarming bark out of bird dogs. Boarhounds were given the bulk to tackle a ferocious tusked beast. Guard work went to the burly Mastiff.

Man has even bred the dog to fight his closest wild kin. This deadly, classic struggle between *Canis familiaris* and *Canis lupus* (as Swedish naturalist Linnaeus classed dog and wolf 200 years ago) echoes throughout literature and folklore. Visitors to the Welsh village of Beddgelert will be shown a monument to Gelert, the legendary wolfhound of Llewellyn, Prince of Wales. Returning to his castle from the hunt one day the prince was met by his favorite hound, with lips and fangs that ran blood. In terror the prince searched inside for his untended son. Finding only gore everywhere, he plunged his vengeful sword to the hilt in Gelert. Alas, only then did he discover his little boy alive and safe, a huge wolf at his side, slain by the faithful Gelert.

Ever wonder why the brass studs on dog collars? These recall earlier times when Rover led a more dangerous life: "To arme them agaynst the Woolfe, or other wyld beastes, you may put brode collars about theyr neckes full of nayles,

"HUNT IN A FOREST," BY PAOLO UCCELLO, 15TH CENTURY, ASHMOLEAN MUSEUM, OXFORD

›y shouting footmen and Greyhounds by the dozen, drove the bewildered quarry into waiting nets.

and iron studdes, lyning it with soft leathers within." So great a threat was this predator that King Edgar in the 10th century demanded annual tribute of "three hundred Wolfes" of the Welsh. Henry II made land grants on condition that the recipients destroy all wolves on their new estates. Combating these stock-killers often took on the character of a military campaign. In medieval Ireland thousands of men and hounds ranged the Mourne Mountains, clearing them of wolves and wild boar. Such hunts took place during months when invasion was least likely, and served to keep warriors and dogs in battle condition.

How different were the hunts of medieval and Renaissance times from today's! The deer drives in the Scottish Highlands, in England's royal parks, and in forests on the Continent were vast pageants that enlivened the entire countryside. Count Gaston de Foix, author of a 14th century book on the hunt, is said to have traveled about with 1,600 hounds. But even this pales before the hunts Marco Polo witnessed in the realm of Kublai Khan:

"The Emperor hath two Barons who are own brothers," he wrote. "Each of these brothers hath 10,000 men under his orders, each body of 10,000 being

GERMAN WOODCUT ENGRAVED BY J. A. LONICER, 1582, BRITISH MUSEUM

Hounds across the sea. Today's well-traveled Rover had his counterpart in the Middle Ages, when dogs of war and the hunt embarked for foreign shores with noble masters. Dogs were favorite royal gifts; Crusaders brought back exotic breeds from the Levant. Here Greyhounds and ring-tailed Afghans travel kennel class with Mastiffs and unshorn Poodles.

dressed alike, the one in red and the other in blue. . . . Out of each body of 10,000 there are 2,000 men who are each in charge of one or more mastiffs. . . . And when the Prince goes a-hunting, one of these Barons, with his 10,000 men and something like 5,000 dogs, goes toward the right, whilst the other goes toward the left with his party in like manner. They move along, all abreast of one another, so that the whole line extends over a full day's journey, and no animal can escape them. Truly it is a glorious sight to see the working of the dogs and the huntsmen on such an occasion! And as the Lord rides a-fowling across the plains, you will see these big hounds come tearing up, one pack after a bear, another pack after a stag, or some other beast, as it may hap, and running the game down now on this side and now on that, so that it is really a most delightful sport and spectacle."

In the Orient as well as in Western lands, royalty favored dogs as prized gifts of state (a Greyhound in 11th century England brought the same price as a serf). In Japan and China toy dogs changed hands as gifts and tribute; in Europe, staghounds, Mastiffs, and the giant wolfhounds of Ireland had greatest renown. Henry IV of France shipped an entire pack of staghounds to

James I of England. But hunting with dogs was not just masculine sport. When England's Henry VIII sent to the Queen of France "hobbies, greyhounds, hounds and great dogs," the queen declared herself "the gladdest woman in the world." And Henry VIII's own daughter Elizabeth delighted in the hunt.

Contemporary woodcuts show the Virgin Queen, dressed in stiff farthingale, in scenes from the chase. Standing on the forest platform from which she shot the deer as hounds drove them past, she receives her Master of the Hunt's report. Attended by her ladies in waiting and her courtiers, she partakes of a hunt breakfast "on pleasant gladsome greene." Baskets bulge with cold loins of veal, cold capon, mutton, beef, and goose, pigeon pie, "gam-bones of the hogge," and "sausages and savoury knacks to set men's minds on gogge." Further to regale the courtly throng, "wagons, cartes, some mules or jades come laden, till they sweat, with many a medicine made for thirsty throats and tippling tongues."

Royalty passed laws to reserve game for its

In knighthood's day dogs wore armor too. This plumed little hunter donned steel to ward off wild boar tusks. Burlier dogs went to war clad in mail and plate, with spiked collars round their throats.

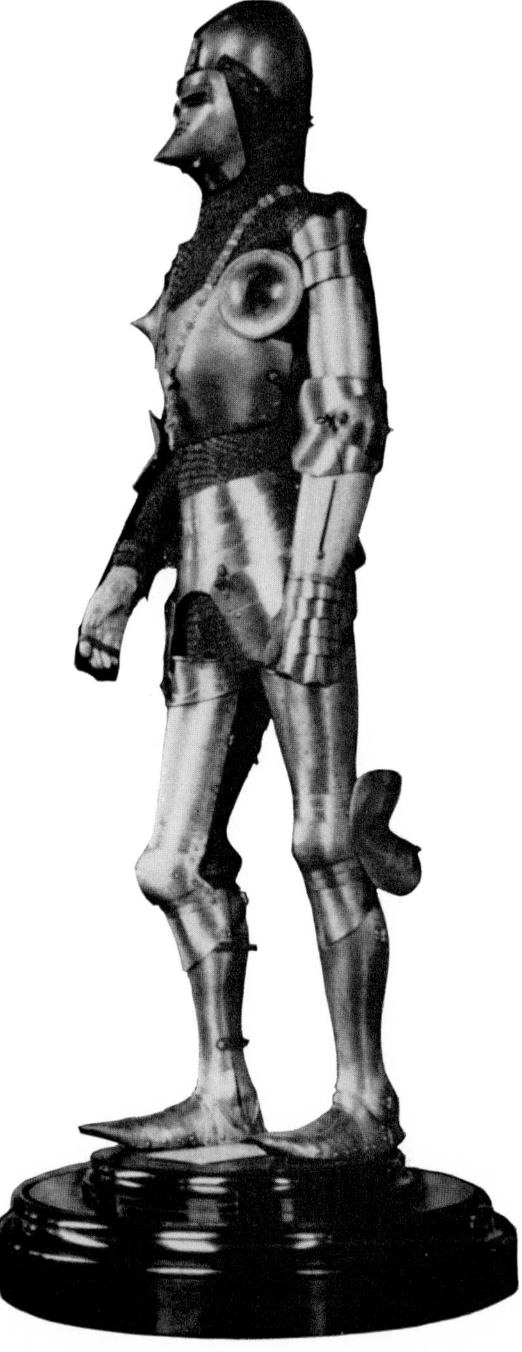

JOHN WOODMAN HIGGINS ARMORY, WORCESTER, MASS.

sole pleasure. King Canute in 1016 decreed that commoners' dogs kept within ten miles of the king's forests must have their "knees cut" to prevent their chasing game. Excepted were "little dogges (al which dogges are to sit in ones lap), because in them there is no daunger." In a later reign these toy dogs had to prove their exempt status by passing through an oval "dog gauge," seven inches by five in diameter.

Tracts of land—"dog tenures"—were granted in return for maintenance of the king's hounds, and by the reign of Charles I no fewer than 69 royal forests and 781 royal parks had been carved out of the English countryside. Though poachers suffered fierce punishment, they took much game from these preserves by stealth, largely with the aid of Greyhound-like dogs known as lurchers. These keen-nosed dogs were trained to run silently; if caught in a snare, to chew their way out. It is even claimed they would withhold recognition of their masters if caught poaching!

Few monarchs were more single-minded in their interests than Louis XI of France. It is said of this unlovable 15th century monarch that he did everything in its proper season; in summer and autumn he carried on his wars, in winter he pursued stag and wild boar, in spring he hunted with the falcon. "In Normandy the army of the English is beaten and disbanded," he wrote in a letter, "and I am returning to Amboise or Plessis to take and kill wild boar, so that I may not miss the season while awaiting the other wherein to take and kill the English." Even when mortal illness finally denied him his cherished hunting and hawking, the monarch enlivened his last hours with cur dogs hunting rats in his bedchamber!

England's kings took their hounds on Continental campaigns and hunted with them between battles. Some dogs also fought at their master's side.

"LA VENERIE," (1561) BY JACQUES DU FOUILLOUX, ADAPTED AS "THE ARTE OF VENERIE" (1576) BY GEORGE TURBERVILLE, LIBRARY OF CONGRESS

"HARE-HUNTING," BY FRANCIS BARLOW, C. 1671. © ASHMOLEAN MUSEUM, OXFORD

*"The timorous Hare, when Started from her seat,
by bloody hounds, to save her life soe Sweet,
with Severall Shifts, much terrour and great payne,
yet dyes she by their mouths, all proves but vayne."*

England's squires hunted the hare, "a wilde and skippishe beast," long before the fox hunt became their favorite sport. This 17th century scene by Barlow shows "deep-mouthed" hounds "hunting under the pole." Flourishing the staff brings the well-trained dogs to a dead stop, even when on the hottest scent.

"The princely Stagge it rangeth through the woods . . . by fullmouth'd Hounds pursued. . . ." Tracking on leash begins the hunt for hart. These staunch Bloodhound types are not fast, so the pack is often posted in couples along the stag's probable line of flight and slipped in relays. Huntsman's horn proclaims success in the chase.

With fire in his eye, a wounded boar lunges at his attackers. Hunting this ravager of the peasants' fields called for the ultimate in courage. The beasts scaled 500, sometimes 700 pounds. Count Gaston de Foix said he had seen men and horses killed by a single stroke of the savage tusks. "Out of fifty hounds that start on a boar hunt often scarcely a dozen return to the kennel whole and sound," writes 16th century huntsman Jacques du Fouilloux. Here baying their prey are German Boarhounds, rough-hewn ancestors of today's magnificent Great Dane. In the heat of the struggle, startled huntsman (left) breaks his spear in the boar. Full foliage is artistic license; the boar hunt was late autumn and winter sport.

"Let slip the dogs of war," cries Mark Antony over slain Caesar's body, and history is packed with dogfights. Since days when Chaldean dogs charged with chariots and dragged the enemy from the saddle, the K-9 corps has aided man in war. In modern conflict dogs have served primarily in scouting, sentry, messenger, and first-aid work, but in former times they were thrown into the attack. Sometimes they wore armored coats of steel plate, mail, or leather,

"BOAR HUNTING," BY ANTHONY VAN DYCK AND FRANS SNYDERS, C. 1616, PINAKOTHEK, MUNICH

with spikes and wicked curved knives protruding from their heavy iron collars.

Cambyses, King of Persia, used large bands of big shaggy dogs trained to attack in formation in conquering Egypt in 525 B.C. Herodotus tells of a battle between the Perinthi and the Paeoni in which "man was matched against man, horse against horse, dog against dog." Roman legions, Attila's hordes, and feudal Japanese warlords all flung troops of savage dogs against their enemies.

In the army Henry VIII sent to Emperor Charles V against the French king "there were foure hundred souldiers that had the charge of the like number of dogs, all of them garnished with good yron collers after the fashion of that countrey." In Queen Elizabeth's reign the Earl of Essex took 800 Bloodhounds with his troops to help suppress rebellion in Ireland.

Canine conquistadores, sometimes armored in quilted cotton against arrows, served the Spaniards in their conquests in the Americas. One ferocious man-killing Mastiff called Bezerillo, "verie cruell, and well flesht upon the Indians," got double rations and earned a salary for his master.

Several Great Plains tribes ate dogs ceremonially before going to war, believing this would imbue them with the animal's bravery and nimbleness.

Dogs not only have fought in battle; they have precipitated and ended it. A 12th century manuscript tells of an Irish Wolfhound named Ailbe, so swift he could run through all Leinster in one day and so renowned the kings of Connacht and Ulster both offered 6,000 head of cattle and more for him. Feeling ran so high in the bidding that kings and retainers took to the sword. Alas, in the bloody battle, Ailbe was killed!

In 1698, near what is now Fredericksburg, Virginia, Indian tribesmen so coveted settlers' fine hunting dogs that their leader Powhatan declared a truce to trade furs, gold, and handicrafts for them. Thus began a colorful tradition: Dog Mart day in Fredericksburg (see Chapter 11).

During the Revolutionary War, while General Washington was dining one night, a large dog, obviously hungry, appeared at the entrance to his quarters. When Washington discovered that the handsome animal's collar bore the name of the British commander, General Howe, he ordered that the dog be well fed and returned to the enemy lines under a flag of truce. For this gracious action he received a grateful letter from General Howe.

TODAY, when some 29,000 veterinarians in the United States alone, backed by the modern facilities of 3,000 small-animal hospitals, minister to dogs' aches and pains, it is easy to forget that once dog served to cure man's ills. The "Spaniell gentle" was held to the abdomen "to succour and strengthen quailing and quamming stomackes." Not only was it believed that "the paine wil depart from the man into the beast," but there is quaint mention in the unwashed Middle Ages of "small ladyes poppees that bere awaye the flees."

In the Germany of old, if you were sick with fever, you would share a bowl of milk with a dog, drink three times alternately, and chant "Good luck, you hound! May you be sick and I be sound!" In Britain you'd cure your cough by putting a hair plucked from your head between slices of buttered bread and feeding the sandwich to a dog. Ancient Chinese believed the blood of a white dog cured lunacy and that of a black dog eased the pain of childbirth.

From earliest times dogs were credited with power to perceive the supernatural and with the gift of prophecy. They could see spirits and, "lightened wyth the lampe of fore-knowledge," foretell death's approach in nocturnal howling. A dog's color held significance to the Chinese; "fortunate" or "unfortunate" markings augured well or ill for his master.

Black dog, black magic—the ancients often linked the two. The devil donned the guise of a big black dog in medieval European accounts of witchcraft. In Wales, a black dog's appearance near the home of a dying person doomed the soul to eternal torment.

Spine-chilling tales have come from Devon's wild and lonely Dartmoor. Wide-eyed travelers have told of unearthly baying from the swirling mists, of hounds racing before a grim dark horseman whose mount breathed smoke and fire. Some said the hounds were headless and bathed in an eerie glow. To Devon folk, all who heard these dogs would die within the year; all pursued by the wild huntsman would lose their souls, for he is Satan.

Persian Greyhounds, members of the noble Saluki clan, course the gazelle on wings of silk.

"PERSIAN GREYHOUNDS," BY JAMES WARD, C. 1807, COURTESY OF MRS. HOPE WATERS

"A HUNTSMAN AND HIS DOGS," BY ADRIAEN CORNELISZ BEELDEMAKER, RIJKSMUSEUM, AMSTERDAM

Wending homeward with pack and prey, a huntsman enacts a timeless theme. A Flemish artist captured the scene in 1653, yet the crossbred hound in the lead might be today's; Greyhounds at right might have pleasured Egypt's Pharaohs; early setters in center, like weapon and garb, are identified with 17th century Europe.

But dogs were not only the hounds of hell, linked with the devil. In many lands, canine symbols were charms against demons. On occasion, guards of China's imperial court dressed as dogs and barked away evil spirits. Europe's nobles displayed the dog as their emblems on crests and escutcheons. Dogs portrayed in sculpture at the feet of crusading knights symbolized Christian fidelity: their masters followed the Cross as faithfully as dog follows master. Dogs are pictured as the companions of Christendom's saints. In France and Belgium, huntsmen still honor their patron, St. Hubert, on his feast day, November 3, when hounds are blessed in colorful ceremony. In the Middle Ages the abbey bearing his name in the Ardennes became famed for its "dogs of black St. Hubert's breed, unmatched for courage, breath and speed."

Such tributes appear through centuries of literature, but the dog's life was not always an easy one. Man long viewed him largely as an efficient tool of the hunt, as burglar insurance, pulling power for a cart, a shepherd that conveniently drew no wages. Prized for his utility, nevertheless he was often used shamefully.

The baiting sports, which pitted dogs against bulls, bears, baboons, horses, even lions, and the spectacle of dog fighting dog to the death wrote dark chapters in man's relationship to his "best friend." Nor was the turnspit's drab life on kitchen treadmill one to be envied. Dog flesh, at least, never grew popular on Europe's menus, as it did in China, on some Pacific islands, and among North American Indian tribes. But many a Continental lady wore dogskin muff, gloves, and shoes with fashionable pride.

Smugglers along France's borders clad their dogs in false skins; concealed beneath were laces and other expensive contraband. The dogs were whipped by uniformed men to teach them to give customs agents a wide berth. The famous contraband-carrying dog Le Diable—sometimes black, sometimes dyed brown, gray, or white—smuggled more than 50,000 francs worth of lace across the border before a customs official's bullet ended his unwitting criminal career.

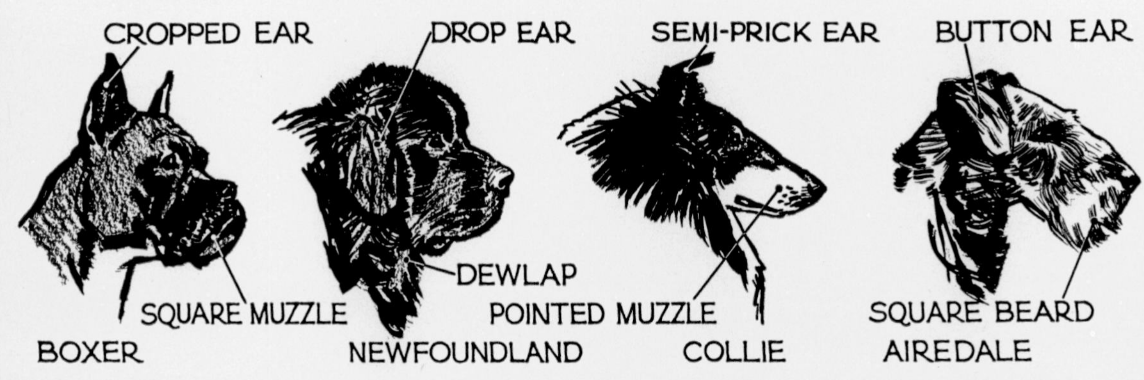

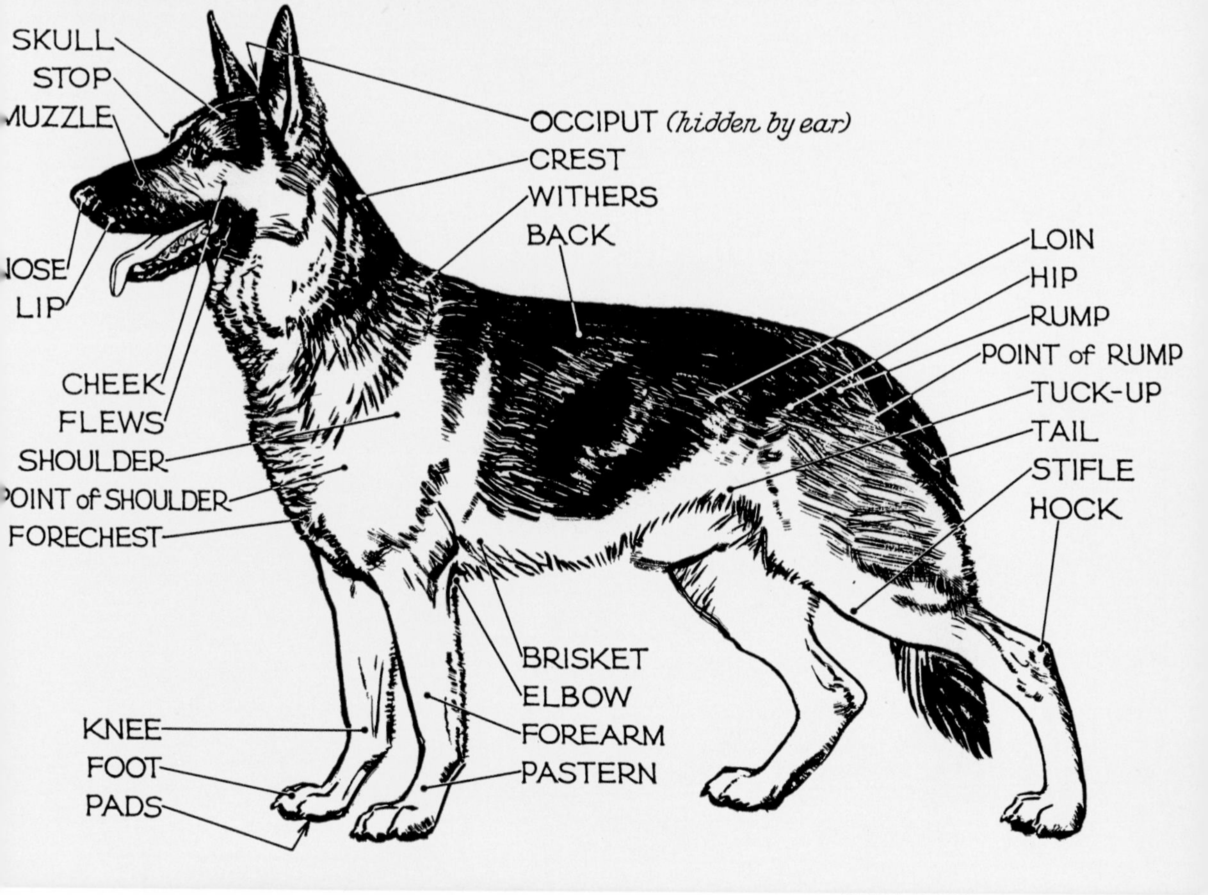

SKULL
STOP
MUZZLE
NOSE
LIP
CHEEK
FLEWS
SHOULDER
POINT of SHOULDER
FORECHEST
KNEE
FOOT
PADS
OCCIPUT (hidden by ear)
CREST
WITHERS
BACK
LOIN
HIP
RUMP
POINT of RUMP
TUCK-UP
TAIL
STIFLE
HOCK
BRISKET
ELBOW
FOREARM
PASTERN
ROBERT E. LOUGHEED

The German Shepherd models for all dogdom. Breeds as unlike as the Yorkshire Terrier and the Irish Wolfhound match it in anatomy. But surface differences distinguish them: the Bloodhound's long ears, dewlap, distinctive color; the Husky's prick ears, pointed muzzle, curled, brush tail; the Greyhound's rose ears, narrow face, curved back, small loins. Prick ears of the German Shepherd are imitated in other breeds by cropping. The practice of "curtailing" dogs stemmed from taxes on long-tailed dogs and the belief that biting off the pup's tail prevented "madnesse." Cropped ears or docked tails cannot be inherited, any more than a parlor trick or a poodle clip. But a good nose, stamina, markings, or other natural characteristic can be passed on and improved by selective breeding.

FEATHERTAIL
RINGTAIL
SETTER
CHOW CHOW
WHIPTAIL
STUBTAIL
POINTER
COCKER

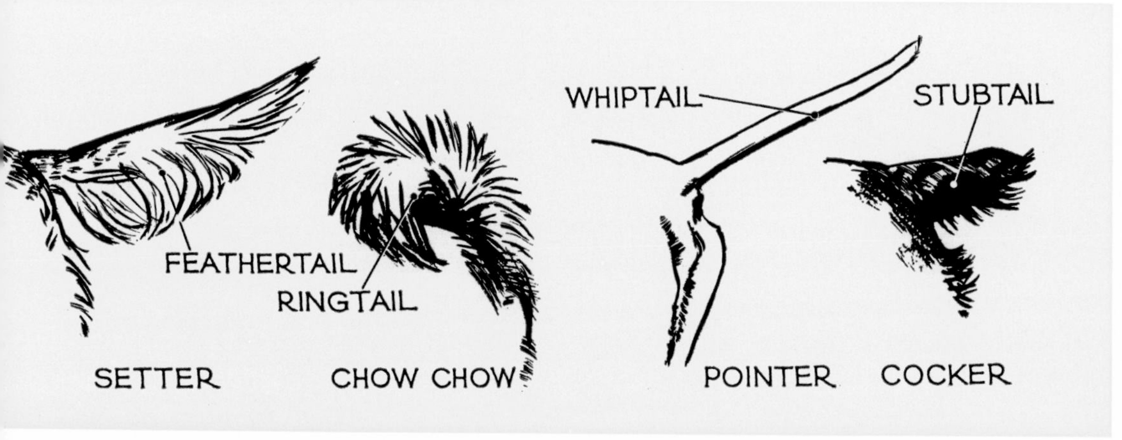

In New Zealand the law finally caught up with a sheep thief and his "accomplice"—a dog trained to open gates at night and drive stolen flocks over remote passes. A court tried the dog, found him guilty, and reportedly hanged him.

When did the change of heart come? No one can say exactly, but the 19th century's surge of romanticism and sentiment certainly brought far-reaching changes in canine status. In many parts of the world man had won new individual dignity, and he shared this with his dog. No longer need a dog be lamed by law to prevent his interfering with royalty's exclusive pleasure. As emphasis on the hunt declined, the dog's role as companion came to the fore.

LIBRARY OF CONGRESS

Praise of the dog as a personality flowed from the pen of novelist and poet and was carved in marble. When financial reverses threatened his estate, Sir Walter Scott's first concern seemed the fate of his dogs: "Poor things," he wrote, "I must get them kind masters." When his dog Camp died, he excused himself from a dinner engagement because of "the death of a dear old friend."

On another occasion Scott wrote: "I have sometimes thought of the final cause of dogs having such short lives and I am quite satisfied it is in compassion to the human race; for if we suffer so much in losing a dog after an acquaintance of ten or twelve years, what would it be if they were to live double that time?"

Romantic artists spared no senti-

Utility created dogs for every need; taste often alters them. The Bloodhound, St. Bernard, Mastiff, Irish Setter, and Pointer dominate this Currier and Ives scene, "House, Kennel and Field." Chihuahua and Pug exchange soprano challenges across a drowsy Greyhound. Just since the 1890's, conformation, trim of coat, and ears of many familiar breeds have changed.

Saved from the wat'ry deep! "Newfoundland dogs are good to save children from drowning," said Josh Billings, "but you must have a pond of water handy and a child, or else there will be no profit in boarding a Newfoundland."

"SLEIGH RIDE," BY JAMES CLONNEY, C. 1845, MUSEUM OF FINE ARTS, BOSTON

Young love creates a sleigh out of a sled, a dappled mare out of a mongrel. What childhood scene would be complete without the ever-patient dog?

ment in attributing the noblest human emotions to the dog. As with Sir Edwin Landseer's famed portraits of Newfoundland and St. Bernard, they immortalized his heroic deeds. Young Abraham Lincoln, however, helped repay man's debt to dog. He braved the icy Wabash River to save his terrier from drowning.

As public sentiment grew, laws banned the barbarous baiting and dogfighting spectacles once so popular. Organizations dedicated to animal welfare came into being: England's Royal Society for the Prevention of Cruelty to Animals was founded in 1824, and its American counterpart—the respected SPCA—in 1866. Where dogs continued to pull merchants' carts, as in Switzerland and the Low Countries, rigid inspection guarded them from mistreatment.

In 1859, Newcastle, England, witnessed an event that was to heighten man's esteem for his dog: owners exhibited fifty pointers and setters at the first modern dog show. (A century later the famous Cruft's Show in London was to draw nearly 7,000 canine contestants.) The grace, beauty, and variety of dogs proudly exhibited at subsequent shows stirred popular interest. Breeders strove to improve and standardize their favorites, recording the dogs' genealogies in stud books to preserve breed purity. Newly evolved dogs like the Sealyham, Boston Terrier, and Doberman Pinscher caught public fancy. Kennel clubs sprang up from Austria to Australia, from Canada to Ceylon.

Queen Victoria enjoyed exhibiting her pets at London shows. But never would she allow her dogs to sleep a single night away from home; the royal canines attended the shows as commuters. All her life she showed her fondness for dogs. Immediately upon returning from her coronation, it is said, Victoria doffed her ceremonial robes—to give her dog a bath! As she breathed her last, 64 years later, a beloved Pomeranian kept watch on her bed.

Man and dog both have come far from the days when Babylonians threw unwanted children to the dogs. If "every dog has his day," surely it must be now: the Animal Rescue League of Boston Shelter provides air conditioning, electronically operated kennel doors, and music piped in to entertain and soothe its doggy tenants!

In this Golden Age of the Dog, 24 million families in the United States alone welcome him into their homes and call him their own. He still hunts for us, but now as a sporting partner whose company we enjoy. His chief role: a companion to be cherished and chided, petted and played with. Secure now in our affections, he makes us want to learn more about him, his groupings, his special talents and ways. . . . And so we shall.

Centuries separate these playful pairs, but sculptured Italian Greyhounds of antiquity and silky English Setters prove the perpetuity of puppy love.

VATICAN MUSEUM AND (RIGHT) EVELYN M. SHAFER

LOUGHEED

The Sporting Breeds

DRY GRASS RUSTLES AS HUNTER AND DOGS roam the yellow fields of autumn. Once of necessity, now for sport they comb the uplands for game. Suddenly a dog stops in his tracks, frozen by a wisp of bird scent; he tenses for his master's shot and command to fetch. Born hunters, bird dogs are called. And with ancestral instincts refined by breeding, they do indeed seem cast "of couragious and fierie mettall, evermore loving and desiring toyle." Spaniel, pointer, setter, retriever—each has special talents, and delights in putting these to test in field trial or hunt. Come out now into the brisk October air with sportsman Roland Kilbon to watch men and dogs work in perfect partnership, and listen for the whir of pheasant wings.

It's nose that counts, with graceful Irish and English Setters. Once they detect the presence of game, these alert hunters freeze to attention.

WALTER A. WEBER, NATIONAL GEOGRAPHIC STAFF ARTIST

CHAPTER THREE

Born Hunters, the Bird Dogs

THE SPANIEL, scrambling up the hillside, pauses. Before him, on the sunny side of a boulder, is the sandy depression in which only a moment ago a pheasant was dusting itself. The scent of game comes heavy to his nostrils; his eager tail flicks faster than ever. Suddenly he plunges into the thicket where the bird sought refuge at the first hint of danger.

With shrill squawks and thrashing wings, the pheasant breaks into the air. The dog sits to watch. A shot rings out; the bird flutters down. At the gunner's command the dog is off like a flash toward the point of fall. In moments he is back, sitting proudly before his master, looking up for the bird to be taken from his mouth.

Here is a 20th century demonstration of the joint effort which in prehistoric times brought about a partnership unique in the animal kingdom—man and dog. Then, as now, the dog, with his superior sense of smell, found the game; the man, using a weapon, brought it down. Together they worked to provide something for the pot.

All dogs then were hunters. Today only a small part of the canine population is trained to hunt. Man, to suit his tastes and mode of living, has reduced many breeds to a size which would have doomed them in times when any animal was prey to larger or craftier creatures. But certain breeds, among them the pointers, setters, spaniels, and retrievers, have remained man's hunting allies. Forebears of modern gun dogs came to England and other countries from Spain; thus the word "spaniel." English prints of centuries ago picture hunting dogs almost identical with our modern pointers, setters, and spaniels.

Pointers and setters, often known as "bird dogs," work mostly with nose in the air. They rely on body scent that drifts from a game bird 20 or more yards away. Watch a fine pointer or setter in action and you will see canine intelligence at its peak. Systematically he quarters the ground, ranging back and forth, but bearing steadily upwind. His delicate nostrils sift the telltale air.

Chesapeake Bay Retriever sloshes ashore with a tame mallard gently held in his mouth. Tied wing and foot, the duck patiently endures its undignified role in teaching retrievers to bring the master's game to hand. Decoy Canada goose bobs in background.

BATES LITTLEHALES, NATIONAL GEOGRAPHIC PHOTOGRAPHER

Briers can't stop his retrieve. Stamina, speed, and the ability to crash through punishing cover have made the English Springer Spaniel a favorite upland hunting dog in the United States.

A good bird dog honors his bracemate's point (below). The Pointer, in the van, has scented birds. The English Setter freezes too. Both will hold steady until the hunter arrives.

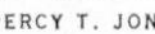

PERCY T. JONES

Suddenly he becomes a statue, a dog of stone. Hot and strong from weeds along the fence the scent of quail is wafted. Motionless, he holds his point when the bird takes flight and his master fires—he is "steady to wing and shot."

The spaniel's job differs. He is not supposed to point but to spring, or flush, the game. And being smaller, he more easily penetrates thickets where pheasants or rabbits find refuge. He works close ahead of his master, nostrils to the ground, searching for foot scent. He pokes his busy nose into every bramble patch until finally, with a bound, he flushes a pheasant. The startled bird flies out with a whir of wings. Without warning the hunter must raise his gun and fire. Tension never lets up when shooting over spaniels.

For all the changes which have taken place over the centuries, one fundamental factor in the man-dog partnership remains: the satisfaction both get from working together. It is all very well for poets and essayists to proclaim the comfort that comes from a cold nose thrust against the hand when one is unhappy or discouraged. But any man who really has worked with his pet will testify that the rewards far transcend those of passive companionship.

Both man and dog are elated at the successful completion of any joint effort, be it a simple parlor trick, an obedience training class, or a hard day hunting. One has only to watch the pride of a gun dog delivering a bird to know that here is the peak of canine pleasure. And what about the man who guides a young dog through the intricacies of field training? On the day the pup, steadied to wing and shot, brings his first bird to hand, his master feels a thrill which comes but seldom in the average lifetime.

FIELD TRIALS PROVIDE a competitive outlet and furnish a yardstick for breeding. In the field champion, the hunting instinct, originally so keen in all dogs, has not been dulled by civilization. When a man tells you his dog has the blood of a Comanche Frank, a Mary Montrose, or a Seaview Rex, you know that dog was born to hunt. The extent to which the hunting instinct is bred into a dog is shown in the story of a New Englander who acquired a Weimaraner, the German dog bred exclusively for hunting for some 200 years and now increasingly popular in the United States. The man liked the dog's looks but was skeptical about all the fine things said of the breed.

He had had no chance to train the dog, already 15 months old when he was first taken into the field. It was the last day of the woodcock season, and he let the Weimaraner come along for company while he explored some likely cover. They had not gone 50 yards when the dog came to a perfect point. The doubting hunter thought the dog had been attracted by a field mouse, but he walked in to investigate anyhow and flushed a woodcock, which he shot.

Just to see what would happen, he commanded, "Go get the dead bird!" The dog quartered a bit, caught the bird's scent, and pointed again. When his master said nothing, he circled the bird uncertainly, mouthed it a moment before picking it up, strutted back and forth with head held high, then sat in front of his master and held up the game to be taken.

In the partridge season which followed, the dog demonstrated that this was no fluke. With no schooling, he proved to be a dependable pointer and retriever. He never again pointed a dead bird but neither did he ever get out of the habit of strutting back and forth, bird in mouth, before coming in to make the delivery! This eccentricity would certainly count against him in a trial, but his master wouldn't swap him for all the field champions in existence. They have worked out their own partnership afield.

Field trials, besides demonstrating hunting qualities, teach sportsmen the part a well-schooled dog plays in conservation. A man with a good dog can put every downed bird into his bag. Thus his allotment truly represents the number

Autumn's tints signal the hunting season in New Hampshire; men and dogs take to the field.

B. ANTHONY STEWART, NATIONAL GEOGRAPHIC PHOTOGRAPHER

of birds shot. He does not leave behind cripples and unretrieved birds. The canine half of the team has three main functions: to find the birds, get them into the air, and retrieve those shot down. While the average gun dog does all these, the various breeds have their specialties.

In the pointing breeds, for instance, the stress is on locating hidden birds and pinning them down with a point until the hunter arrives. With the nonslip retriever (one whose leash is not slipped until just before he is ordered to get the bird), ability to retrieve rather than locate or flush is emphasized. Spaniels are expected to do all three things—locate the birds, get them off the ground, and fetch them after they have been shot.

Trials for the pointing breeds lead by far in number. The pointer and setter folk hold trials in what amounts to a grand circuit, starting on the Canadian prairies in summer and working southward toward the goal of all top bird dogs, the National Championship at Grand Junction, Tennessee, in late February. As

On point at the sudden scent of quail! Tail rigid, legs in mid-stride, muscles tensed like steel spring.

each event covers an extensive area, the judges and handlers are usually mounted.

But field trials have their sand lots too, and on these, as in baseball, the big majority get a chance to participate. In the parlance of field trial folk, such events are one-course trials, because in successive heats dogs must cover the same ground. It is necessary to plant birds for these, otherwise the first dogs down would have too great an advantage.

In all trials, regardless of the breeds tested, it is customary to work dogs in pairs, thus shortening the time required to give each dog a fair chance and reducing the number of birds needed. Each pair works a stretch of open country where the judges can observe their eagerness to hunt and their thoroughness. Then they are brought into the bird field where game is certain to be located.

This artificiality is not without its advantages. The spectator, without having to climb into a saddle to follow the judges, usually can find a vantage point to see the bird field and part of the course. He can also experience the thrill of the breakaway—the moment when the contestants, fresh and eager, are cast off. No race horse leaving the barrier is away with more drive than the good pointer or setter when his handler slips the leash and orders him out.

e Pointer makes a picture of frozen energy.
DAVID W. CORSON, A. DEVANEY

The sedentary spectator, of course, misses some things. Not for him is the beautiful picture of the smooth-gaited dog racing along, head high to catch the faint scent of a bird that may be hiding along a hedgerow. He cannot see the dog hesitate as it catches wind of a lark or possibly a rabbit, and then race on. A remarkable thing is the speed with which a good bird dog can distinguish between all other wild creatures and the game birds it seeks. To find a seasoned setter pointing a songbird would be unthinkable.

At the bird field the brace dashes into open view. The lead dog gets the scent and freezes to a point; his bracemate also freezes immediately—or commits the cardinal sin of ignoring his partner's find. They hold their point until the handler comes up, gets his command from the judges to flush the bird, and fires a blank pistol to test the dogs' steadiness to shot.

Excitement and tension run high. The

charged atmosphere communicates itself to the dogs and sometimes they break under the strain. Freeman Lloyd recalled such an episode during field trials at the Duke of Portland's estate in England. "A fine Pointer, Champion Saddleback, had been kept all day awaiting his turn," wrote Lloyd in the *National Geographic Magazine*. "For hours he had heard the men and the guns, and the air must have been full of scent.

"When at last Saddleback was 'put down,' a hare got up in front of him. Now in no case may a Pointer chase a hare, and the sight of one so far forgetting himself is enough to raise every eyebrow in the county. But as soon as Saddleback saw that hare, off he went as hard as he could run, disturbing game all over the place and finishing trials for that day. The assembled sportsmen commiserated with the owner as solemnly as if he had just had a death in the family."

A trial which utilizes a bird field cannot, of course, test the contenders as thoroughly as one held on a preserve large enough for the dogs to be put down in hour-long heats without covering the same ground. There they may range far before the cry "Point!" from the handler brings the mounted judges and gallery galloping up. The dog may have to hold his point for some time, severely trying steadiness and stamina as well as bird sense.

Just how long a bird dog will hold a point is a moot question. I saw an informal test out on Long Island. A setter, let out of her master's car for exercise,

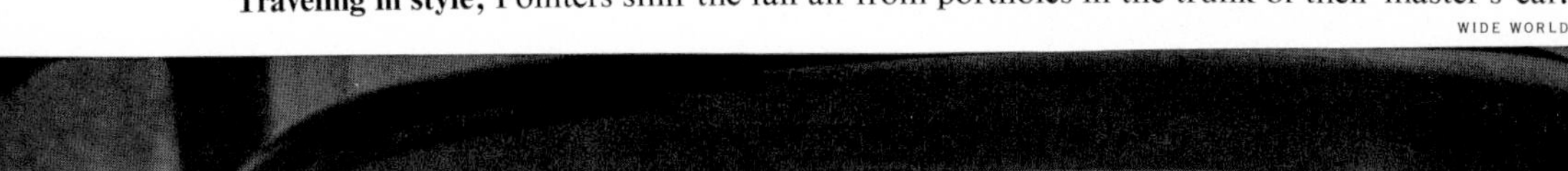

Traveling in style, Pointers sniff the fall air from portholes in the trunk of their master's car.
WIDE WORLD

KATHLEEN REVIS, NATIONAL GEOGRAPHIC PHOTOGRAPHER

Ready contestants, quartet of English Cockers arrives for spaniel field trials at Herrin, Illinois.

caught the scent of birds in a crate waiting to be taken out for planting. At once she froze to a point and refused to be distracted by dogs and men moving about her. At the urging of bystanders, her owner let her hold the point. She might have held it indefinitely, for she hadn't budged for minutes when her master decided she had had enough and called her to him. (There may be some truth in that old tale of the hunter who lost his Pointer and found him on the moors months later, a skeleton dog pointing a skeleton bird!)

This setter looked as if moths had been having a field day in her coat, and she would not have gotten a second look from a judge at a bench show. But there was no denying her proficiency in her own sphere of competition.

Performance, not beauty, is what counts most with the hunting fraternity. Take the case of Drudaig Bess, a diminutive English Cocker Spaniel certain to be ignored by anyone seeking an ideal specimen of her breed. But she was a most eager hunter. The minute the bird flushed she would sit erect on her haunches so she could mark its flight and fall. On the command to fetch she

Field trial badges studding their hat bands, sportsmen gather for spaniel trials at Crab Orchard Wildlife Refuge, Herrin, Illinois. It's crisp, early December and participants and spectators are keyed up at the sight of brilliant dogs in top form.

For several days the spaniels are put through their paces under conditions approximating an ordinary day's rough shoot adjoining water. In certain stakes English Springers may compete against Cockers and English Cockers, but not in championship stakes.

In advance of the trial the name of each dog is drawn and assigned a number which determines his order of running. The judges test two dogs simultaneously working parallel beats or run the dogs singly. After all have run, the judges call back selected dogs for further runs and water tests until they decide on the winners.

Eager contestant here is an English Cocker.

would be off like a flash and struggle back with a cock pheasant as big as she. One judge who placed her over a number of far more impressive-looking dogs explained, "She'd have my bag full before the others knew what it was all about. She's a hunting fool if I ever saw one."

Bess is gone now, but I can still see her in memory, sitting up, quivering with excitement, eyes sparkling as she watched the flight of her bird.

SPANIEL AND RETRIEVER TRIALS differ from pointer and setter trials in that the birds are shot and the dogs are required to bring them to hand. Also, the spaniels and retrievers are at all times under close control, while pointers and setters range far afield, gliding along hedgerows and freezing to a point when they find their quarry. Everybody walks at spaniel and retriever trials and spectators can get close enough to see the dogs in action.

While all trials have their special appeal, I admit partiality to spaniel trials, solely because they most closely approximate conditions encountered in a day's hunting. Although open to all spaniels but water spaniels, which are tested as retrievers, and the Brittany, which is tested like a pointer or setter, spaniel trials have become pretty well monopolized by the Springers.

For the type of cover found in upland hunting in the United States, the

Canine gallery of Cockers keeps a keen eye on the competition while waiting a turn to hunt.

KATHLEEN REVIS (OPPOSITE) AND VOLKMAR WENTZEL, NATIONAL GEOGRAPHIC PHOTOGRAPHERS

VOLKMAR WENTZEL AND (OPPOSITE LOWER) KATHLEEN REVIS, NATIONAL GEOGRAPHIC PHOTOGRAPHERS

A pheasant is flushed! The spaniel drops to mark its loud flight; his master takes hurried aim.

Back after a quick retrieve, the little Cock

bulkier Springer is regarded by many as a better bet than the Cocker. But fanciers of the latter breed maintain that the Cocker Spaniel, one of America's favorite house pets, can give a good account of himself in the field. He is best adapted for hunting woodcock, from which he takes his name. One of the best trial performers I ever saw was an English Cocker, a breed somewhat longer in leg and muzzle than his American cousin.

A veteran trial spaniel will quarter back and forth, covering a rectangular piece of ground approximately 50 yards in front and on either side of his handler. At his master's order he will plunge into an almost impenetrable wall of briers to get into a thicket where a bird might be hiding. When with cries of alarm and whirring wings a pheasant breaks into the air, the dog drops to mark its flight and fall. Then, on command, he will dash out and bring the bird back, the more gently mouthed the better.

A "hard mouth" is a serious mark against a spaniel or retriever.

As in all other trials, the spaniel must honor his bracemate's work, no matter what the temptation. He must remain steady even when, as I have seen happen, the bird shot for his bracemate falls not more than a dozen feet from his own nose. Occasionally a judge will order a severe test. The first dog has flushed a pheasant and the gun has brought it down in a nearby brush patch. The dog sits on his haunches, eagerly waiting for the word to fetch his prize. But the judge pointedly ignores him and gives the rival dog the cherished errand.

Imagine what is running through the first dog's head, what an urge to shuck off all his training and rush out to get the

roudly sits, holding the pheasant for his master to take.

Shooting over water calls for a well-trained spaniel or retriever quick to plunge in after fallen gam

bird! After all, it's his, isn't it? Didn't he sniff it out and flush it? What right has that other fellow to go after his bird?

But the true champion will hold his ground, fighting off temptation and swallowing his hurt pride with a show of self-discipline few men could match. This steadiness, as long as it does not arise from laziness, is a great attribute in a spaniel. The natural instinct—inherent in most dogs—is to pursue at once the bird he has flushed. The dog that breaks into a wild dash after a bird can strip the whole course of its game and leave it barren for the next contender. This is a cardinal sin in a field trial dog, yet I have seen the best of them commit it. I remember one time when a great Springer was so overwhelmed by the instinct to get his bird that he broke like a puppy. His crash into a clump of cover sent a big cock pheasant whirring. Up to then, his capture of the spaniel event of the year, at Fishers Island, New York, had seemed a cinch.

Nothing so tests a spaniel's merits as a bird which has been winged rather than killed and is able to run from the spot where it was brought down. This tests not only the dog but the handler's faith in him, since the handler ordinarily has no way of knowing that the bird is not where it landed. If he loses faith in his canine partner and tries to call the dog back to where he thinks the bird is, the retrieve may never be made.

I recall once when a pheasant was brought down in marsh grass near a road. A moment later, in sight of dog and handler, another bird scurried across the

"Fetch!" A Chesapeake Bay Retrieve

KATHLEEN REVIS, NATIONAL GEOGRAPHIC PHOTOGRAPHER, AND (BELOW) RALPH CRANE, BLACK STAR

'he handler directs the dog by hand, voice, or whistle signals in this water test at Herrin, Illinois.

road into the brush near where the pheasant fell. When the dog reached the spot, he scented the running bird, hesitated a moment, then started on toward the fall. Instead of letting him go, the handler turned him on the trail of the runner. Several times the dog tried to come back and each time he was ordered off.

Finally, the judges directed that he be taken up and the hunt proceeded down the road. There at the edge of the grass was the dead bird which the dog would have brought back quickly if the handler had not been sure he knew more about the situation than the dog did.

One of the most spectacular performances I ever watched developed out of the pursuit of a runner. A pheasant, flushed by a little black

aps into water, eager to get his duck.

English Cocker was brought down on a steep hillside. It had been winged but could run as fast as ever. The dog picked up the trail at the point of fall and began the chase. The pheasant zigzagged back and forth up the hill, wisely moving downwind away from the dog. At times the bird was not more than a dozen feet above the dog. If only he had looked up, he could not have missed seeing his prey. His friends on the gallery almost prayed that he would lift his eyes. But he was on the job, keen nose to the fresh track, not sight-seeing.

I would like to report that he made the retrieve. None doubted that he could have done it, but to meet the time schedule of the trial he was called up after the bird went over the hilltop and a gamekeeper was sent after it.

Since water may present a problem in any hunting, spaniel trials also have water tests to prove that a dog will not hesitate to enter water when necessary. As a shot is fired, a bird is thrown into the water and the dog ordered to retrieve. If he refuses to make the swim, he cannot qualify for a field title.

FOR RETRIEVERS, water tests play a far more important role. In the National Championship Retriever Trials, held early in December, land and water tests are evenly divided—five of each. But the straight water work, it always seems to me, shows the retrievers at their best. On a wintry day, when the spectators huddle in their warmest hunting clothes, it is thrilling to watch a good retriever unhesitatingly plunge into icy water after a brace of ducks.

The retriever is a canine specialist. His job is not to locate game but to bring it swiftly and gently to hand after it has been downed. When out duck hunting with his master he may lie for hours in the blind until the command "Fetch!" sends him leaping.

Ordinarily, one duck poses no problem. The dog marks it from the blind and goes directly to it. Getting a second is something else, especially if wind and tide have carried it away from the fall. Then the dog may have to swim a long way in a chop that breaks over his head, especially when returning upwind, duck in mouth. If the dog can deliver the bird smartly, shake himself, and wag his tail in pride at a job well done he is worthy of being classed with champions.

Since the dogs are not required to flush game, retriever trial judges enjoy broad latitude in planning tests.

An English Springer smartly delivers the good

KATHLEEN REVIS, NATIONAL GEOGRAPHIC PHOTOGRAPHER

They can direct how far ahead of the dogs and in what type of cover the birds are to be released and shot down by the expert "guns" for a land test, or how far out in the bay or stream for water work. Tests can be made progressively more difficult as competition narrows. In the final series of one national championship the judges ordered a triple retrieve—two ducks shot down in front of the decoys and a third dropped in high reeds about 150 yards away in the marsh. The sensation of that meet was the manner in which a Labrador marked and remembered the falls. With a minimum of direction he got all three with a speed and dash no one who saw him is likely to forget.

The dog with such a memory has an advantage over other competitors. But the dog lacking that faculty can offset it to some extent by the readiness with which he follows his handler's directions. While retrieving one bird a dog may lose its marking on another. Then it must rely on the man, turning at the sound of a whistle and promptly following the hand signals, left, right, or straight ahead, as the case may be.

The sportsman hunting waterfowl does not want to send his dog out continually, especially when birds are coming in fast. This has led to the inclusion in virtually every stake of at least one difficult "blind retrieve." For this, dead birds are planted and the dog is sent after them. In the course of such a test the retriever usually must cross one or more bodies of water and proceed some distance ashore. He has no way of knowing whether he is seeking a duck floating on a wind-whipped bay or a pheasant in the brush ashore, since there was

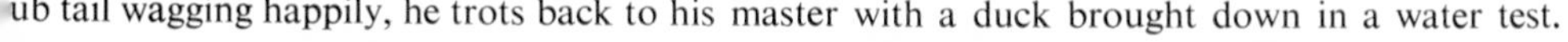

ub tail wagging happily, he trots back to his master with a duck brought down in a water test.

VOLKMAR WENTZEL, NATIONAL GEOGRAPHIC PHOTOGRAPHER

It won't be long now. Future Cocker champions store up the energy they'll need in the field.

no fall for him to mark. Under such conditions a dog that will not take direction readily from his handler is at a tremendous disadvantage.

There are tense moments for the handler and the spectators when a dog, forced to swim against wind and tide on such a search, circles uncertainly before he catches the handler's signal and plunges ahead to the opposite shore. Once a good retriever knows that this is a land instead of a water test, he casts about for the scent, since the cover usually makes further hand direction impossible. Then suspense mounts until the dog, bird in mouth, reappears on the far shore and plunges in to bring the game to hand.

With eager bounce, English Spring

Sometimes, since the best of gunners is not infallible, a duck will have been merely winged. This can work to the dog's advantage, since a moving bird is easier to spot than one floating dead. But the retriever is in for a race that can be both taxing and spectacular. I recall one contest in which the bird could swim and dive but not fly. It would go down as the dog was almost on it and then reappear behind or far to one side. It was a grueling contest for the dog, but he won. This is why conservationists contend that a dependable retriever should always be used when hunting waterfowl.

One of the great appeals of field trials is that participation need not involve much expense. Some sportsmen, of course, have invested huge sums in building up kennels of top dogs under the care of professionals. But they are few compared with those with one or two dogs they have bred and trained themselves.

The sensation at one autumn's spaniel trials was a Springer owned by a mechanic who had trained her in his own back yard. Unable to afford live birds on which to teach her retrieving, he schooled her on pigeons which, thanks to refrigeration, he could use over and over. After scoring impressive victories in the Midwest, he worked overtime at the factory to get the money for a trip east to compete in the big stakes. His reward was a beautiful collection of silver trophies, topped by the winning cup in the national amateur stake of the English Springer Spaniel Field Trial Association, the blue-ribbon event of spaniel competition held each autumn.

To be sure, this Cinderella touch is not encountered every day, but it happens often enough to emphasize the democracy of field trials. Hunting clothes in themselves are leveling, since weather-resisting qualities—rather than style or cut—are what interest their wearers. Then, too, at a trial, participants and members of the gallery have this in common: all are dog lovers, most are dog owners, and who can remain unimpressed at autumn's crimson glory?

In woods and fields the game birds are in proud plumage. All summer they have feasted, growing strong in body and power of wing, and they are cunning and wary. The dogs are eager; excitement pervades the fresh, crisp air. Little wonder so many of us love to watch these splendid animals compete against a background of russet and gold and the dark green of the conifers.

A Portfolio

Following are the sporting breeds, painted in full color for the National Geographic Magazine by Staff Artist Walter A. Weber and James Gordon Irving. Heights and weights show the range between the smallest average female and the largest average male.

paniels drive a pheasant whirring into air. Superior size and energy make them ideal all-round hunters.

WALTER A. WEBER

◀ *English Springer Spaniel*

IN AN ECSTASY OF SUPERLATIVES, the 17th century author of the *Art of Fowling* observes that "to search is the perfectest charracter of the most perfectest spaniel."

Whereas pointers and setters freeze, their task accomplished once game scent strikes their nostrils, the smaller spaniel pursues the scent to its ultimate source.

This unflagging zest for the search has given the English Springer Spaniel his very name. Bounding eagerly back and forth through underbrush and patches of cover, the Springer flushes—or, more graphically, springs—game out to the hunter.

Pheasant, ruffed grouse, and the lightning-fast woodcock are the principal objects of the Springer's dashing probes. If encouraged, the graceful brierhopper will forsake his breed's preoccupation with "anything that hath wings" long enough to scare out rabbits.

However, the dog's method of quartering after his game makes him most adept at hunting pheasant. Before taking flight this wily bird often zigzags along the ground in an attempt to divert the hunter's attention from its young. But the Springer's ceaseless questing leaves no square foot uncovered.

Once his startled quarry takes wing, the well-trained spaniel sits quietly through the crack of his master's firearm. Then, carefully marking the bird's fall, he awaits the command to fetch.

Retrieving is one of the Springer's most spectacular talents. A strong swimmer, he will plunge into the coldest stream without hesitation in pursuit of birds shot down over water. His toes are slightly webbed—as with his cousins, the water spaniels—enabling him to range swamps or tidal flats with assurance. His muscular neck bears with ease the quarry he carries in his jaws.

The English Springer, in short, is close to the ideal all-around bird dog. Alert in appearance, he has a broad, deep chest that bespeaks stamina. Powerful hindquarters combined with unusually long legs impart lunging speed. His glossy white coat, marked with liver, black, tan, roan, or liver-and-tan, is waterproof, weatherproof, and thornproof.

Although the English Springer was not recognized as a separate breed in his homeland until 1902, he has an ancient and honored lineage. First known mention of his name occurs in a book published in 1790, but a picture dating from 1637 shows a dog that mirrors the modern Springer in all essentials.

The spaniels—whose name derives from their supposed origin in Spain—were trained for the hunt in England and France almost 600 years ago. The Springer no doubt gained his first field experience working with Greyhounds, falcons, and huntsmen armed with nets. Since then, generations of sportsmen have lost their hearts to this "dogge of perfit and good sent . . . naturally addicted to the hunting of feathers."

The flop-eared, wistful-eyed Springer is a friendly companion whose gentle ways are a children's delight. More than a century before the discovery of America, Count Gaston de Foix neatly summed up the spaniel disposition: "They love their master well."

Shoulder height 18–21 in. Weight 40–50 lbs.

WALTER A. WEBER, NATIONAL GEOGRAPHIC STAFF ARTIST

Extra-heavy coat makes an all-weather spaniel of the Welsh Springer, rarely seen in America.

Welsh Springer Spaniel

THE ACTIVE, MERRY WELSH SPRINGER makes himself at home in many lands around the world, for he adjusts easily to a range of climates. This ability to endure extremes of temperature, coupled with his sturdy build and vigor, enables him to retrieve through cold waters, hunt long hours, and adapt to life indoors and out.

Midway in size between an English Cocker and an English Springer, the Welshman is solid, compact, and symmetrically shaped. He is clothed in a thick, straight silky coat colored the deep red-and-white that so readily distinguishes the breed. His red-and-white ancestors are recognizable in English sporting paintings from the 18th century. His ears are comparatively small, and taper toward the tip.

The Welsh Springer Spaniel is sometimes known simply as the Welsh Spaniel, and in his native country is often called a Starter. Built strictly for work, he is a relative stranger to the show bench.

Bred for centuries specifically for "springing" game in the rugged terrain of Wales and western England, the Welshman is a hardy, all-round gun dog. He finds no cover too difficult, no weather too severe. He is not only an able and versatile hunter but an excellent water dog and retriever as well.

The Welsh Springer also makes a good, sensible pet, convenient in size, companionable in personality. Gentle with children, he knows when to be a stern guard.

However even his disposition, the Welshman has an independent streak that makes him a bit hard to train. This is one reason he lags behind other spaniels in popularity and is seldom seen in the United States. But if taught early, he will learn well and remember faithfully.

Shoulder height about 17 in. Weight 35–45 lbs.

WALTER A. WEBER, NATIONAL GEOGRAPHIC STAFF ARTIST

Longer legs, longer muzzle give England's favorite an edge over his American cousin in the field.

English Cocker Spaniel

"HE LOVES ME BETTER than the sunlight without," wrote the immortal Elizabeth Barrett of her Cocker Spaniel Flush.

Miss Barrett quickly discovered the dog's loyalty, as did her suitor Robert Browning. Not once but twice Flush nipped the poet whose energetic presence shattered the Victorian tranquillity of the Barrett household.

The English Cocker traces his ancestry to a broad category of the parent strain known as field spaniels (the two other groups were water spaniels and toy spaniels). Smallest of these upland bird hunters, he gained the name "cocker" because of his skill in routing woodcocks out of dense cover.

The name is not mentioned in any publication prior to the late 18th century, but a spaniel resembling the modern English Cocker appears in a 17th century Van Dyck portrait of the Prince and Princess of Wales.

The English Cocker is taller, stronger, and longer of leg than his American-bred cousin. His head, shaped somewhat like a setter's, features a long muzzle, enabling him to cope with the largest game birds. No member of the breed is able to qualify as a bench champion in England without first displaying skill in a field trial.

The dog's intelligence and warm response to affection catapulted him into first place in popularity in recent years among all breeds in his homeland. The British so forsake their customary reserve where he is concerned that one firm even elected its Cocker watchdog to the board of directors; his right front paw mark appears on contracts.

The American Kennel Club did not recognize him as a separate breed until 1946, but already the hard-working import has made a name in field trial competition and won a legion of admirers on this side of the Atlantic. *Shoulder height 15–17 in. Weight 26–34 lbs.*

Cocker Spaniel ▶

CITY COUSIN to the English Cocker Spaniel is the apartment-sized American Cocker. The smaller dog's effervescent personality as pet and his achievements in show ring and field made him the United States' most popular breed for a record 17 years, until overtaken by the Beagle in 1953.

The affectionate, flop-eared Cocker ingratiates himself with every member of the household. Active by nature, he particularly loves to romp with children. The playful little dog does not accede to full spaniel dignity until relatively late in life.

This versatile dog's roots go back to the Spanyell mentioned in England as early as 1386. But it was not until around 1870 that Britain's breeders began to develop the Cocker strain in its modern conformation. Both English and American breeds are named for their ability to plunge into heavy cover to flush woodcocks.

American breeders, with an eye on the show ring and pet marts, have since shaped their Cocker into a more compact, heavier-coated version of his English prototype, with more luxuriant feathering.

Distinguishing the American dog are a squarer head and muzzle, and somewhat shorter legs. He has also developed a larger eye that adds much to his appealing expression. However, the Cocker still retains all the hard muscles needed for field work.

The color of his soft, dense coat may be black, red, liver, or lemon; or any of these combined with white. Ideally, the colors should be clear and pronounced, rather than washed-out in appearance.

In his drive to the top of the pet parade, the American Cocker proved unusually adaptable to the whims and professions of his 20th century masters.

Chota Peg, a tan Cocker owned by the skipper of the *S. S. United States* logged 13 years and 2,000,000 nautical miles at sea. Another Cocker, Sergeant Bode, hit the silk 16 times with his paratrooper master—convincing proof that his breed is at home in the air as well as on land and sea.

While the American Cocker has made his mark primarily as a pet, he still possesses a proud hunting heritage. A minimum of competent training can transform virtually any member of the breed into an accomplished sporting dog.

Like the English Cocker—who has never forsaken farm and field—the little gamester excels both in flushing and retrieving birds. The Cocker's comportment in the field is all exuberance, and he shows his delight in his work by the incessant, enthusiastic wagging of his tail.

The amazing case of Prince Tom III, first member of the American breed ever to win the National Field Trial Championship, vividly illustrates the Cocker's inbred affinity for the hunt. Prince began life as a house pet, with at least four generations of pet stock behind him, and was three years old before he flushed his first bird. The astonishing dog received no professional field training of any kind, and was handled in his championship effort by his master, a non-hunter.

Shoulder height 14–15½ in. Weight 22–28 lbs.

Friendly American Cockers, smallest of sporting spaniels, have long been United States favorites.

◀Ideal family pets, these lively little dogs seldom see enough of the field work they enjoy so much.

WALTER A. WEBER, NATIONAL GEOGRAPHIC STAFF ARTIST

Sussex Spaniels, built close to the ground, are hardy hunters, but often bark when on the scent.

Sussex Spaniel

THE STOCKY LITTLE SUSSEX sports a rich golden liver coat that distinguishes him from all other spaniels. It is also a sign of the breed's purity, for a darker liver denotes a recent cross with the Field Spaniel, a similar breed.

He also differs from his cousins in his inclination to "speak" while hunting, a most unspaniel-like quality. But while field judges may frown on this houndlike tendency to give tongue, it has proved an advantage in the heavy cover he was bred to hunt.

The Sussex was developed in the late 18th century to suit the special conditions of the county in southeast England from which he takes his name. An abundance of game concealed in dense hedgerows and woods choked with undergrowth called for a powerful, short-legged dog that worked his ground carefully not far ahead of the gun. And here the low-slung Sussex admirably fills the bill.

He hunts close to earth, tramping under and pushing through cover rather than leaping and scurrying about like the faster-paced spaniels. His ringing bark lets the sportsman know where the dog is working.

Exhibited at England's first dog show in 1859, the Sussex was also one of the first breeds to be recognized by the American Kennel Club.

Keen of nose, and a sensible, hard-working companion for the upland game hunter, he makes a first-rate retriever. Even so, the Sussex has yet to make his mark in the United States, where his chunky build slows him in the hunt and his bark when on the scent is considered a serious fault in bird work.

But the Sussex has won support from those who have come to know his cheerful disposition. He makes a fine pet and an excellent choice for children.

Shoulder height 14–16 in. Weight 35–45 lbs.

Clumber Spaniel

ONE DAY IN THE 1760's the Duke of Noailles, in France, presented to his friend the Duke of Newcastle several large spaniels he had bred to high hunting skill. Newcastle kenneled them at Clumber Park, his English country estate, and there developed the dogs that were to become one of England's notable breeds.

Spaniels from Clumber began to make their appearance on the pheasant-shooting estates of persons of highest rank. A royal favorite through several reigns, the Clumber became known as the "aristocrat of the spaniel family."

The breed was long hunted in teams. Ten or more Clumbers working abreast, like an advancing line of soldiers, made an impressive sight. The dogs, steady and not too fast for the following guns, would find every head of game, feather or fur, and push it out without giving tongue. They would drop in unison at the sound of wing or shot, the Clumber nearest the fallen game retrieved it, and the field would move on in military array.

First brought to America by British regimental officers in Canada's Maritime Provinces, the slow-moving Clumber has yet to achieve wide popularity in the New World.

With long body and short, strong legs, the Clumber is to the spaniels what the Basset is to the hounds. Only an inch or two taller than our familiar little Cocker, he will weigh as much as 40 pounds more!

Heaviest of land spaniels, the Clumber is nevertheless full of movement, with the merry tail carriage of the good-tempered dog. He is easily trained and has a keen nose for game birds. He also makes a gentle, affectionate pet. His straight, silky coat is white, with small lemon-colored markings about the head.

Shoulder height 16–20 in. Weight 35–65 lbs.

An English name belies the French origin of the sedate Clumber Spaniel, heaviest of land spaniels.

WALTER A. WEBER

Field Spaniel

THE WHIMS OF FASHION once dealt the Field Spaniel a body blow, but the sturdy dog has bounded back in splendid form.

He was developed for hunting in heavy cover. Welsh Cocker stock was crossed with the Sussex Spaniel to produce a heavier, more powerful version of the Cocker. Sportsmen began to take to the new breed.

Then late Victorian exhibitors remade him as a show dog with long body and short legs. Specimens of exaggerated length and lowness brought high prices. Sportsmen scathingly dubbed them "caterpillar dogs" and turned to other breeds.

Fortunately the breeding style changed markedly after World War I and the Field Spaniel became longer in leg, more compact in body. Today he is a well-proportioned hunting companion and an able retriever from land or water. Some fanciers consider him the perfect combination of beauty and utility. And with his silken coat, "even as the sheen on the raven's wing," he is indeed a most attractive fellow.

Not as flashy a field trial performer as the Springer or the Cocker, the Field is nevertheless a dependable worker. He can take rough workouts and has the brawn to break through heavy brush, yet is small and agile enough to weave under shrubbery to flush game. He deserves a wider public.

Shoulder height about 18 in. Weight 35–50 lbs.

Brittany Spaniel ▶

FROM FRANCE'S PROVINCE OF BRITTANY comes this distinctive spaniel to win the hearts of American sportsmen. The Brittany is a spaniel with a difference. While other spaniels flush their game, he chooses to point his like a setter. And he further departs from spaniel custom by being born with just a stub of a tail, if any at all.

Relatively new to America, his is one of Europe's oldest hunting breeds. His ancestors ranged the Breton coast of France, some say, in early medieval times. Doubtless he stems from the same Spanish breeds that gave us England's spaniels. But he was bred longer in leg, and his hunting style anticipated that of the setters; he may even have shared ancestry with the Irish Setter.

The first tailless Brittany was born in the Breton village of Pontou less than 150 years ago. So expert a hunter was he that his owner used him to found a tailless or stub-tailed strain.

Many years of inbreeding caused the line to degenerate. But around the turn of the century a French sportsman, Arthur Enaud, introduced the blood of French and Italian pointers to restore the breed to the vigor and excellence of its Breton ancestors.

Today's agile, long-limbed Brittany wears a dense white coat, marked with orange or liver. The flat or wavy hair is never silky, as with other spaniels. Looseness of the skin prevents injury by brier or thorn.

In the short decades since this unusual pointing spaniel made his United States debut he has created a fine reputation in the field, on the bench, and in the home.

Height $17\frac{1}{2}$–$20\frac{1}{2}$ in. Weight 30–40 lbs.

he Field Spaniel, big brother to the Cocker, is ıilt to work heavy cover. Usually black, his ɜek coat is sometimes liver, mahogany, or roan.

Rangy Brittany Spaniels are hunters' favorites in New England and French Canada. ▶

WALTER A. WEBER, NATIONAL GEOGRAPHIC STAFF ARTIST

WALTER A. WEBER

Irish Water Spaniel

WHEN AN IRISH WATER SPANIEL comes up to you for the first time, you'll probably smile, for he looks as though everything he has on was borrowed from friends. He has the Afghan's flowing topknot, the curly coat of the old English "water dogge," the Pointer's clean cheeks and tapered tail, and the ears and gait of a large Poodle.

Yet he is an old-line spaniel whose ancestry, like that of his land spaniel cousins, goes back to the Iberian Peninsula. For centuries there have been close ties between Spain and Ireland and the Irish Water Spaniel's basic makeup (largely from the Portuguese Water Dog, some authorities believe) has probably been long established.

The breed's known history begins in the early 19th century with the work of Mr. Justin McCarthy, who developed the wholly liver-colored "south country" strain. The breed has changed so little that the description McCarthy wrote a hundred years ago still fits accurately:

"The head should be crowned with a well-defined topknot, not straggling across like that of the common rough water dog, but coming down in a peak on the forehead. The body should be covered with small, crisp curls which often become clogged in the moulting season. The tail should be round without feather underneath, rather short, and as stiff as a ramrod; the color a pure puce liver without any white."

Across the Irish Sea in England the Irish Water Spaniel has never achieved popularity. But on the other side of the Atlantic he has become firmly established, particularly in the southern United States. He is seen both in the field and at shows.

The Irish Water Spaniel is a powerful swimmer and his coat offers protection from the coldest water. Some use him as a land spaniel, but his size (he is tallest of spaniels) slows him in brier and thicket. Give him a marsh or tidal flat and a chance to plunge in after a downed duck and your Irish Water Spaniel will be in his glory.

Shoulder height 21–24 in. Weight 45–65 lbs.

American Water Spaniel

EQUALLY AT HOME in the water is a rural American of obscure origin, recognized today as the American Water Spaniel. One of the few dogs of purely American development, he achieved popularity as an all-round hunting dog shortly after the Civil War, especially in the Midwest, where he has been bred true for generations.

This hardy, versatile dog flushes game from marsh or upland thicket, and as a retriever he has few peers. In densest brush and through icy river currents he swiftly and surely seeks out fallen game—rabbit or quail, ruffed grouse, pheasant, or duck.

Shorter and about 20 pounds lighter than his Irish cousin, he looks a good deal more spaniel-like. His dense, protective coat is less tightly curled and is smooth on head and legs; its color ranges from dark chocolate to liver. The almost constant motion of his feathered tail signals his cheery disposition. Always a hard-working field dog, he did not make his show debut until 1940.

Here is a well-proportioned, handsome dog, an enthusiastic and thorough hunter, and a most agreeable family dog and guardian.

Shoulder height 15–18 in. Weight 25–40 lbs.

WALTER A. WEBER, NATIONAL GEOGRAPHIC STAFF ARTIST

Clown of the spaniel family, the topknotted Irish Water Spaniel is nevertheless a serious and efficient worker. His American cousin (lower) is somewhat smaller, with feathered legs and tail. Developed for all-round hunting, he is one of the few dogs of American origin.

Rigid point of keen-nosed English Setters alerts ▸

English Setter

THE ENGLISH SETTER is one of the world's most beautiful purebred dogs, and his beauty is more than skin deep. From the finely chiseled head to the tip of the feathered tail, every line reflects grace and intelligence. His gentle dignity bears witness to a lovable disposition and aristocratic lineage.

For four hundred years or more such dogs have been valuable hunting companions. Long before the day of the shotgun the ancestors of our English Setters, known as "setting spaniels," were spotting game birds for hunters with nets. The dogs were taught to approach quietly and "set"—sit or crouch—while the net was dropped over the birds.

Later these "setting spaniels" were trained to point as gun dogs do today. Some Spanish

WALTER A. WEBER, NATIONAL GEOGRAPHIC STAFF ARTIST

ɹnter to quail camouflaged in covert (lower right).

or English Pointer blood may have been introduced at that time to create a rangier dog for working open fields and to increase the pointing instinct. In any event, the setters became distinguishable from the spaniels by their taller, leaner proportions, longer heads, and plumed tails.

A born hunter, the English Setter is a dependable shooting dog under all conditions of terrain and climate, though in hot climes a shorter-coated dog might be preferred. In bird-dog field trials the English Setter is always among the most popular entrants. His performance is best when training has not been hurried or forced. Once a setter learns a lesson he is not apt to forget or disregard it.

Two men were instrumental in bringing the English Setter to the height of his beauty and hunting ability. One was Edward Laverack, an Englishman who began his work on the breed in 1825 with a brace of setters whose strain had apparently been kept pure for some 35 years. The other was his Welsh friend R. L. Purcell-Llewellin, who crossed other English Setter strains with those of Laverack.

The Laverack type is generally preferred for the exhibition ring, the lighter-built and racier Llewellin for hunting.

Physically, the English Setter has changed little in the last hundred years. Performance is such a necessary foundation for appearance that the setters will probably never deviate widely from the present standard. They are built much like a Pointer, except that they lack the springy arched legs and back, being more careful but less rapid workers than these rangers of the open fields. Viewed from front or back, the stifle is straight, not free and turned out.

The setter is a one-man dog, admiration for his master showing in his expressive and intelligent eyes. His forehead is broad and his hair is long, fine, and nearly straight, with a full feather along the back of the legs and the lower side of the tail. The body ground color of the English Setter is white with black, lemon, liver, or orange; or has black, white, and tan markings distributed in flecks. Heavy markings are not considered desirable for show purposes.

Under his soft and silky coat the setter should be hard, finely muscled, and compact. None should be allowed to get fat and lazy, as they so often become in the hands of indulgent owners. No dog has a more wheedling way with him, and it takes a firm nature to withstand his wiles.

Shoulder height 23–26 in. Weight 50–70 lbs.

Beauty and brains mark the silky-haired Irish Setter, alert hunt of upland game birds. Often bred just for show, he is a popular co tender in the ring. Gentle, cheery disposition makes him a perfect pe

WALTER A. WEBER, NATIONAL GEOGRAPHIC STAFF ART

Irish Setter

HAPPY-GO-LUCKY, loyal, and likable, the red Irishman is blessed with a winning personality as well as good looks and abounding vitality. In the field, where his job often demands toughness, endurance, and courage, he is not found wanting, yet he makes the most gentle and affectionate of companions. He lives to a ripe old age.

Mystery surrounds the Irish Setter's origin. Some say the breed was developed by crossing an Irish Water Spaniel with an Irish Terrier. More common is the belief that it sprang from a combination of spaniels, pointers, English and Gordon Setters.

Many of the first Irish Setters were not red but white with red markings. Prizes still are offered in Ireland for white-and-red-marked setters, but such dogs are few. The rangy, silky-haired, mahogany setter we know first appeared early in the 19th century. He was known as the "red spaniel," in Gaelic, *madradh ruadh* (red dog).

When paraded at shows in the United States and the British Isles, no dog is received with more acclaim by the audience than a champion Irish Setter, in which canine beauty reaches its peak. Yet this enthusiasm is aroused not only by the rich and shining glory of his coat—like a ripe chestnut fresh from the bur—but by the spirited way the aristocratic red-coat strides around the arena. He steps like a drum major, carries his head high, and pulls his handler along. The public likes action and gets it when an Irish Setter is on the move.

The Irish Setter is more finely drawn and usually higher at the shoulder than the English or the Gordon Setter. He is slim and fast, long legged, and has the sloping shoulders—and sensitivity—of a Thoroughbred race horse. Since Irish Setters are highstrung and often temperamental, they require more patient training than do some other breeds. Nevertheless, they are born field dogs, found wherever the shotgun is carried.

The Irish Setter should be allowed to develop naturally until he is mature enough to understand his trainer's aims; this may be as young as six months or as old as 18 months. He should never be crowded, and necessary punishment should be administered in small doses; harsh treatment may break his spirit and kill his desire to hunt. His first love is his master's companionship, not finding birds, and when treated as a close friend he is easy to control.

Breeders are trying to correct the Irish Setter's tendency to point with lower tail than the English Setter or the Pointer. The Irish can't match these two breeds in dash on breakaway or extreme range, but he covers his more restricted territory thoroughly and always works to the gun. In autumn woods abounding in russet browns and deep shadows the dark coat that makes him so beautiful is a disadvantage, for he is sometimes harder to see than the white breeds.

The rich golden chestnut color should have no trace of black. White on chest, throat, or toes, a small star on the forehead, or a narrow streak or blaze on nose or face should not disqualify.

Shoulder height 25-27 in. Weight 60-70 lbs.

Gordon Setter

A NATIVE SCOT, the handsome black-and-tan Gordon Setter is as gifted as he is good-looking. He is eager to work hard and long for his master, has good bird sense and memory. And what a joy he is to watch as he quarters the field, tail wagging gaily!

Tradition says that nearly two centuries ago the Duke of Gordon heard of a Highland shepherd's dog which was remarkably successful in finding game, and he crossed this black-and-tan Collie with the setters at Gordon Castle. Whether the breed actually started then or had already developed from the "black and fallow setting dog" described as early as 1620, the Gordon Setters established themselves as hunters of red grouse in the heathery uplands.

In 1842 George Blunt brought Rake and Rachel, bred at Gordon Castle, to America. They were white with black-and-tan markings, in contrast to present-day Gordons, which are coal black marked with tan. Mr. Blunt gave Rachel to his friend Daniel Webster and presented one of the puppies bred from the pair to Henry Clay. In accepting it, Clay wrote from Washington, D.C.:

"I have no great attachment for dogs, because they kill sheep, but some of my family like them better, and I sometimes overcome my repugnance to them, and get attracted by their fidelity. If it should be convenient to send the one you offer me to William A. Bradley, Esq., of this city, I will carry her with pleasure to Ashland, and thank you for her. If convenient she ought to be here by this day week. I am truly and faithfully yours, H. Clay."

This Gordon evidently won his stubborn heart. She or a setter very much like her appears in a portrait of Mr. Clay.

In the middle eighties a lighter, more finely built type of Gordon Setter arrived in the United States. More active than the older Gordon, it proved an excellent hunting as well as show dog. Today no distinction is made between field and show types, and the official breed standard still allows considerable range in size to suit sportsmen in various parts of the country.

A slow but sure hunter, the Gordon can handle heavy cover and is especially good on ruffed grouse and woodcock. He has the nose and brains, a temperament for training, and is easily broken to retrieve. Breeders are seeking to develop greater range and speed in the Gordon while maintaining his dependable bird-finding ways.

Loyalty is the Gordon's most endearing quality. He lives for his master, a devotion which makes him a responsive gun dog as well as an eager-to-please pet. He gets along splendidly with children. Wary of intruders, he will have occasional run-ins with other dogs as a result of his guarding his family jealously.

Slightly heavier than the two other setters, the Gordon resembles the English Setter in build: wide across the forehead, deep in the chest, sturdy, well muscled, with plenty of bone and stamina. The characteristic mahogany markings on his shiny black coat are above the eyes, on chops, ear linings, chest, belly, legs, and feather.

Shoulder height 23–27 in. Weight 45–80 lbs.

WALTER A. WEBER, NATIONAL GEOGRAPHIC STAFF ARTIST

Rugged as their native Scottish moors, Gordon Setters were named for the Duke of Gordon, reputed to have developed the breed from setter and Collie blood. Dependable companion in field or home, the soft- and silky-coated Gordon is gentle with children and "a most pettable dog."

Pointers (above) hunt with speed and steadiness, ra

Pointer

WITH NOSE AQUIVER and every muscle taut, the Pointer eagerly anticipates the whir of partridge wings, the shot, and his master's command. A first-rate bird dog, the Pointer is built on lines that suggest his speed and superlative staying powers.

His forebears, which appeared in England about 1650, were used to locate hares for Greyhounds to chase. Early in the 18th century, when wing shooting grew popular, the "shorthair" gave up his supporting role and became star of the bird-hunting show.

English sportsmen had tried blending in the old Spanish Pointer with its strong pointing instinct, but this strain proved too slow. Crosses of English Foxhound, Bloodhound, and Greyhound created a fast dog that carried its head high to seek scent from the air as well as the ground. Later, setter blood was introduced.

So widely distributed is the English Pointer now that the "English" has been dropped; he is known simply as "Pointer."

What Westminster is to the show dog the National Bird Dog Championship Trials held annually since 1896 in Grand Junction, Tennessee, are to the field dog, the Pointer in particular. A dog must run three hours and finish as strongly as he started. He must exhibit speed, eagerness to hunt, bird sense, and constant attention and obedience to commands. These may be whistled or yelled from as much as a mile away. When birds are found, the dog must display style and

WALTER A. WEBER, NATIONAL GEOGRAPHIC STAFF ARTIST

JAMES GORDON IRVING

wider afield than smaller Vizsla (right).

steadiness on point, good gun manners, and readiness to back his bracemate. In all these the Pointer excels; no finer upland bird dog exists.

The Pointer has long been bred for show as well as field ability. His short-haired coat shows off his lithe, muscular conformation in the ring. Its smart white color, marked with liver, lemon, or black, is easy for the hunter to follow.

Gentle in disposition, he makes an ideal family pet. *Shoulder height 24–27 in. Weight 50–70 lbs.*

Vizsla

ANCESTORS of this light-footed upland bird dog loped into history as the companion-hunters of Magyar hordes that swarmed onto the plains of Hungary 1,000 years ago. Tenth century stone etchings depict the huntsman with his falcon and a dog that resembles the Vizsla.

Down the centuries Hungarian warlords and nobles developed the Vizsla (the name stems from a word meaning "to examine") into a close-working dog, keen of nose and expert at pointing and retrieving. Through two world wars he narrowly escaped extinction. In 1945 Hungarian refugees spread the breed throughout Europe. In 1960 the American Kennel Club admitted it to registry.

This powerfully built aristocrat wears a short, smooth, rusty-gold coat that has not changed in 500 years. Because of it he is often called the Yellow Pointer. He is a robust hunter and an affectionate, fearless friend.
Shoulder height 21–24 in. Weight 35–55 lbs.

Fine hunters, the Weimaraner and the Short-haire

Weimaraner

FROM HIS BLUE OR AMBER EYES to his sleek and lustrous coat, from his stern ducal past to his sudden popular favor, everything about the "Gray Ghost" is amazing.

Nobles of the Court of Weimar developed this versatile sporting dog for their Thuringian game preserves. Chief contributor to his hunting skill was the old Schweisshund, a solid-red Bloodhound.

The Weimaraner first stalked deer, bear, and the savage wild boar. When big game grew scarce in Germany, he took to pointing and retrieving birds. He reached his present refinement in the early 1800's but was so closely held he was long unknown outside his native duchy.

Master of the Weimaraner's fate was an exclusive club of sportsmen-owners who followed rigid rules. Only dogs which met highest standards were bred, and only their choicest offspring were kept. "Breed wardens" traveled over the land decreeing which puppies should be destroyed.

Owners were limited to three or four of the breed at a time. Weimaraners were not entered at bench shows or field trials, and three club members voting "No" would prevent any outsider from acquiring one.

In 1929, Howard Knight, a sportsman from Providence, Rhode Island, was admitted into the German club, and for the first time Weimaraners came into Yankee

WALTER A. WEBER, NATIONAL GEOGRAPHIC STAFF ARTIST

•inter came to America from Germany.

hands. The brace he brought to this country and the six he later imported became the foundation stock of the carefully controlled breed in America.

Gaining American Kennel Club recognition in 1943, the exotic silver-tinged hunter has surged up the ladder of popularity. Dwight D. Eisenhower's Weimaraner Heidi was the first canine in the White House since Franklin D. Roosevelt's Scottie Fala.

Keen scent and intelligence make training easy for the powerful, rangy uplander. He matures early, and is also a gentle pet. Kennel life wounds his dignity, for he is a proud and home-loving family dog.

Shoulder height 23–27 in. Weight 55–75 lbs.

German Short-haired Pointer

"BIRD DOG BY DAY and houn' dog by night" is one apt way American fanciers have described this versatile breed from Germany.

The extremely useful Short-hair stems from a cross of the old German Pointer with the English Pointer.

The old German Pointer came from Spanish Pointers brought into Germany some 300 years ago. The Germans crossed them with Bloodhounds to get a hunting dog that could point birds in daylight and track animals in the dark.

The English, on the other hand, crossed the Spanish breed with Foxhounds and even Greyhounds to give their Pointer speed.

In the late 19th century, Continental sportsmen cast envious eyes on the speed and dash of the Pointer in American field trials and began to breed their German Pointer with his flashier English cousin. They would produce, they reasoned, a faster dog for bird-shooting that would still retain his keen nose and hound voice, or tongue, for night hunting.

The resulting Short-hair is still not a speedy dog, and is seldom seen in open field competition with Pointers and setters in the United States. But he works his ground carefully, and his all-round ability and common sense have won him a respected role, especially in the Midwestern States. He not only points and tracks but retrieves from land or water. Webbed feet and water-repellent coat make him a favorite with waterfowl hunters in the Great Lakes region.

Color and docked tail distinguish this attractive, tractable breed from the Pointer. The flat, hard coat is solid liver, or liver and white, spotted and ticked.

Shoulder height 21–25 in. Weight 45–70 lbs.

JAMES GORDON IRVING

German Wire-haired Pointer learns quickly, may prove adept at pointing at one year of age.

German Wire-haired Pointer

RUGGED best describes this German import, with his tough, armorlike coat and a constitution to match.

One of the younger breeds of pointers, he developed as a distinct form beginning in the mid-1800's. German breeders and trainers had become impatient with specialized gun dogs. They determined to create an all-purpose hunter hardy enough to pursue any kind of game on any type of terrain, even to fetch waterfowl from the frigid North Sea.

Blends of Pointer, Foxhound, and Poodle produced their ideal: the *Deutsch-Drahthaar*, a sturdy, courageous animal of superior nose that not only pointed birds but retrieved from land or water with equal enthusiasm. He also proved dependable on four-footed game.

Brought to America in 1920, the breed won special favor in the Midwest. In 1959 it gained American Kennel Club recognition.

A great asset to the Wire-hair is his remarkable double coat. An outer layer of wire hair (*drahthaar*)—straight, coarse, and 1½ to 2 inches long—lies flat and shields him from the cruelest brush. In fall and winter a dense, soft undercoat insulates him from the cold. Bushy brows and whiskers protect eyes and face.

Color varies from liver and white to liver roan and solid liver. The brown head may sport a white blaze. The tail is docked.

Energetic and intelligent, the Wire-hair may seem aloof but often exhibits clownish ways. One of these pointers reportedly runs in front of any camera she sees, sits down, and waits to be photographed!

Shoulder height 22–26 in. Weight 55–70 lbs.

WALTER A. WEBER, NATIONAL GEOGRAPHIC STAFF ARTIST

Wire-haired Pointing Griffon, developed by a Dutch banker's son, sports a short bristly coat.

Wire-haired Pointing Griffon

THE CREATION of this striking dog caused a father and son to quarrel. In 1874 young E. K. Korthals deliberately set out to produce a new sporting breed. His preoccupation so displeased his banker father that he was obliged to leave his Netherlands home.

Moving to Germany and then to France, he continued to experiment. He traveled extensively, taking every opportunity to extol the virtues of his Griffon. His enthusiasm over the breed generated wide interest, especially in France, where it became known as the Korthal's Griffon.

What the banker's son finally produced was a distinctive and useful gun dog. It proved to be an able pointer and retriever possessed of a first-class nose. This is not surprising, since blood of the Otterhound, setter, pointer, and some larger spaniels is believed to have been added to the basic rough-coated Griffon stock.

As a wide-ranging dog for quail, Hungarian partridge, and other outlying game, the heavy-set Griffon is more deliberate than the Pointer or setter. His best talents lie elsewhere—as a strong swimmer and fine water retriever. Here his unkempt coat, "harsh like the bristles of a wild boar," stands him in good stead. It well adapts him for rigorous winter duck hunting in marsh country.

Mixed colors of this bushy-browed exotic are steel gray, gray white, and chestnut—never black. The nose is always brown. The unplumed tail is generally cut to a third its natural length.

Although the breed came to America in 1900, it is seldom seen in the United States. *Height 19½–23½ in. Weight 50–65 lbs.*

Golden Retriever

FROM THE WARM COLOR of his coat to his broad and sensitive face, every aspect of this dog reflects his gentle and friendly disposition. But good looks and winning personality do not detract from his efficiency in the field. He has proved as hardy as any other retriever or large spaniel, even retrieving ducks during bitter Canadian winters.

The Golden appeared in his present form in England in the 1860's, although his lineage is in dispute. The prevalent story is that Sir Dudley Marjoribanks (later Lord Tweedmouth) so admired a troupe of Russian performing dogs that he bought the lot.

These big taffy-colored dogs were of a breed renowned for independence and intelligence and used in the Caucasus for tending sheep. Lord Tweedmouth, to reduce their size and increase the sense of smell, reportedly crossed them with Bloodhounds.

Not true, cry the dissenters. Lord Tweedmouth purchased a yellow puppy, the only one of a litter of black, wavy-haired retrievers. He later got another of these rare pups and, by selective mating, established the breed.

In any event the Golden Retriever first appeared in America in the early 1900's and has risen in popularity here since the 1930's.

His water-resistant coat is flat or wavy and golden in color. At home as a retriever on land or in water, he is equally at home as a member of the household. Of all retrievers the Golden is most often a family pet. *Shoulder height $21\frac{1}{2}$–24 in. Weight 60–75 lbs.*

Golden Retriever is hardy and expert in the field, affectionate and companionable in the home.

WALTER A. WEBER, NATIONAL GEOGRAPHIC STAFF ARTIST

A powerful and eager swimmer, the Chesapeake Bay Retriever has webbed feet and waterproof coat.

Chesapeake Bay Retriever

IN 1807 the American ship *Canton* met a brig flying the British flag off the coast of Maryland. The latter, outbound from Newfoundland, had been driven off course by storms and was foundering. Quick action by the Americans saved captain and crew.

Also rescued were two pups. The male—destined to be the Adam of a new breed—was liver colored; the female was black.

The progeny of stock introduced into Newfoundland long before by fishermen, probably from Spain, the puppies were presented to his American rescuers by the grateful master of the abandoned brig. Tractable, they developed into just the sort of dog needed for duck shooting along the shores of Chesapeake Bay.

Bred with local Maryland dogs, and perhaps with each other, Sailor and Canton produced a race of fearless retrievers. By 1885 a clearly distinguishable type had emerged, known for its skill and stamina working the wintry tidal flats of the bay. In those days a dog might be called on to retrieve 300 ducks in a single day!

A capable retriever of upland game as well, the Chesapeake today is popular among hunters throughout the United States, Canada, and Britain. His reddish-tan or dead-grass color is of marked advantage. It blends with marshland cover and shields him from the eyes of ever-wary wild fowl.

The Chesapeake loves to go swimming on his own accord. One dog insisted on retrieving his master's young daughter by gripping her bathing suit when he thought she was going into water too deep.

Shoulder height 21–26 in. Weight 55–75 lbs.

Labrador Retriever

NO ONE SEEMS TO KNOW just how the Labrador got his name, but one thing is sure: this powerful, short-haired retriever came not from Labrador but from Newfoundland.

There he was generally known as the St. John's dog, to distinguish him from the somewhat larger Newfoundland. His only known connection with Labrador is that the fishing boats which first brought him to England in the early 1800's often carried catches from the cod banks off that bleak and desolate coast.

For some 300 years before this, Basque and Portuguese fishermen had frequented the Newfoundland and Labrador banks. Canine salts who shipped with these adventurous sailors earned their keep. A powerful swimming dog could sometimes retrieve a dropped cod or broken nets or tackle. This same dog could help a shore party hunting wild fowl for meat.

It was only natural that Newfoundland settlers should keep and refine this excellent dog, and that the rigorous task of retrieving waterfowl in a climate so severe should produce a robust breed.

In England the Labrador's excellence as a sporting dog was soon recognized. "Their sense of smell is scarcely to be credited," wrote the British sportsman, Colonel Hawker, in 1830, "and their discrimination of scent in following a wounded pheasant through a whole covert full of game, or a pinioned wild fowl through a furze brake or a warren of rabbits, appears almost impossible."

In this respect the Labrador has changed not a bit. His scenting powers now are as phenomenal as they were then.

The Labrador is shorter of leg than other retrievers, and generally more solidly built. Nevertheless, he is a very agile performer on land or in water.

The alert and friendly breed can be trained to follow the most complicated signals by hand or whistle. Generally, he is kept only for retrieving, as he is considered too high at the shoulder and too bulky in body to enter readily dense coverts or thickets that a spaniel could penetrate with ease. But the Labrador is also used as a rough all-round shooting dog if a pointer, setter, or spaniel is not available.

The Labrador is easily recognized by his distinctive tail, which is round and tapered like that of an otter, and by his coat. Short and dense, it turns off water like oil, gives admirable protection from cold, and sloughs off ice, mud, and brush. The Labrador's coat is usually black, free from rustiness and white markings, except perhaps a small spot on the chest.

Other whole colorings are permissible, and yellow is becoming increasingly popular. The breed seems to carry a gene for yellow, and a light-colored pup will occasionally appear in an otherwise all-black litter. The eyes, regardless of coat color, can be yellow, brown, or black.

The breed was first recognized by England's Kennel Club in 1903, and since has frequently won that club's cup for best in show. Off to a late start in the United States, the Labrador has risen to great popularity and has come to lead the field of retrievers. He is truly the hunter's friend.

Height 21½–24½ in. Weight 55–75 lbs.

WALTER A. WEBER, NATIONAL GEOGRAPHIC STAFF ARTIST

Sleek coat shedding the icy water, a Labrador Retriever speeds to his master's hand. The heavy-set but light-footed breed actually came from Newfoundland, not Labrador, and was originally called St. John's Newfoundland or St. John's Water Dog. Fishermen brought him to England.

At home in marsh or upland cover, Curly-coated (

Curly-coated Retriever

NAMED FOR THE CRISP, tight curls which cover his body from occiput right to the point of his tail, the "Curly" is a handsome dog indeed.

He probably derived from a cross between the St. John's Newfoundland and the Irish Water Spaniel, and Poodle blood was likely introduced to increase the tightness of curl.

The first breed actually to be classified as a retriever in England, the Curly-coated has existed as a true breeding strain from about 1855. The breed had a separate classification in Birmingham as early as 1860.

The United States caught its first glimpse of the crinkle-coated beauty in 1907; today he has a small but devoted following.

His coat protects him from the rigors of cold and water and enables him to tackle the most punishing brush. But it has a tendency to pick up mud and twigs, and re-

WALTER A. WEBER, NATIONAL GEOGRAPHIC STAFF ARTIST

and Flat-coated Retrievers are in eclipse today.

quires much regular care. His color is solid black or liver.

Among retrievers the Curly has the longest legs and the lightest build. But he is hardy, and a lively performer in the water.

Steady and affectionate, he is easy to train. He shares not only the teachability and endurance of the other retriever breeds but makes an equally splendid companion.

Shoulder height 22–25 in. Weight 60–75 lbs.

Flat-coated Retriever

CANINE HISTORY contains many references to the early use of Europe's poodles and spaniels for retrieving waterfowl. But today those breeds that specialize in retrieving derive mainly from the water dogs of Newfoundland.

The Flat-coated Retriever is no exception. He apparently stemmed basically from the island's stocky St. John's dog, or early Labrador. Evidence exists that his flat, slightly wavy coat was gained by infusion of Gordon Setter blood. Irish Setter may also have been used.

He made his first English show appearance at Birmingham in 1860, along with the Curly-coated Retriever. The Flat-coated quickly became popular and flourished as a field and show dog until the early years of this century, when he lost ground first to the Curly-coated, then to the modern Labrador.

He was once known as the Wavy-coated Retriever, but a straighter coat was evolved until he became more accurately known by his present name.

The Flat-coated Retriever has been seen in the United States for many years but has never mustered widespread support. Nevertheless, he can hold his own against the other retrievers, and as a companion he is unsurpassed. He is a strong swimmer, a natural water dog that loves his work, marking, retrieving, and delivering with admirable style. At one time he was reputed to have a hard mouth, but this is not generally the case today.

His distinctive coat is dense, fine-haired, and sleek, either solid black or liver in color. A few white hairs are allowable on the chest. The eyes are expressive, medium large, and set well apart. They should be dark brown or hazel.

Shoulder height 21½–24 in. Weight 60–70 lbs.

The Hound Breeds

THE SPORTSMAN THRILLS, to be sure, to his bird dog's quivering point
and the explosive whir of wings. But equally tingling is the headlong chase to the hounds.
"I never heard so musical a discord, such sweet thunder,"
says Shakespeare's Hippolyta of the hounds of Sparta baying bear.
Others we see speeding after antelope "as silently as death."
Reliving his own long decades in the field,
author Freeman Lloyd brings us the magic world of hounds—
a world as varied as regal Afghan and merry Beagle;
as vast as Canada's prairies; as colorful as pink coats
flashing over English downs. The hounds are ahead.
Let us follow with huntsman Lloyd to marvel
at their grace and speed, and wonder at their chorused cry.

ROBERT F. SISSON, NATIONAL GEOGRAPHIC PHOTOGRAPHE

CHAPTER FOUR

Hark to the Hounds

Of all the stirring sounds in nature, none to me has a deeper elemental appeal than the bugle music of a hound pack in full cry. Take even a confirmed city dweller and set him down in an English meadow or on a Missouri hilltop when the hounds are running and he will probably confess to a quickening of the pulse and a prickly sensation along his spine as the mournful notes come ringing through the air.

This sense of suppressed excitement, this lifting of the hairs on the back of the neck, is doubtless a throwback to the time when a man had to run down his meat on the hoof with his dogs instead of buying it by the pound at the supermarket. Or perhaps it harks back to an even earlier time, when he himself was often the quarry of the pack, before he succeeded in capturing and training the young of his canine neighbors and winning their allegiance.

Broadly speaking, there are two kinds of hounds—the coursing hounds and the tracking hounds. Both are hunters, but one depends more on eyesight and speed; the other has keener scenting powers. The fleetest legs in all the canine world are in this first group, represented by the long-headed, small-eared, rangy Greyhounds of Europe and the long-eared, fringe-tailed gazelle hounds of Asia and North Africa. These swift coursing dogs find their game by sight, not scent, and run as silently as death, using all their breath in driving their marvelous legs.

ers and foxhounds jog to a hunt near Aiken, South Carolina.

Blue Ridge Hunt rides forth from the grounds of Carter Hall, in Millwood, Virginia. A glorio

The true tracking hound is a heavy-skulled, long-eared, long-lipped type—like that majestic-looking old master, the Bloodhound, with the best trailing nose in the business. When on the scent the tracking hound gives vent to his feelings in rich, melodious baying. In the wily fox the lighter, faster members of this clan found a worthy opponent, and the pack has been chasing Reynard for centuries.

Fox hunting has been a national sport in England for more than 300 years, and before that, early in the 14th century, the huntsman for King Edward II gave written instructions on methods to be followed. In England a man would be considered a scoundrel if he killed a fox in any but the legitimate way—mounted behind a pack of hounds.

Many years ago while I was shooting woodcock in Wales a fox suddenly broke cover ahead of my spaniels. Without thinking I gave a shout, "Hou, hou, hou!" and

JUSTIN LOCKE

utumn day calls hunters and hounds to the chase.

my Greyhound, which had followed me from home without my knowing it, shot past, quickly collared the fox, and killed it. I was overcome with shame. Furtively I concealed the victim in a hedge and that night I came out and buried my sin, making it a perfect crime. Had it become known that I killed a fox while hunting woodcock, I would have been ostracized.

In America the English type of fox hunting has won popularity, especially in the Middle Atlantic States where horsemen and women in smart hunting pink ride to hounds and thrill to the shout of "Tallyho, the fox!"

One Maryland hunt club fences in farmland, pays farmers for chickens killed by foxes, and once a year, on "Farmer's Day," entertains all nearby landowners. With its drag hunts, Aiken, South Carolina, spares the fox. A horseman pulls a fox-scented sack through woods and fields. Hounds trail the odor and riders gallop after. But in many States the fox is hunted as vermin with single hound and gun.

An American form of fox hunting with genuine appeal for the dog lover—and for the friend of the fox as well—is described with great feeling by MacKinlay Kantor in *The Voice of Bugle Ann.* The "hunters" sit around a campfire while the chase goes on through the dark countryside around them; by the quality of the distant tonguing they follow every move in the contest of wits and speed. At last the tired fox slips into a hole and lives to run another night.

SOME YEARS AGO I was going up to Winnipeg to judge a Canadian dog show and I decided to go on to Alberta where two nephews of mine had a cattle ranch called "Trevallen," after the old family homestead in Wales. Knowing they lived miles from the nearest railway station or store, I wrote asking what I could bring them from the outside world. A radio? A box of cigars?

B. ANTHONY STEWART, NATIONAL GEOGRAPHIC PHOTOGRAPHER

"Yoicks! Yoicks!" echoes over the North Carolina countryside as huntsman, in the lead, spurs on his pack with traditional cry. Members, guests, and master of the Tryon Hounds follow. Famed Bywater and Walker blood courses the veins of these American Foxhounds.

Back came the answer, by telegraph: "A hunting horn." With their horses, hounds, and a hunting horn the brothers Lloyd would be content.

I found a short copper horn of English make at a saddler's shop, and once I arrived the boys lost no time in putting it to use, teaching their hounds the time-honored calls which are as full of meaning to a well-trained pack as bugle calls to a soldier. Various combinations of long and short notes mean specific things: that the quarry has been located and the chase is on; that the prey has broken cover, or "gone away"; that the hunt is over and it is time to return.

My rancher relatives, I found, were using dogs of Greyhound and Deerhound bloods to hunt the coyote, or prairie wolf, a pest fully capable of killing a calf.

These outcasts of the plains are amazingly fast and elusive, and one of their favorite pastimes is to tease a pack of slow dogs by loping just ahead of them, then opening the throttle and drifting away like wisps of smoke. A Greyhound's speed is needed to cope with them, but other qualities are desirable too.

In the prairie provinces of Canada, accordingly, the Greyhound is crossed with the Scottish Deerhound and sometimes with the Russian Wolfhound—the English dog for speed, the Scot for hardiness, the Russian for biting and holding powers. These "long dogs," as they are called, can track not only by sight but also, because of their Deerhound blood, by scent. That they possess keen olfactory powers I was able to observe for myself. One of the six long dogs running ahead of our party suddenly stopped as game scent reached his nostrils. Like pointers and setters, the five others froze in their tracks.

Dismounting, we walked on past the dogs. About 30 yards beyond we flushed a covey of prairie chickens. Here were wolf-hunting hounds with bird-dog manners, one of the strangest combinations I have ever observed.

Thanks to their Greyhound blood, these hounds were keen-sighted, able to spot a coyote about as far away as the human eye could see it. Usually, however, one of the riders, being higher, was first to spy the quarry—a tawny shadow popping out of the plain. With a "Hou, hou, hou!" and a pointing wave of his arm, he could direct the hounds' attention. One sharp-eyed dog would sight the loping form and stretch out, top speed, the others swiftly joining him. During the chase, like true Greyhounds, they gave no tongue whatever. The coyote had a fighting, or rather a running, chance for his life, as his smooth and effortless

"D'ye ken John Peel . . . with his hounds and his horn?" England's hunting men still carol the feats of the immortal huntsman who seemingly "came into this world only to send foxes out of it." Peel, who died in 1854, kept a pack of hounds at his home in Cumberland for 55 years.

These men and hounds await the start of a hunt over the hills and vales of Somerset. Horseman, known as "the whip," will keep the pack in check. When they catch the scent of the fox, the hounds will give tongue. And the chase is on!

KATHLEEN REVIS

Over the fence in joyous cry scramble the eager hounds, for the fox is getting "sweet." Its sce

s heavy and fresh, full of promise for the tonguing pack, hot on the trail on the English downs.

"PICKING UP THE SCENT," PAINTING BY THOMAS BLINKS, COURTESY OF MRS. PARKER POE

WESTERN WAYS, BY TOMMY LARK

A chorus of howls tells the Arizona hunter his pack has treed a snarling mountain lion. These speedy, clear-voiced Plott Hounds will bay for hours, if necessary, until the hunter arrives.

Fox hunt in the Ozarks centers around a campfire. The hunters stay put, following the progress of the night chase by the distant music of their foxhounds. Horns recall the hounds.

action sometimes enabled him to wear out his rivals, especially if he had a good start and the dogs had already been running hard. And when cornered, a coyote can give a good account of himself.

For coursing the big gray wolf in the western wilds, the Greyhound was crossed with some hard-bitten breed such as Bulldog, Mastiff, or Great Dane. Even at that there were many casualties, for a wolf can snap a dog's leg like a carrot.

Perhaps the most spectacular workman of all coursing dogs is that handsome Russian, the Borzoi. Nowadays, of course, most Russian Wolfhounds live and die without ever seeing a wolf. But their heritage of hatred of all things lupine is ever-present. I well remember the hubbub Russian Wolfhounds set up at a New York dog show when a dog of wolflike look and remote wolf ancestry was led past their stall. Although reared in luxury, these canine aristocrats were carried back in a flash to the wild steppes of Russia. And the object of their hostility, from his cold-eyed expression, returned their hate with compound interest.

In their coursing days in Russia these fleet and tenacious dogs were trained not to kill the wolf but rather to pin him by the throat and hold him until the hunter

A. DEVANEY

could come up and either dispatch the beast or muzzle him for capture alive. Czar Nicholas's aggregation of Borzois was reported to contain at least one dog that could perform this feat alone, but usually two or three were run at a single wolf. Loping up alongside, one would collar the beast with a quick bite just under the ear and hang on while his running mate found a similar hold on the other side. Together they held the wolf powerless until the deadly jaws could be tied shut.

We can better appreciate the strength and tenacity required for this feat of the Borzois when we remember that a wolf is so strong in the neck he can toss a sheep over his back as easily as a fox can carry off a chicken.

Unusually interesting coursing breeds are the fleet and graceful Afghan Hound and the Saluki, with their long and feathered ears like a spaniel or setter. In the United States today there are many excellent specimens of these two exotic breeds. The Afghan, wearing a long, silky coat to suit the high altitudes of his native Afghanistan, is a favorite where a smart appearance is admired.

Both are very old breeds, treasured favorites of kings and sheiks in their native lands, where they were used for coursing the gazelle. Where the soil was sandy

gal beauty marks the Afghan Hound, once hunting partner of mountain kings.

Desert aristocrats, lithe and swift Salukis grace a London show.

ERNEST PALINKAS, PIX (LEFT); AND KEYSTONE PRESS AGENCY

and more fitted for the hoof of the gazelle than the foot of the dog, hawks were sometimes used to fly at the head and eyes of the quarry, baffling and delaying the animal until the coursers could overtake it.

SWIFTEST RUNNER in the world of dogs is the Greyhound. In fact, for limited distances, the Greyhound is one of the fastest animals on earth. From early times and in many lands sportsmen have bred and trained these long-legged, deep-chested speedsters for coursing hares and other game, and more recently for racing. Archeologists have unearthed monuments showing ancient Egyptians releasing their dogs at hares, using a collar device similar to that with which Greyhounds are "slipped" today at coursing meetings.

Britain had its Greyhounds even before the reign of King Canute, and no one of lower station than "gentleman" might keep one. "A gentleman is known by his horse, his hawk, and his Greyhound," went a saying in Wales. King John of England often accepted a brace (two) or a leash (three) of Greyhounds in lieu of tax money or in return for a royal favor. And down to the 20th century each Duke of Cornwall, by custom, has been presented with a brace of rare, all-white Greyhounds by the people of his duchy.

A good commentary on the rather reserved bearing of the Greyhound is the story told about King Charles I. "Sire," said a retainer, "I perceive you love the Greyhound better than you do the Spaniel."

"Yes," answered the King, "for they equally love their masters, and yet the hound does not flatter them so much."

At one time in South Africa, Umbandine, titular king of Swaziland, would trade a wagon and a span of 16 fine oxen for a Greyhound fast and hardy enough

Racing Greyhounds catapult into stride as the barrier flies upward. Hunting instinct spurs the speedsters into hot pursuit of a mechan rabbit whizzing around the track 20

Swifter than racehorses, Greyhounds cle

to pull down a springbok. And my own travels in a sparsely populated part of the Orange Free State impressed upon me the high value placed upon a fast dog in that land of antelope. My train stopped at a siding on the veld. I noticed a native with an *assagai*, or spear, and a "long dog," or crossbred Greyhound, on a horsehide lead. He was going on a long journey through wild country, he said, alone except for his dog.

Would he sell the animal?

"No, no!" he cried and actually ran away, his long dog bounding at his side. On such a trek his fleet-footed mongrel, the meat-winner, would be priceless.

Today Greyhounds have come into prominence because of the popularity of dog racing in many countries. In modern Greyhound racing the live hare of the coursing meetings has been replaced by a mechanical rabbit. The bunny is utterly uncatchable, and devoid of all nourishment anyway, yet the dogs spend their lives in its pursuit.

An offshoot of the Greyhound is the Whippet, a smaller dog produced by breeding Greyhounds with terriers. Terrifically fast for 200 yards, a first-class Whippet can cover the distance in approximately 12 seconds—nearly 17 yards a second! The little racers are often lured into showing their best speed by waving towels or sounding a siren or steam whistle just beyond the finish line.

More maligned and misunderstood than any other dog, perhaps, is the solemn-faced, deep-voiced Bloodhound. His sanguinary-sounding name may have had something to do with this, and no doubt *Uncle Tom's Cabin* and various detective tales have helped create the impression of fierceness and give the dog a bad name. The Bloodhound is not by nature a savage dog—quite the contrary. Some years ago I had occasion to observe this while visiting an owner of English and American Bloodhounds trained as man-hunters.

About 6 o'clock one morning I was aroused by hard knocking on the door. "Come on!" a voice cried. "A man has been stabbed and the police have asked us to put Moses and the new hound on the culprit's trail."

The hounds were allowed to smell the fugitive's crumpled felt hat. They acknowledged the scent with sonorous baying and were off, tugging their handler along at a dead run. The trail led to a factory near the river, where the fleeing man evidently had tried to escape by boat. Finding no oars, he had turned back and finally hidden in an old barn.

When the quarry was found Moses simply bayed his loudest, showing no inclination to attack the man. The other hound, however, gave indications that she might do so if not restrained.

ead. Muzzles keep them from biting ch other in the heat of the chase.

ORLANDO, THREE LIONS

e air with jackknife strides as they streak nearly 40 miles an hour down the track at Phoenix, Arizona. ▶

HY PESKIN, COURTESY OF "THE SPECTACLE OF SPORT FROM SPORTS ILLUSTRATED"

Rhodesian Ridgebacks, named for cowlick on spine, are newcomers to America.

JOHN GAJDA, DPI, AND (ABOVE) EMORY KRISTOF, NATIONAL GEOGRAPHIC STAFF

Dachshund, increasingly popular in America, is nimble, alert, companionable.

Asked why this difference in temperament, the handler said the new hound was penitentiary-trained. Some institutions, he said, ordered prisoners to kick the iron fences around the kennels, thus making ardent enemies of the dogs.

Today many handlers train their Bloodhounds to track silently, so as not to warn a fugitive or alarm a lost child.

Many years ago I saw the famous dog show at Birmingham, England, with a dog authority. My mentor pointed to a magnificent black-and-tan Bloodhound and said: "There you see the pillar of the Stud Book. From such a hound came the other varieties of tracking hounds. Is there any wonder he is benched on the No. 1 stall in the world's greatest exhibition of hounds?"

The Bloodhound remains at the head of the hound family. And what a proud family it is.

In imagination now, hark to the choir of the hounds! Here they come, in full cry, with joyous tongue—the deep-throated basso-profundo of the Bloodhound and Otterhound, the baritones of the Foxhounds and Bassets, and tenor baying of the little Beagles.

Here, too, come the coursers, the swift, silent ones, skimming the earth like swallows. Wonderful creatures all! Let's look them over, one by one.

DAVID W. CORSON, A. DEVANEY

Basset Hound's ears are as long as his pedigree. This old French breed is a cousin of the sad-eyed Bloodhound.

A Portfolio

Following are the hound breeds, painted in full color for the National Geographic Magazine by Edwin Megargee and other artists.

Sad-eyed sleuth leads a state trooper along an invisible trail. Boastin dogdom's keenest nose, the Bloodhound has followed human scent mo than four days old; some courts consider his findings legal evidenc

EDWIN MEGARG

Bloodhound

A PATRIARCH among the dogs that hunt by scent, the venerable Bloodhound combines the canine world's most solemn countenance with its most efficient nose.

A hound of extraordinary scenting power and determination was described in Roman times. But the Bloodhound's known lineage begins in the eighth century with the black-and-tan hounds St. Hubert used to hunt stag in the Ardennes, and a strain known as the Talbot Hound. Norman conquerors brought the Bloodhound ancestor across the Channel to Britain. In following centuries, when every monastery had its kennel and even bishops rode to hounds, clergymen guarded the breed's purity, giving rise to the name "blooded hound."

The Elizabethan authority, Dr. Johannes Caius, offered another explanation. The dog was properly called "Bloudhounde" or *Sanguinarius*, he said, for its skill in following the blood scent of wounded game. Even then, when cattle thieving flourished on the English-Scottish border, Dr. Caius admired the long-eared hounds as unerring trailers of man: "Creepe they never so farre into the thickest thronge, they will finde him out notwithstandyng he lye hidden in wylde woods, in close and overgrowen groves, and lurcke in hollow holes apte to harbour such ungracious guestes." Later the Bloodhound tracked deer poachers in England's great parks and preserves.

Though British-developed, the breed won its greatest fame—and undeserved ill repute—in the United States. Abolitionists painted a grim picture of relentless Bloodhounds mauling runaway slaves. Actually, the purebred Bloodhound is the gentlest of dogs, far more inclined to be shy than aggressive.

The friendly hound has tracked down fugitives from a mink farm and sniffed out gas leaks in underground pipelines. But his main job still is to follow human scent to find the lost and the fleeing. This the Bloodhound does with zeal. One pet wandered out of his yard, singled out a scent, and happily pursued it for 20 miles—to the door of a marathon runner training for a race!

Any dog can distinguish human perspiration diluted to one part in a million, but no breed excels the trained Bloodhound on a "cold" trail. Nick Carter, a Kentucky hound whose radarlike nose led to more than 600 arrests, once successfully tracked an arsonist who had fled 105 hours earlier. Such a feat requires ideal scent conditions: damp ground, little breeze, moderate temperatures. A Bloodhound courses a fresh trail with head chest-high, catching the odor from the air. On a faint track he may rasp nose and lips raw against the earth.

His great head often measures more than 12 inches from nose to occiput; blanketlike ears sometimes span 30 inches. Deep folds of skin about head and neck slip into near-blinding brow wrinkles when he sniffs the ground. His muscular body is coated in black and tan, red and tan, or tawny.

Other breeds may look more like house pets, but few enjoy human company more. The Bloodhound is lavish in affection and sensitive to every kindness or correction. *Shoulder height 23–27 in. Weight 80–110 lbs.*

Edwin Megargee

Basset Hound

MEET THE CYRANO of dogs! Long nose and mournful visage impart an air of comic sadness, but beneath the Basset's loose-fitting coat beats a gallant heart. And for beauty of expression, this Frenchman's song on the scent matches the magic of Cyrano's lilting verse.

The Basset descends from old St. Hubert hounds, used not to run down game so much as to trail and drive it out. Thus he shares ancestry with the Bloodhound, from which his head seems borrowed. Among today's breeds only that master sleuth excels him in scenting skill. Bred by generations of huntsmen, this sturdy little hound courageously tracked roe deer, wolf, and boar in northern Europe's forests, and often went to ground in pursuit of fox and other prey.

Titled sportsmen of 16th century France hunted badger with Bassets in truly grand style. A writer of the day listed among the necessities at least a dozen well-trained Bassets, each wearing a collar three fingers thick, with bells attached; rugs to lie on when listening to the dogs give tongue as they pursue their prey underground; and a dozen strong men with digging tools and tongs to excavate the badger from its hole.

"Further, to do the thing properly," he added, the nobleman "must have his little cart in which he will ride. . . . The sides and posts of the cart should each be furnished with flasks and bottles, and at the end should be a wooden case full of cold Indian game fowls, hams [and] beef tongues. . . . And in winter time he can have his little pavilion brought along in which a fire can be lit to warm him."

Through centuries many varieties of Basset Hound evolved in France—smooth-coated and rough, straight-legged and crooked. Although the Continent had long known the

A hunter of ancient French lineage is the Basset, with his Bloodhound head, Foxhound coat, and

Basset, few Englishmen had seen one prior to 1863, when the low-slung dog captured visitors' fancy at the first dog show held in Paris. Shown in England 12 years later, the breed quickly won favor. British royalty fell under its spell; both King Edward VII and Queen Alexandra were Basset admirers.

The strain most often seen in the United States is known as Le Couteulx, after a noted 19th century French breeder. This type still fits a portrait Shakespeare drew in *A Midsummer Night's Dream:* ". . . Their heads are hung with ears that sweep away the morning dew; crook-knee'd, and dew-lapp'd like Thessalian bulls; slow in pursuit, but match'd in mouth like bells. . . ."

The maxim that "no good hound is a bad color" applies to the Basset; most often he wears foxhound hues. From pendent ears "like the softest velvet drapery" to gaily carried tail his body is borne on sturdy legs only a few inches off the ground. This stubby running gear proves no disadvantage; it keeps his keen nose close to earth and enforces a pace leisurely enough to follow on foot. Sportsmen in the United States use him on fox, raccoon, opossum, and squirrel, but chief among the Basset's assets is his skill in flushing pheasant and rabbit. His thorough, unhurried conduct in the field moves game to gun without startling it into panicky flight. He trains easily, and can be coached to retrieve as well.

For decades the Basset enjoyed a modest number of devotees on this side of the Atlantic. Recently, however, his popularity as a family pet has soared (registrations leaped 68 percent in a single year), spurred in part by canine television stars. Once seen, the frank friendliness that shimmers in his soulful eyes proves irresistible.

Shoulder height 11–15 in. Weight 30–55 lbs.

ınning gear of a heavy-boned Dachshund. He sniffs the earth for scent, then gives melodious tongue.

EDWIN MEGARGEE

Heads come up as a well-matched pack catches fox sce

English Foxhound

THE SWEET-TONGUED English Foxhound begins and ends life as part of a skilled team, the foxhound pack. His finest moments are spent caroling across misty English meadows with his fellows.

Hunting has been his job since medieval monarchs followed his bulky staghound ancestor after wild deer. Cromwell's iron hand destroyed many deer parks and forced Restoration "bloods" to set their hounds after foxes.

One story says an 18th century Duke of Beaufort, trotting home from a stag hunt, let his pack swing off on the scent of fox. The duke was caught up in a tumultuous cross-country scamper that stirred his spirit. Such enthusiasts spread fox hunting into the lives of earls and farm hands, squires and clerks.

The rigors of the sport—"a dead fox or a broken neck"—and its scrupulous etiquette added fiber to Britain's soldiers and diplomats. Ruddy-cheeked huntsmen gallop through the pages of literature and galleries of sporting prints. "'unting is the sport of kings," quoth the fictional Mr. Jorrocks. "All the excitement of war without the guilt and only 25 per cent of the danger."

Careful breeding tuned the English Fox-

EDWIN MEGARGEE

ıd leads pink-coated huntsmen over fence and fen. Some 200 packs still chorus across Britain's farmlands.

hound to his work. Greyhound blood added long, straight legs, speed, and stamina. A good pack may lead a field of hedge-jumping horses 75 miles over rough country. Square-chested and cat-footed, the hound is bred to order by his Master of Hounds. Sizes and speeds vary slightly from England's rolling central shires to hilly Wales or stone-walled Ireland.

Black and tan splotch the dog richly or give way to white. Many breeders strive for packs of uniform color. All seek harmonious voices in their hounds. Sir Rodger de Coverley, ideal squire of 18th century fiction, turned down the offer of a hound because it was a bass and he needed a countertenor!

Fox hunting has followed Englishmen around the world. Lord Fairfax brought English hounds to Virginia in 1738. An occasional foxhound pack still bays across Australian or New Zealand pastures after an imported fox. Hounds with the trimmed ears and erect heads of proper English packs gallop over Canada's frosted turf on the trail of fox scent planted by a man on horseback.

English meets gather as always before the village pub, riders and onlookers with expectant air. Now the pack arrives, 18 or 20 couples, so John Masefield says:

"Intent, wise, dipping, trotting, straying,
Smiling at people, shoving, playing,
Nosing to children's faces, waving
Their feathery sterns, and all behaving."

Shoulder height 23–25 in. Weight 55–75 lbs.

American Foxhound

SLIGHTLY LEGGIER AND LIGHTER than his English cousin, the American Foxhound boasts enough speed and endurance to give the elusive fox the race of his life.

De Soto reportedly brought the first hounds to the New World to track down Indians. In 1650, Robert Brooke settled in Maryland with his pack of foxhounds. George Washington bought part of a shipment of English hounds in 1770 and received a gift of tall, long-eared French staghounds from Lafayette in 1785. Washington's two varieties, crossed, may have been the fountainhead of today's American Foxhound.

Colonists were eager to carry on the fox hunting they knew in England. But the wilderness forced changes in the sport. Hard-riding Marylanders and Virginians gave little thought to British hunt etiquette. Following the pack at breakneck pace through thicket and ravine, across deer pasture and up mountainside, a huntsman glimpsing the quarry would let out an exuberant falsetto yipping. This cry, caught up and carried by the whole field, perhaps gave birth to the bone-chilling rebel yell of Civil War battles.

Dashing horsemen chased the fox through the outskirts of young Philadelphia and the farmlands of upper Manhattan. The Brooklyn Fox Hunt disbanded only 100 years ago.

The sport also shaped regional varieties of foxhound. Isolated packs, each of a jealously guarded breeding strain, sprang up in the South. Each bore the breeder's name: Maupin, Walker, Trigg, Birdsong, and others. All met special demands of the hunt.

Filling the night with music, American Foxhounds streak off on a fresh scent while hilltop "hunte

New World fox is scarcer than England's, and scent lies poorly in heavy woodland and rocky terrain, so the American Foxhound needs an especially keen nose. Courageous and eager, the close-tracking hounds follow the speedy fox at full tilt through the roughest country, their hare feet driving them faster than horsemen can follow.

Riders are guided by the pack's distant chorusing, so breeders have favored a deep, carrying voice. Washington's French hounds were said to sing "like the bells of Moscow."

The rich hound tones inspired the purely American pastime of "hilltopping," wherein "one-gallus" hunters around a campfire listen for their own hounds "speaking to the line" as they chase Reynard through the night. Such hunts end when the fox dives into its burrow. If not recalled by horns, the hounds trot back miles to their own farmyards, thanks to an inbred homing instinct.

In New England, armed hunters stage a similar chase. Then, led by the baying, they slip through the woods to ambush the fox.

In the Middle Atlantic States, California, and a few central states, horsemen don formal regalia to follow more than 100 traditional-style hunts. They enjoy a good day's run, even if the lure is not live fox but a scented bait dragged over the ground by a rider.

Long-eared and sober-eyed, the American Foxhound pads before them. He can't take a ribbon in a British show, but he'll find his fox and give tongue in an echoing melody that thrills dirt farmer and millionaire alike. *Shoulder height 21–25 in. Weight 45–65 lbs.*

isten in. Experts judge positions of Old Jubilee or Melody by the way they "throw their tongues."

EDWIN MEGARGEE

Rough-coated Otterhound leaves a drenching chase to meet two Harriers, followers of an equally ancient sport, hare hunting. American strain of Harrier, left, has more slope to his neck than his English colleague.

Otterhound

LOOKING LIKE A BLOODHOUND in sheep's clothing, the Otterhound is woolly from heavy head to straight tail. His deep-set eyes glint from the matting, and wide nostrils emerge between mustache and tufted beard.

Rare in America, this well-muscled hound has chased otters along Britain's fishing streams since Plantagenet days. No one can pin down the Otterhound's ancestry with certainty. Not only the Bloodhound but the Southern Hound, Welsh Harrier, Water Spaniel, and Vendeen Hound may all share in it.

Whatever his origin, the Otterhound is well equipped for the cold, wet, exhausting sport that gave him his name. Webbed feet lend him surging power as he swims. An oily undercoat keeps him warm. His highly tuned nose works over stream banks at dawn, seeking scent left by the night-traveling otter. Once he strikes the trail, his basso profundo reverberates, warming the chilled huntsmen who follow on foot.

One hunt covered 23 miles and lasted 10 hours. When the otter makes for his lair, terriers are often used to dislodge the prey while men, knee-deep in water, bar its escape.

More than 20 packs of Otterhounds worked British rivers in the 19th century. Enthusiasts still follow the sport during fox hunting's off season. Today, foxhounds and crossbreeds are included in Otterhound packs.

Ranging in color from blue and white to black and tan, the Otterhound remains happiest splashing and baying through the cold backwaters of secluded brooks. But raise him in the home and he becomes a patient, affectionate companion for children.
Shoulder height 24–26 in. Weight 50–70 lbs.

Harrier

THE GREEK HISTORIAN Xenophon described qualities a hound should have for the sport of hare hunting. Had the Harrier existed in 400 B.C., Xenophon would have had his dog.

The Harrier looks like a small English Foxhound—same head and nose, same cat feet, level back, straight legs, and square chest. Colors are identical, except that some Harrier strains have a mottled blue coat. In fact, experts suggest that the Harrier is no more than a foxhound bred down in size.

Bounding over an English farm, Harriers raise melodious echoes as they unravel the tangled trail of the European hare. Leaping a hedge, the pack may overshoot the wily hare, which has doubled back and leaped to one side. The quarry has a bagful of tricks that befuddle all but the wisest hound. Sometimes a winded hare will rest beside a companion in the selfish hope that when the Harriers flush them, the innocent bystander will draw the pack.

If the Harriers finally drive the hare from its own terrain, it simply runs straight ahead, lost, until it drops from exhaustion. Few hunts cover more than five miles.

In medieval England, hare hunting thrived as a poor man's pastime. Ploughmen gathered with their dogs and sprinted after them on foot. The aristocracy tried the game on horseback and found it good. An item about James I notes that "live hares in baskets, being carried to the Heath, made excellent sport for His Majesty." Huntsmen are usually mounted today.

The Harrier has been known in America since colonial times but is seldom seen here today. His smaller relative the Beagle is better suited to hunt American rabbits.
Shoulder height 19–21 in. Weight 35–55 lbs.

Sounding off, a brace of handsome Beagles spri

Beagle

FEW DOGS HAVE MATCHED the Beagle in popularity in the United States. Thousands of Americans find life incomplete without this happy little hound to share it, and in 1953 he replaced the sad-eyed Cocker as top dog.

In field trials he delights watchers with his alert tracking sense. On farms across the Nation he is an eager hunting companion, ecstatic at the smell of a gun and the crunch of dry leaves under his pads.

Apartment dwellers marvel at his adjustment to city life. He is neat and clean, and seldom barks indoors. Short tail wagging and ears flapping, he roughhouses gently with adoring children, somehow avoiding ornamental glassware. He returns painful proddings by infants with a generous lick of his tongue. Yet on a weekend visit to the country, the same good-natured pet will slash through swamp and brier with single-minded recklessness, tonguing his high-pitched warning to all cottontails.

Rabbits and hares are the Beagle's age-old quarry. His British ancestors hunted them long before Elizabethan days. Queen Bess herself kept "singing Beagles," and English yeomen raced on foot after the tuneful little hounds. As the pastime developed, the breed improved. In the mid-19th century, Parson Honeywood of Essex hunted with so fine a pack that the world of art took notice. An engraving of "The Merry Beaglers" caught the eye of sportsmen and brought wide popularity to the sport and the dog.

Honeywood's hounds are considered the first modern Beagles. Looking like an English Foxhound in miniature, the Beagle keeps game on the move, yet does not outdistance running men. He stands on strong, straight legs and wears a coat of foxhound colors. His ears nearly reach the tip of his nose. Wide-set eyes are soft and pleading, yet sparkling with some secret joke.

Turned loose in hare country, the Beagle

…er darting cottontails. The breed's name is believed to stem from an old French word for clamorous.

pack fans out, probing for the scent. Sterns wave wildly. A veteran hound finds the line, or track, and "speaks to it" with contagious excitement. Huntsmen and whippers-in, often dressed in green coats and white breeches, move forward.

Overrunning the line, the Beagles check. The huntsman gestures in a new direction. Instantly the pack is off again in full cry, the field racing breathlessly after it:

"Was there ever sweeter music?
What is there can compare
With the wailing of the beagles
As they press the bounding hare?"

Less expensive and easier to organize than mounted fox hunts, beagling caught on in the United States after modern Beagles were imported in the 1860's. Then, in 1890, New Englanders discovered a new diversion: Beagle field trials.

In these tournaments the dogs compete in pairs in a rabbit patch. Avidly, they seek a line and trace its meanderings as they sing their tenor duet. A Beagle need not make a kill to win. Judges watch for technique, penalizing the hound that putters, swings in hit-or-miss circles, or babbles at a cold trail. Elimination produces the champion.

Beagles compete in two size classes: 13 to 15 inches tall, and those less than 13 inches, counterparts of England's "pocket Beagles."

Large or small, the Beagle gives every last ounce of effort in field trial or hunt. Huntsmen sense his inner frenzy when rabbit lies close at hand. Yet he is so tractable he will flush quail or pheasant or race a fox to earth with little training. In Australia, Beagle packs chorus after medium-size kangaroos. A Beagle in Michigan plunges off a dock to catch fish.

And in thousands of American homes, winsome little Beagles are content to track down only their masters' slippers.

Shoulder height 11–15 in. Weight 20–40 lbs.

Edwin Megargee

rking up the right tree for coon, Black and Tans reach trail's end er a race through dark woods. Developed in the South, these relatives the Bloodhound were the first coonhounds to join purebred ranks.

N MEGARGEE

Black and Tan Coonhound

THE CAR JOUNCED down the dark country road and stopped. Four men and a brace of dogs, on leash, piled out into the chill October night. The men carried kerosene lanterns and five-cell flashlights. Twigs snapped underfoot as they scrambled over an old stone fence and plunged into the woods.

A few hundred yards in, the hunters released the dogs and sat down in a lantern-lit circle. Snuffling about in the leaves, the dogs padded off. Soon they could be heard no more. The men stopped talking and listened.

Now, finally, a yelp, deep and mellow, comes from off in the woods.

"They've got a trail, let's go!" The men hurry after, lanterns cutting circles of light in the gloom. From time to time they stop to listen as the hounds change direction, come closer, or bay deeper into the woods.

Suddenly the hounds' voices rise and sharpen; they are "barking up." The men hasten to the scene and hang their lanterns in a wide circle around the tree. Flashlights beam up into the branches. Two beady eyes come afire with light. Deep in the night woods the hunter is face to face with his quarry; the chase has reached its climax.

But the real hunters in this scene are the Black and Tan Coonhounds barking and jumping at the tree in the desperate hope they can grab the rascal whose scent rises out of reach.

What sort of dog is this nocturnal expert, unleashed in dark woods to track and tree the wily raccoon?

First, he's as American as the woods he roams. One of many tracking dogs developed in the South, he stems from the American Foxhound, the Virginia Foxhound of colonial days, and the Bloodhound, whose line harks back to the Talbot Hound of Norman nobles. Indeed, with his pendulous ears and pendulum tail, the Black and Tan looks much like his Bloodhound cousins, though he's lost both weight and wrinkles. His color is the hound's classic black and tan.

He nosed into his specialty quite naturally, for he's one of the best of the tracking hounds—not speedy but determined and thorough—and he has the strength and stamina to cope with rugged terrain. He knows what he's after and invariably gets it. No veteran coonhound will be lured away from his raccoon scent to chase porcupine or rabbit. Black and Tans have also been trained successfully to tree bear and bobcat.

As a result of breeders' careful work in standardizing the alert and eager hunter, the Black and Tan in 1945 became the first coonhound to gain American Kennel Club recognition. But renown had come long before. It was a Black and Tan Coonhound that inspired the famous tribute in the late 19th century by United States Senator George Vest of Missouri:

"The one absolutely unselfish friend that man can have in this selfish world is his dog. He will kiss the hand that has no food to offer, he will lick the wounds and sores that come in encounters with the roughness of the world. He guards the sleep of his pauper master as if he were a prince. When all other friends desert, he remains."

Shoulder height 23–27 in. Weight 55–70 lbs.

Dachshund

MORE FUN has been poked at the low-slung Dachshund than at any other dog. Jokesters say he is "sold by the yard," stands "two dogs long and half a dog high," and can be

Sausage-shaped but lionhearted, Dachshunds beard

patted by all members of the family at once!

Actually, a well-proportioned Dachshund is three times as long as his shoulder height. Translating his German name explains why: *Dachs*, badger; *Hund*, dog. He was bred to track a burrowing animal to earth and squeeze in after him. Such a dog needs low clearance, strong legs, loose skin to allow free

dger in its den. Wire-haired strain is often gray. Long-haired and Smooth generally wear red or black.

EDWIN MEGARGEE

play in tight quarters, powerful jaws, and the reckless courage to face a cornered foe. His bark tells hunters where to dig.

In medieval Europe any dog so equipped was known as a badger dog, just as any informally bred dog good on rabbits becomes a rabbit dog.

Gradually the German Dachshund evolved, combining qualities of hound and terrier. He has the hound's tracking nose, long ears, and affectionate disposition. He packs a terrier's self-reliance, determination, and bravery into his sleek and tapered head. His deep, well-muscled chest lends digging power to his short forelegs.

Germans called their breed *Teckel*, possibly for Tekal, a similar dog on a Pharaoh's statue; and they founded the first Dachshund association, the *Teckel Klub*, in 1888.

Breeders have developed smooth, wirehaired, and long coats. The original badger hunters of close to 35 pounds have been bred down in size. Miniature Dachshunds, weighing less than 8.8 pounds at 12 months, rate special classification in Germany.

Europe's Dachshunds still hunt, though seldom the badger. They bolt rabbits and occasionally go to earth after a fox. They also slip through underbrush and close in on deer without frightening them off.

The United States has long cherished the Dachshund as a pet. By 1958 the breed had risen to fourth place in popularity. Clean, odorless, friendly, and comical, the Dachshund greets visitors with an authoritative bark. Then, seeing an old friend, he rolls over to have his belly tickled.

On a country stroll, he seesaws beside his master, scampering aside after wayward scents. He romps endlessly with children, and when laughed at, laughs right back.

Shoulder height 5–8 in. Weight 8–22 lbs.

Norwegian Elkhound

WHEN STONE AGE MAN hunted in the wooded mountains of Scandinavia, Norwegian Elkhounds padded beside him. These robust northern dogs left skeletons in a stratum that dates from 4000 to 5000 B.C.

The Elkhound has changed little since then. Strong and stocky, with broad, deep chest and wide-browed face, he looks somewhat like a compact German Shepherd. His hard, thick coat is silver-gray, lighter on the underside. His bushy tail curls forward.

Centuries ago these dogs hunted bear for Viking masters. Now they stalk the European elk, counterpart of North America's moose.

On a hunt, the Elkhound ranges far, nose searching the frosty air, sharp ears cocked for distant sounds. Hunters claim the dog can scent, or sense, his quarry three miles away; the dog may suddenly whimper, warning that the unseen elk has started to run. Turned loose, the dog seeks to cut across the line of flight and intercept the elk.

Face to face with his antlered prey, he dances in and back, holding its attention. If a bull elk attacks, the dog handles it like a skilled torero. He darts aside at the last moment, teases the bull to charge again, and all the time barks furiously for his master.

Scandinavians have also used the adaptable Elkhound as sled dog, shepherd, and guard. He keeps predators away from a farm, announces strangers, and escorts them to the house.

Not until about 1880 did the Elkhound leave his native mountains to try his luck as gun dog, otterhound, and show dog in Great Britain. He has come to the United States primarily as a pet.

Scrupulously clean, loyal, and trustworthy, he adopts his family wholeheartedly. But on a walk in the park he is still apt to range afield, as if to remind city dwellers that he remains captain of his soul.

Height 18½–20½ in. Weight 45–60 lbs.

EDWARD HERBERT MINER

"We've found your quarry. Now you take over." What huntsman could fail to read the message in those fearless brown eyes? Proud dog of the Vikings, the Norwegian Elkhound adapted millenniums ago to the rigors of the northland clime. Isolation kept the sturdy breed pure.

Rhodesian Ridgeback

NOT FOR TEN YEARS had the American Kennel Club opened its stud books to a new breed when in 1955 it recognized the Rhodesian Ridgeback as 112th in purebred ranks.

But a distinguished African reputation heralded the sturdy newcomer. On his native

Circling and feinting, courageous Rhodesian Ridgebacks bay a lion for the hunter's coup de grâce

veld his valor in baying the king of beasts had won him the name African Lion Hound.

When Dutch, Germans, and Huguenots settled in South Africa in the 17th and 18th centuries they brought their dogs with them. These Great Danes, Bloodhounds, and other European dogs interbred with the half-wild hunting dogs of the Hottentots. The African dogs carried the cowlick that was to mark and name today's Rhodesian Ridgeback.

This ridge of dorsal hair grows from hip to shoulder in a direction opposite that of the

e cowlicked breed originated in South Africa; its extraordinary nose follows the faintest lion scent.

WALTER A. WEBER, NATIONAL GEOGRAPHIC STAFF ARTIST

rest of the Ridgeback's short glossy coat.

Selective breeding by the Boers eventually produced a dog ideal for life in the African bush. A fleet and brave hunter, he could endure insects, daytime heat, and nighttime cold, and go 24 hours without water. He guarded isolated farmstead and gave gentle company to the women and children.

Necessity bred this stalwart dog but sport brought him fame. In 1877 a missionary introduced the breed into Rhodesia, where big-game hunters enthusiastically adopted it. The dog's stamina, courage, and keen scent and sight here came into full play, for sportsmen used him in packs to track down lion. He would besiege the mighty prey until mounted hunters came in for the kill.

Fanciers in Rhodesia standardized the breed in 1922, and the first specimens arrived in the United States in the late 1930's. Here he has utilized his African experience to hunt cougar, and when properly trained has qualified as a bird dog. But more often the rangy hound fills the role of pet in his adopted land.

Quiet and well-behaved, he adapts well to town or country life. He is easily trained in obedience and is fond of children.

The Ridgeback's color is light wheaten to red wheaten with some white occasionally showing on chest or toes. In the show ring excessive white is not desirable. He has high-set drop ears and long tapered tail. *Shoulder height 24–27 in. Weight 65–75 lbs.*

EDWIN MEGARGEE

Barkless Basenjis wear bells for driving antelope in the Sudan. Wrinkled brow gives puzzled look.

Coursing full tilt, Salukis overtak

Basenji

ONE OF THE MOST ANCIENT of breeds yet among America's newest; a dog that doesn't bark like a dog, and cleans himself like a cat—this is the exotic Basenji.

Egyptian carvings of 5,000 years ago depict the proud little dog with his perky ears and tightly curled tail. Then the one-time companion of Egypt's nobles dropped from sight, only to be "rediscovered" by late 19th century explorers in the Congo.

But the Basenji had not spent the intervening centuries in idleness. He beat game for tribal masters. They often hang bells or gourds around his neck to create a din in the bush and sometimes call him the "jumping-up-and-down dog" for his habit of leaping high to see over tall elephant grass.

Introduced into the United States and England in the 1930's, the Basenji has quickly gained a following. About a Fox Terrier's size, he is often compared to a tiny deer for his agile grace. His glossy hair is copper, black, or black and tan, with white markings.

He keeps his short, odorless coat immaculate and makes an ideal pet—devoted, playful, and normally quiet—for city or suburb. Though barkless, however, he is not mute. He murmurs, chortles, snarls, yodels. One Basenji brought stunned silence to a London show when he broke a 5,000-year-old tradition by going "Woof!"

Shoulder height 16–17 in. Weight 22–24 lbs.

Saluki ▶

TO THE DESERT SHEIK he is *el hor*—"the noble one"—a sacred gift of Allah. He is not a dog at all, for dogs are unclean, Moslems believe. Certainly the sleek Saluki, swiftest and likely the oldest of purebreds, must be in a class by himself.

Through countless centuries with nomad masters he has coursed deserts from Sahara to Caspian Sea. No breed excels him in the hunt on sand and rocky waste: "My Saluki will catch gazelle and bring them down even if they should gallop over the stars," boasts the Arab, and treats his hound accordingly.

The Saluki sometimes rides athwart the saddle (or in recent years, aboard a jeep) to keep fresh for the chase. No other dog sleeps in his Arab master's tent; no other's pedigree has been handed down in song and chant for perhaps a thousand years. News of a litter brings visitors hopeful of the gift of a puppy, for in the desert this highly-prized breed is not for sale. A Saluki's demise is mourned almost as a death in the family.

This high regard appears as old as the breed itself. Sumerian and Egyptian murals and carvings 5,000 years old or more immortalize the lithe Saluki figure. His remains lie mummified, like those of his royal masters, in long-dead cities on the Nile. Even his name rings with antiquity, for it is thought to come from a vanished Arabian town, Saluk.

A picture of grace and symmetry of form, the Saluki displays a long, refined head, deep chest, and silky coat ranging in color from pure white to black and tan. Soft feathering adorns his long ears, tail, and legs, although a smooth variety is known. Arched hindquarters drive him in a graceful gallop timed at more than 40 miles an hour. He turns as swiftly as his prey.

Although Crusaders are said to have brought these dogs to Europe as exotic proof of pilgrimage, few appeared in the West until the late 19th century. England's Kennel Club recognized the Saluki in 1922, America's in 1927. Owners prize the breed not only for its striking beauty and heritage but for its gentle, companionable nature.

Shoulder height 23–28 in. Weight 50–55 lbs.

›et gazelle as Arabian hunters gallop in for the kill. Trained falcon harries the prey until the dogs bring it down. ▶

ROBERT E. LOUGHEED

EDWARD HERBERT MINER

·yhounds were favorites of Egypt's Pharaohs. British miners bred the smaller Whippet a century ago.

His every slender line proclaims his function as a running machine. His short, smooth coat (in almost any canine color) cannot hide the rippling sculpture of the muscles beneath; he seems built of spring steel and whipcord. Finely chiseled head, delicate ears, and arched neck give him an air of distinction and quality.

Greyhound coursing as a competitive sport found favor in Britain as early as 1576; a hare would be released and a brace of hounds slipped after it. In the western United States, homesteaders imported Irish and English Greyhounds to put down plagues of crop-devouring jackrabbits. Inevitably, proud owners boasted of their dogs' speed and pitted them against others.

But dog racing with a mechanical rabbit as widely practiced today did not become popular until the 1920's. So keen is the Greyhound for the chase he will eagerly pursue even this man-made bunny around an oval track with 15-foot strides at speeds sometimes topping 40 miles per hour.

Some observers don't think the Greyhound is being very smart. When Fox Terriers were raced after a mechanical rat, they circled the track just once. Thereafter they simply waited at the finish line for their prey to arrive, then demolished it!

Greyhound fanciers have a ready reply: their breed has been clever enough to win man's favor for 50 centuries or more.

Shoulder height 26–30 in. Weight 60–70 lbs.

Edwin Megargee

llen roebuck testifies to the Scottish Deerhound's hunting prowess. ce no lesser rank than earl could own this wiry-coated Greyhound clans- n. Modern firearms signaled the breed's decline; dog shows revived it.

N MEGARGEE

Scottish Deerhound

HIS STATELY CARRIAGE and rugged look suggest a romantic past, and this the Scottish Deerhound has. Once the dog of nobility, he coursed the fleet stag over Scotland's hills and, at hunt's end, reposed at his laird's feet in torchlit castle halls.

Time obscures the breed's origin, but there is no mistaking the Greyhound family in its graceful lines. Certainly the dog was well known in Britain in 1570, when Dr. Johannes Caius wrote of the Greyhound: "Some are of a greater sorte, some of a lesser; some are smoothe skynned and some curled, the bigger therefore are appointed to hunt the bigger beastes, the buck, the hart, the doe." This "greater sorte" went by many names—Scotch Greyhound, Rough Greyhound, Grew, and Highland Deerhound.

Pageantry and splendor attended the 16th century hunt to Scottish Deerhounds. In 1529 the Earl of Atholl invited King James, the Queen Mother, and Rome's ambassador to a hunt; a richly furnished palace "three houses height" was built in the forest for the event. In three days of hunting "there were slain 30 score of hart and hind with other small beasts such as Roe and Roebuck, wolf, fox, and wildcat." When the King and his party left, "there rose behind them leaping flames, for all that palace the Highlanders did set on fire and burn to ashes in a reckless gesture of farewell."

So highly did early Scotsmen prize their Deerhounds, they went to battle over a dog stolen by a band of Picts. "Of the Scots there died some three score gentlemen, besides a great number of the commons. . . . Of the Picts there were about one hundred slain." A noble condemned to death could buy his freedom with three of these dogs.

The great hunting pageants to hounds ended in the early 18th century, closing the most glorious chapter in Deerhound history. About a century later, when the nobility lost exclusive right to deerstalking and it became a popular sport, the "Royal Dog of Scotland" flourished anew. But as game thinned, so did Deerhound ranks. Interest sparked by dog shows saved the breed.

Using dogs on antlered prey is illegal in the United States, but the Scottish Deerhound has run down wolf and coyote, and smaller game. His deep chest houses capacious lungs; powerful hindquarters give him stamina and driving speed. His lean outline conceals the strength that once downed 250 pounds of stubborn stag.

A crisp, wiry coat three to four inches long on neck and body inures him to Highland chill and dampness. Color ranges from dark blue-gray to yellow.

A true Scot, the Deerhound possesses great dignity and sensitivity; he remembers "with accuracy both benefit and injury." Although he craves human companionship, do not expect the lavish affection of a lap dog from this giant. Be content with unswerving loyalty and a warm gaze from his honest Scottish eye.

Those fortunate enough to know this splendid dog echo in feeling the tribute Sir Walter Scott paid to his beloved Maida: "the most perfect creature of Heaven."

Shoulder height 28–32 in. Weight 75–110 lbs.

Tallest of dogs, an Irish Wolfhound stands victorious after battle. Rivali[ng] a Shetland pony in stature, the shaggy-browed vanquisher of Irelan[d's] wolves here sets his hunting prowess against western America's coyo[te].

EDWIN MEGAR

Irish Wolfhound

KING OF CANINES by virtue of his size and majestic bearing, the Irish Wolfhound boasts a proud lineage that extends back into the mists of Celtic legend and romance.

His debut in Classical history had appropriate impact. "All Rome viewed them with wonder," wrote the Consul Symmachus when seven of the giant dogs from Ireland fought in the imperial circus, A.D. 391.

Clan chieftains in Ireland enlisted the mighty breed as their companions in arms; and as with Scotland's Deerhound, at least one war was fought over the Wolfhound himself. But the dog traditionally was protector of flocks and man against wolves, a role already old when the Jesuit Edmund Campion, in 1571, wrote in his *History of Ireland:*

"They [the Irish] are not without wolves and greyhounds to hunt them, bigger of bone than a colt. The Irish wolfhound is similar in shape to a greyhound, bigger than a mastiff and tractable as a spaniel."

Fleet in the chase, the Wolfhound also had the power of jaw to dispatch a full-grown wolf. The rangy giant did his work so well that he destroyed the last of his hereditary enemies in his native land in the 1780's.

So great was his prestige, so popular did he become with royalty abroad that in 1652 the export of Wolfhounds was forbidden; depletion of the breed had increased the ravages of wolves on Ireland's herds.

But with the ultimate extermination of the Irish wolves, the great hound had apparently outlived his usefulness and was allowed to languish. By the early 19th century his kind was all but extinct.

In 1862, a British officer, Capt. G. A. Graham, set out to revive the breed. Collecting the last survivors, he skillfully crossed them with the Scottish Deerhound, Great Dane, Mastiff, and Borzoi to restore Ireland's Wolfhound to his traditional appearance and stature. Today's Irish Wolfhound, with his rough, hard coat in gray, brindle, red, black, fawn, or pure white, is the image of his stately ancestor.

Surprisingly, the first of these great dogs to cross the Atlantic apparently did so with Christopher Columbus. Records of the fourth voyage tell of an attack Columbus's Panama garrison repulsed with the aid of an Irish Wolfhound. The Indians, "punished by the edge of the sword and by the dog who pursued them furiously," fled.

So well established is the breed in American life that two huge, shaggy mascots of the old Fighting 69th Regiment led the annual St. Patrick's Day Parade down New York's Fifth Avenue. A Wolfhound graces the Gettysburg monument to the heroes of Meagher's Irish Brigade who died there in 1863 to preserve the Union.

The big hound still runs down coyotes on the western plains. His lightning speed and agility also make him effective against smaller game. Yet this powerful giant is the best mannered and most companionable of dogs, with a reservoir of affection and good will as vast as his body. He is aptly personified in his old Gaelic slogan:

"Gentle when stroked,
Fierce when provoked."

Shoulder height 30–38 in. Weight 105–160 lbs.

Edwin Megargee

EDWIN MEGARGEE AND (OPPOSITE) EDWARD HERBERT MINER

Gazelle hunter of ancient line, the silk-coated Afghan Hound surveys his rocky land for game.

Afghan Hound

A CRUMBLING PAPYRUS and pictographs on tomb walls survive to tell us that the "monkey-faced hound" of ancient Egyptians originated on the Sinai Peninsula and coursed game in the Nile valley 5,000 to 6,000 years ago. As if this were not old enough, tradition holds that a pair of Afghans represented dogdom aboard Noah's ark!

Desert sheiks kept the rangy breed pure through centuries, but no one yet has bridged the gulf in its history that placed it in Afghanistan, whence comes the Afghan's name. There this regal member of the Greyhound family has hunted since 2200 B.C., rock carvings show, though he was little known outside that land until the present century.

A heavy standoff coat shields him from the intense heat and cold in rock-strewn plains and mountains. It clothes his legs in feathery trousers and crowns his long, aristocratic head with silken visor. Broad feet and high powerful hindquarters make him a champion hurdler and climber that moves with liquid gait. He usually hunts gazelle and hare, but his boldness, speed, and strength arm him even against leopard.

He has also herded sheep and served as frontier sentry. British army officers helped popularize the breed in India, Iran, Arabia, and England. Winning Best in Show at Westminster in 1957 spurred the Afghan's career as a dog of fashion in America, where he is prized for beauty, dignity, and grace.

He wears a haughty look, but when he lets his hair down in his family circle he is an affectionate, playful pet.

Shoulder height 24–28 in.
Weight 50–60 lbs.

Borzoi

HIS NAME SPELLS SPEED—Borzoi means "the swift one"—and his every curving line confirms it. But he couples fleetness with striking beauty. From long Roman nose to low, arched tail he looks every inch the aristocrat, bred to please Russia's czars and nobles.

Although he often hunted smaller game, his descriptive name, Russian Wolfhound, discloses his traditional use. Coursing the wolf was long the favorite sport of the Imperial court.

A pack of smaller hounds would drive the wolf out of the forest to waiting horsemen, who slipped two or three Borzois to run it down. Racing alongside, the dogs seized their prey by ears or neck and held it powerless until the hunter came up for the kill.

Mystery long clouded the Borzoi's origin. Modern findings, however, reveal that early in the 17th century a Russian duke imported a number of Greyhound-type dogs, possibly Salukis, from Arabia for hunting. The thin-skinned dogs could not withstand the north's fierce winters until he crossed them with a heavy-coated Collie-like native breed. The swift, hardy dog that resulted sired the magnificent Borzoi of today.

Britain and the United States first saw the Borzoi in the late 19th century. Fortunately the breed was well established outside its homeland by 1917. Symbols of the hated aristocracy, Russia's finest Borzois were slaughtered in the revolution.

The slim and deep-chested speedster has used powerful jaws to dispatch calf-killing coyotes on America's western plains. One Borzoi in Alaska that helped kill 62 wolves died trying to save an Indian girl attacked by wolves. But more often his silky-coated brethren grace the show bench or lend a glamorous white accent to Park Avenue strollers. *Shoulder height 28–31 in. Weight 75–105 lbs.*

Grace and poise mark these regal Borzois, which boast a fighting heritage. Their foe: the savage wolf.

The Working Breeds

DOG'S DEBT TO MAN? He owes us, true, for biscuit, bone, and bed; but the companionship he provides is alone reward enough. To reckon his full worth we must also count in the unsung service of those we call the working breeds. From Collie herding wayward sheep to Husky harnessed to arctic sled; from Doberman stalking jungle sniper to Shepherd gently guiding the blind, dogs on the job ease man's lot. In return for "working like a dog" he asks nothing but direction, and perhaps an approving word. Edward J. Linehan of the National Geographic staff has watched man's faithful ally toil in sunlit pasture and patrol night-darkened alleyway. Here he renders his account of man's debt to dog. Then let us go to the Swiss Alps with George Pickow to meet the canine rescue squad that brought fame to the St. Bernard name.

Police dog's keen ears and nose equip this German Shepherd to detect criminals on his nightly Baltimore beat.

ELWOOD BAKER, WASHINGTON STAR

EDWARD J. LINEHAN

CHAPTER FIVE

Working Dogs of the World

AN EERIE DRAMA UNFOLDS inside one of New York's largest department stores. Night lights bathe empty aisles and laden counters in a faint glow. The din of shopping crowds has surrendered to stillness, punctured only by distant traffic clangor.

Enter, as if from nowhere, a spectral black creature.

Swiftly it pads down the central aisle, explores each corridor, weaves past shrouded showcases and skeletal clothing racks. Mannequins, frozen in lifelike pose, stare as the big dog trots by—seeking, always seeking.

The trim Doberman Pinscher stops abruptly, swings his narrow nose like a settling compass needle. Ears twitch erect; muscles tense beneath the ebony hide. A growl rumbles from his throat.

Behind a counter . . . *there!*

A few bounds and he confronts a cowering figure in dark raincoat and cap: a thief who hid at closing time, to loot the store and walk out boldly with the morning crowds. Crisp, ringing barks fetch the dog's uniformed handler at a run from a distant doorway.

The handler orders the intruder to lean, facing a wall, hands high. He points and gives the dog an urgent command: "*Watch him!*"

For long minutes Red Star, pride of Macy's dog guard force, holds his post a yard from the prowler's heels, a study in canine vigilance. He seems chillingly eager for his captive to attempt escape.

"Okay, Red," the handler says finally. "Heel!" The dog trots to his side and wags at his reward for a job well done, an affectionate pat on the head.

This purposeful drama, in which another handler portrays the thief, is part of a constant training program to keep the dogs alert, efficient, and interested in their lifetime career.

To watch man's oldest animal ally at work today, I began with a visit to brisk, gray-haired Francis X. Fay, Macy's Director of Security. Fay told me the store was once plagued by nighttime thefts, one alone including $12,000 in furs. He suggested Macy's try canine detectives.

In October, 1952, four dogs began patrolling the store's 2,000,000 square feet. "To our knowledge we haven't lost a penny in merchandise to burglars since," said Fay as we stepped out onto a windswept roof 20 floors above the street, possibly the loftiest dog kennel in the United States.

A fierce clamor broke loose from wire-fenced runs.

"They don't see many strangers," Fay apologized. "We discourage them from 'fraternizing' with anyone but their handlers and me. It might save a dog some night from a prowler with a knife or poison."

Each 20-foot pen enclosed an insulated doghouse and a sleek black-and-tan Doberman. The dogs writhed with delight at seeing Fay and fixed me with cool brown-eyed stares. All were magnificent specimens. Five had been sired by a two-time winner of the Westminster Kennel Club's Best in Show award.

At the last pen, handler Steve Muller was taking six-year-old Cash out to work off pent-up energy and sharpen discipline. After a bit of rough-housing he gave a few basic commands: "Come," "Heel," "Sit," "Down," "Stay." Next he sent the dog around an obstacle course. Cash bounded through hoops and over barriers with the precision of a steeplechase horse.

"Each of these dogs is like a loaded pistol," Fay said. "To make sure it doesn't go off accidentally, we rehearse and rehearse, repeat and repeat." So absolute is the dogs' obedience, they won't eat food placed before them until granted permission. When ordered, they will stop eating instantly.

"See that wall?" Fay pointed to a low parapet bordering the roof edge. "Any of them could clear twice that in one jump." To forestall such accidents, each dog was held at the edge for a long look at the awesome canyon below and commanded: "No!" None has forgotten the lesson.

Sgt. Muller was now sparring with Red Star.

"Watch him," said Fay admiringly. "That dog runs on steel springs!" Time after time the big Doberman lunged at his handler with mock ferocity, twisting at the last instant to deal him only a glancing blow on the shoulder.

"He loves to play this game," Muller grinned. "Often he'll sit back and eye me as if to say: 'I can take you if I really want to!'"

Claws filed for stealth, eager Dobermans patrol Macy's in quest of thiev

Red Star proved his point later. In a mock encounter a "prowler" and the dog faced each other several yards apart in a broad aisle.

"Get him!" Muller hissed suddenly. Red sprang like lightning for the intruder's gun arm. It was heavily padded; without protection bones might have been broken. Grimly the 85-pound dog hung on, though hoisted off the floor and whirled in a circle. My spine tingled at his deadly determination.

"Okay, heel!" Muller called finally, and Red trotted submissively to his side.

"These dogs are trained to attack only if a prisoner they are told to watch tries to escape," Muller said, "or on the command G-E-T H-I-M." He spelled out the words guardedly, for Red Star was watching intently.

Though trained to detect only strangers, fire, or smoke, Macy's dogs in-

M. WOODBRIDGE WILLIAMS

stinctively warn of open windows, leaky radiators, running water—anything departing from the normal sights and sounds of the store.

Once, on a routine patrol, Suzy detected a broken steam hose that might have caused hundreds of dollars' damage if left unchecked. Investigating an office one night, Cash bristled and growled. His handler found nothing. The dog was insistent. Checking again, the guard lifted the cover of a costly accounting machine. It was silently running, and overheated. Damage could have resulted, but for an alert dog.

Asked what training principles were used, Fay jotted down a name and address. "See John Behan," he told me. "John and his brother Bill trained our first four dogs, and we have used his methods on the rest."

A DAY LATER I pulled up to a neat farmstead amid wooded hills near West Redding, Connecticut, for a look at the "campus" of Canine College. Its four-footed graduates are each worth up to $1,500.

John Behan, a youthful-looking ex-Coast Guardsman who trained sentry and scout dogs during World War II, gave me a rapid-fire history lesson. Dogs have served man, he pointed out, ever since primitive hunters thousands of years ago grew dimly aware that these wild creatures possessed more virtues than might appear on the end of a roasting spit. Quickly Behan traced the dog's evolution from scavenger (Rover's tendency to tip over garbage cans "should be respected as the world's oldest franchise," one writer put it) to warning device, and eventually to man's working partner.

"What we do here is to use the dog's natural instincts and abilities," he said.

Topper shows how it's done as famed trainer Winifred Strickland drills him in obedience. "Stay," says the silent hand; even from afar the signal roots the German Shepherd to the spot. "Hup!" she calls, and Topper clears the bar; this readies him for the trial ring, where dogs must retrieve dumbbells over a barrier and leap the slotted broad jump without trainer or leash. Well-schooled dogs often find uses for their skill; Mrs. Strickland's lug bundles, fetch slippers, deliver notes, even swim with the family as lifeguards.

BRUCE DALE, NATIONAL GEOGRAPHIC PHOTOGRAPHER

U. S. AIR FORCE AND (RIGHT) LONNIE WILSON, GILLOON

Fur flies over Labrador as a sled dog begins his parachute descent in a rescue rehearsal. The U.S. Air Force devised Operation Paradog for mercy missions over difficult arctic country.

"Our training puts nothing in and takes nothing out. We merely develop a little more finely what nature has placed there." The Behans base their training on three "A's": Affection, Approval, and Authority.

At eight or nine months a potential guard dog is ready for obedience training. I watched Bill Behan work a handsome young German Shepherd.

"To teach a dog anything you first have to let him make a mistake," said Bill. He ordered the frisky dog to heel and led him on a slack leash up and down the cork-floored stable. Carelessly the dog chose the wrong side of a post. Bill jerked lightly on the leash, thumping the dog's head against the post. Unhurt but surprised, the Shepherd came around to his master's side.

"He's made a mistake. He's been corrected. And he's learned something. Now watch." He led the dog past several more posts, leaving scant room. Each time the animal squeezed by on the proper side and got an approving word.

The worst punishment the Behans inflict on a student is a light slap across the muzzle. "It doesn't hurt him," said John, "but it touches his dignity."

More advanced training takes advantage of a common canine characteristic:

"A dog is wary of anything he doesn't understand. We put him in a familiar setting, then introduce an intruder or something else unexpected. The dog reacts by barking—and we reward him with praise."

Once a multimillionaire asked Behan for three of the biggest, most savage dogs obtainable to patrol his estate against possible kidnapers. "Try just one, first," Behan counseled. "And take a well-trained dog, not a vicious one."

The advice paid off when a watchman on the estate carelessly left a kennel gate open; the 100-pound Shepherd roamed loose somewhere on the grounds. The dog was found—gently playing on the lawn with the children!

Much of the Canine College curriculum is for "problem" dogs that bark excessively, bite, fight, or are inordinately shy. Often the trainers find the owner is the problem. One matron urged the Behans to treat her horribly pampered pet gently because "he's the reincarnation of Buddha."

Behan recalls two Collies that arrived in separate cars, so deadly was their enmity; and a Boxer so shy he crashed into doors while running from people.

"It was easy to see that the Collies fought simply to get attention," Behan

"Get him!" cry the handlers. Leashes strain as German Shepherds leap to attack. Daily agitation, part of eight-week training course for Air Force patrol dogs, sharpens aggressiveness.

said. For a few weeks he corrected them whenever they snapped at each other, and they rode home together, the best of friends. The Milquetoast Boxer, once he learned that humans needn't be feared, actually took to growling at strangers.

But John Behan is proudest of the case of the Opera Fan and her Crippled Pet. A New York woman brought the Behans her small mongrel. An encounter with an automobile had left it unable to walk. She was loath to leave it alone, yet she sorely missed Verdi and Wagner. What to do?

Behan mulled the matter over and set to work. In a few weeks he had the bright little creature trained to lie perfectly still, no matter its position.

The dog's delighted owner seldom missed an opera thereafter—with her pet contentedly draped around her neck as a living scarf!

BEHAN, with his experience in the military use of dogs for scout, sentry, and attack work, believes any police department would find them ideal additions to the force. First to agree would be officers of Baltimore's 40-dog K-9 Corps who nightly patrol trouble spots with leashed German Shepherds.

"When I hunt a prowler in a dark building," one patrolman told me, "I'd rather have Kejn, here, than my gun." The dog at his feet thumped the floor with his tail. During my visit I learned about the deterrent effect of police dogs on such offenses as purse-snatching, pocket-picking, and auto thefts. "Some nights we'd need extra men on one particularly bad post," an officer told me. "Now one man and his dog do the job more effectively."

The K-9 Corps tallied nearly 800 arrests in a single year's operation. Dog-supported officers captured eight burglars in one weekend.

In a typical case, a patrolman and his dog saw two thugs beating and robbing a man. The officer sent his dog after one fleeing suspect and pursued the other himself, but lost him. Returning 15 minutes later, he found the dog holding his man at bay in a doorway. The Shepherd wrapped up the case by sniffing out the victim's wallet, thrown away during the chase.

In a course averaging 14 weeks, the police dog learns basic obedience and how to guard a prisoner. He learns to pursue a fleeing suspect and to attack on command, even in the face of gunfire. Advanced training teaches him to follow a person's trail, even to scent out evidence such as drugs or explosives.

Off duty, the dog lives in his patrolman master's home not only to save costly kenneling but to foster a strong bond between man and dog.

I cruised on night patrol with Sgt. Irvin Marders. His dog Victor paced the car's seatless rear, ever alert. Victor's muzzle probed the back of my neck with disquieting interest; finally he swiped at my ear with his huge tongue.

"You've been accepted," Marders grinned.

Minutes later I saw Victor in a different mood, responding to a burglar alarm

Fangs bared, German Shepherd guard lunges at the photographer at the U.S. Naval Base on Guantánamo Bay, Cuba. Superior nose and ears enable a dog to do the sentry work of four men. Some patrol with handlers; others, staked out alone, bark at approach of trespassers.

W. E. GARRETT, NATIONAL GEOGRAPHIC STAFF

J. BAYLOR ROBERTS, NATIONAL GEOGRAPHIC PHOTOGRAPHER, AND (TOP) ELWOOD BAKER, WASHINGTON STAR

in a garment factory. He didn't get a chance, however, to repeat his achievement of a few nights before, when he had captured two thieves in a furniture store; there was no burglar this time—the alarm had been tripped by a window left ajar. But as the big dog ranged through rows of machines, ink-black storage rooms, and basement crannies I recalled the sergeant's words:

"These dogs do a real job for us. Yet all they want is meals, medical care, and affection. It's the cheapest protection in the world."

In Morristown, New Jersey, I saw canine service of another sort, on its most inspiring plane. I sat in a car watching two blind students traverse a tree-shaded suburban street. At each curbstone their Seeing Eye dogs stopped smartly and awaited the command "Forward."

As one dog stepped into the street I asked my companion, a Seeing Eye official, how it would cope with a careless driver.

JAMES F. LALLY, BALTIMORE NEWS-POST

Ladder-scaling Shepherd (right) answers a Baltimore jewelry store burglar alarm. When officers found nothing amiss in the store, they sent the dog through an open second-floor window in a neighboring building. Dog and officers investigated two upper floors and finally the roof; there the animal flushed three prowlers who meekly surrendered.

Police dog (above) cruises Baltimore's streets and alleys in a prowl car; between night shifts he frolics as the officer's household pet. His annual "salary": $700 in meals and medical care.

Quilted armor shields a trainer (left) from teeth of a "rookie" learning to attack and release his hold on command. German Shepherds of Baltimore's K-9 Corps average 80 to 85 pounds, enough to fell a fleeing criminal.

A Pennsylvania State Trooper (top left) demonstrates police dog discipline as his charge braves a circle of fire.

Learning A B C's of a Seeing Eye career, three Shepherds and a Boxer rehearse the "Sit" command. Trainers at Morristown, New Jersey, grade each on intelligence, willingness, and performance.

Bond of trust and a harness link Seeing Eye guide and student for life; trainers, like marriage counselors, study personality of each to insure happy match.

He replied by shifting into gear and careening around the corner, squarely into the pair's path!

We squealed to a halt. The dog calmly checked his master within arm's length of the car and led him around it.

At Seeing Eye, Inc., nearly 4,000 blind persons since 1929 have learned to rely on patient, gentle dogs to guide them through a sighted world.

The dogs learn first. Many are raised from puppyhood by youthful 4-H Club members, to familiarize them with people, automobiles, and other animals.

At 14 months they return to the Seeing Eye to train for a life's work that will average more than eight years.

I watched Seeing Eye trainers gain the dogs' confidence by playing and walking with them, and drill them in fundamental obedience. Weeks of harness drill follow. In harness, each dog was learning to move left, right, or forward on command; to stop automatically at each

J. BAYLOR ROBERTS, NATIONAL GEOGRAPHIC PHOTOGRAPHER

curb; and to lead his master at a brisk, 3½-mile-an-hour gait. He would learn to avoid pedestrians and obstructions on busy city streets—even to gauge the height of the person he leads. The trainer deliberately bumps obstacles until his pupil realizes that dog-size clearance is not enough.

"A traffic-wise dog sometimes alarms people by seeming to come too close to cars," one trainer told me. "He simply has learned to judge distances accurately without endangering his master. He can see anything that moves, such as a car, far better than you or I can."

Throughout his education the Seeing Eye dog meets the distractions of loud noises, the challenge of a cat chase, the nuisance (and allure) of doggy strangers—and learns to ignore them all. Not until he has safely led a blindfolded trainer through the busy streets of Morristown is the animal judged ready for training with his new blind master.

"The transition from trainer to new master is the most difficult part for the dog," Seeing Eye's G. William Debetaz, told me. "Some dogs actually lose weight during this period."

I asked what kind of dog makes the best Seeing Eye guide.

"Big enough to pull a man out of danger; small enough to fit under a train or bus seat; healthy enough to work in all weather," he replied. "He mustn't be a fighter, and must have a strong sense of responsibility."

The Seeing Eye has successfully trained 29 breeds. But eight out of ten guides are German Shepherds, a versatile breed with a heritage of guardianship.

"Sometimes," Debetaz reflected, "I think it's the man who belongs to the dog. In a good relationship there's no limit to what the dog will do to safeguard his

Entrusting his life to a Seeing Eye dog, a blind student skirts sidewalk construction. The dog, always at his left, obeys his direction commands except when they lead into danger.

master." He shows this in what the Seeing Eye terms "intelligent disobedience"—calculated refusal to lead his master into danger. "We encourage the dog to use his own head," Debetaz said. "He'll often have to make his own decisions."

A dramatic example occurred several years ago while a German Shepherd led his sightless mistress home through a Connecticut city. A crowd had gathered near a theater where two bandits and police had fought a pitched battle. The dog balked at leading his mistress through the milling throng where she might be jostled. Despite her commands of "Forward," he detoured four blocks, skirting a cloud of stinging tear gas, to bring her safely back on her route.

Those who come to the Seeing Eye for a dog must learn, too. Often a person without sight arrives with stooped and tentative shuffle. But in the month that follows, the blind person comes to "see" through a dog. He learns to read the sensitive signals of his dog's harness, and to praise his dog as it leads him safely from curb to curb. He learns to care for and to love the companion that will seldom leave his side until death. And he leaves the school erect and confident, with the quick stride of one newly liberated and unafraid.

More than mobility awaits the blind person with a dog. Said one graduate: "When I came to the Seeing Eye I had little interest in life. My dog did what I never believed could be done—she made me over mentally."

Executive Vice President George Werntz, Jr., put it this way: "The newly blind person tends to mourn his lost sight. His dog furnishes him with a constant companion; he must go out of himself to praise him and give him affection. This is a major step in learning to live with a handicap."

There are eight schools like the Seeing Eye; some provide free services. Seeing Eye's fee of $150 for the first dog falls far short of actual costs. The applicant pays the fee, spread over years if necessary. Nobody else may pay for him. Says Werntz: "The idea is to spur him on to make his own way."

As one Seeing Eye graduate said in tribute to his four-footed guide, "Blindness has at last come out of the tin-cup stage."

SINCE MAN first domesticated livestock he has recognized the worth of a dog to guard and move his flocks and herds. This specialized task has molded a variety of herding dogs. The rough-coated Komondor protects—and even resembles—the semiwild sheep of Hungary's wind-swept plains. Half a world away the agile Kelpie shuttles flocks across Australia's outback.

For centuries the stumpy Welsh Corgi, favorite of Britain's Royal Family,

"This is the hand that feeds him; this the voice he obeys." Guide and master constantly tend one another. Dog leads blind man to dinner; at night, harness doffed, he sleeps by his bed.

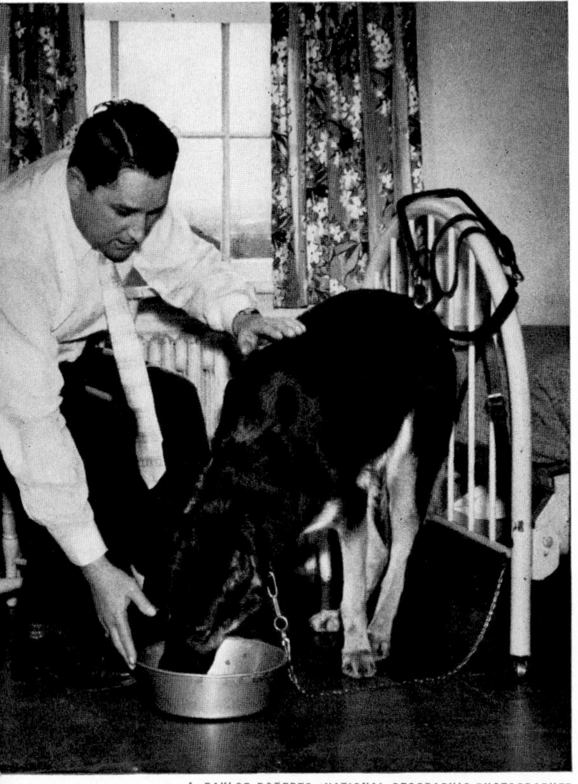

J. BAYLOR ROBERTS, NATIONAL GEOGRAPHIC PHOTOGRAPHER

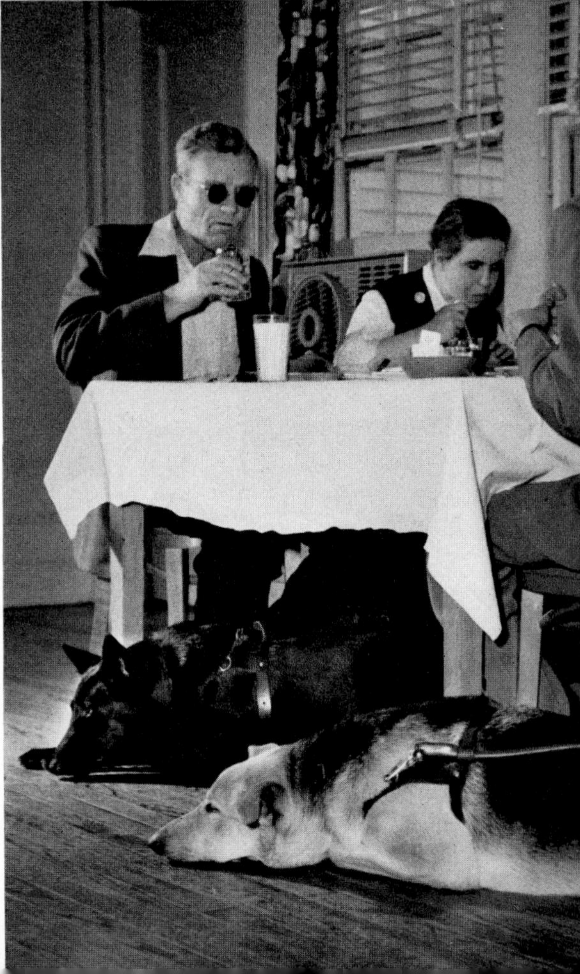

Six sheepdogs ring a huddled flock as Carl Bradford demonstrates Border Collie discipline and tea

has nipped at laggard cattle's heels. So have Germany's Rottweiler, a remnant of Roman invasion; France's Briard; and the Low Countries' Bouvier des Flandres. Even dogs of Russia's Laika breeds tended reindeer herds long before a mongrel by that name gained renown as the world's first space dog.

But the most worked shepherd's dog in English-speaking countries today is a canny little Scot known as the Working, or Border, Collie.

Dr. Johannes Caius, a learned English physician who in 1570 wrote the earliest treatise on the dogs of Britain, said this of the shepherd's working partner: "This dogge either at the hearing of his masters voyce, or at the wagging and whisteling in his fist . . . bringeth the wandring weathers and straying sheepe, into the selfe same place where his masters will and wishe . . . wherby the shepherd reapeth this benefite, namely, that with litle labour and no toyle or moving of his feete he may rule and guide his flocke . . . either to have them go forward, or to stand still, or to drawe backward, or to turne this way or to take that way."

Aside from whistling through a gap in his lower teeth, Carl Bradford of Wooster, Ohio, might well illustrate the old doctor's remarks. This specialist in sheep research at the Ohio Agricultural Research and Development Center happily joined his work with his hobby—breeding and training Border Collies.

J. BAYLOR ROBERTS, NATIONAL GEOGRAPHIC PHOTOGRAPHER

ork; one dog can easily control this band. Creeping dog at right shows his breed's hypnotic "eye."

"Move!" barks a bossy Border Collie, leaping aboard to unravel a woolly traffic jam.

I watched Bradford work Roy, then the black-and-white pride of his kennels, on a flock of ewe lambs. He first scattered the sheep out of sight behind a low rise. Then, with a snap of his fingers, he dispatched Roy to bring them back.

The dog sped low across the meadow. With two whistles, one low, the other high, Bradford corrected his course a bit to the left. Roy vanished over the rise. "Now he's on his own," Bradford said. "A good herding dog needs initiative as well as obedience, for he often works out of sight of his master."

A minute later a sea of dust-stained wool flowed like heavy sirup over the brim of the hill. Patiently, never approaching too closely except to head off an errant sheep, Roy darted in an arc behind. When the flock edged toward a fence, Bradford split the air with two low-pitched whistles. Roy shot instantly to his right, heading off a difficult situation. By stops and starts the sheep approached like a company of awkward recruits. At each halt Roy crept closer with a crouching, almost hypnotic movement to start them again.

"That's what we call 'eye,' " Bradford said. "All good herding dogs have it to some degree. It's the ability to creep up with trancelike attention and force the flock to move without stampeding." It was an astonishing display—a 40-pound dog silently pushing balky sheep hundreds of times his weight.

Training sharpens the long-inbred herding instinct which the Border Collie generally shows even as a puppy. Basic obedience comes first—except for the command "Heel." The last place a shepherd wants his dog is at his side.

Bradford teaches his dogs to respond to whistles, voice commands, or hand signals; sometimes all three. Most often used is the order "Down," which brakes an over-eager dog threatening to panic a skittish flock. Roy's response to this command while running was so quick that the trainer first had to whistle

Reluctant ducks retreat to pen. A trained poultry dog can gently herd a 1,000-turkey flock.

B. ANTHONY STEWART AND (OPPOSITE) J. BAYLOR ROBERTS, NATIONAL GEOGRAPHIC PHOTOGRAPHERS

Cattle dogs by tradition, pet Pembroke Corgis amuse their mistress in their Maryland home. Ancestors of these working dogs migrated to Wales with Flemish weavers in 1107 and drove beef to market for centuries. Low-slung build enables them to nip a hoof and dodge the ensuing kick.

a slow-down warning to keep the dog from injuring himself in the sudden stop.

Through constant repetition and correction the dog learns to move right and left; to "gather" a flock toward his master, and to "drive" it away. Fifteen minutes a day for six months trains the dog for most herding work.

A cattle dog needs courage to nip at the heel of a kicking heifer. Swine are the hardest of all to move, Bradford told me, requiring a forceful dog. Sheep usually prove the most tractable. Herding poultry, particularly turkeys, the dog can work closest of all, using slighter movements to control the flock.

Carl Bradford, Jr., and his brother Jerry demonstrated the difficult feat of working three dogs simultaneously. The subjects were four reluctant ducks; oddly, a large flock would have handled more easily than this handful. With whistles and commands for each dog, Carl directed his charges as they herded the quacking quartet back and forth between wooden barriers.

Even an unpracticed eye could discern differences in style. Fly, veteran of dog shows and state fairs, pursued her duties with flair. Nan tended her business with grave concern. Venerable Towser let the others tire themselves on the flanks as he ploddingly shut off escape to the rear.

Ancient Welsh law said a good herding dog was worth a prime ox; in recent years one Border Collie sold for $1,500. Whatever the cost, it is fully repaid

Huk! Huk!—Go! Go! Muzzles down, paws churning, Huskies strain to the Eskimo command to squeeze a sled through an icy labyrinth on the Arctic Ocean. Fan of dogs, hitched Greenland fashion, gets helping yank from drivers. Tumbled mazes of ice and temperatures that plummeted to 65° below zero thwarted the Bjørn Staib expedition's dash

BJØRN STAIB NORTH POLE EXPEDITION

to the North Pole from Ellesmere Isand in 1964. Men and dogs struggled to within 200 miles of their goal, at that time achieving the farthest north on foot since Peary's epic trek in 1909.

in loyalty. Many are the tales of a dog driving his woolly charges home and returning to the fields to guard a helpless lamb.

A memorial stone was erected at an English roadside some years ago in tribute to Tip, a Border Collie. Her master, an 85-year-old shepherd, took her along on his last winter's walk on the lonely moors, where he died. Not for 15 weeks was either seen again, until searchers found the feeble, emaciated dog standing vigil by her master's body.

HISTORY'S PAGES, from the book of Marco Polo to the polar journals of Peary and Amundsen, record still another service the dog has rendered man: transporting him across the earth's frozen wastelands. In exploration, sled dogs' shoulders bracing against harness opened countless thousands of ice-locked miles never visited by man before. During war, dog teams hauled ammunition and supplies through blizzard-swept France and rescued downed fliers from the Greenland Icecap. During peacetime they have carried Alaskan mails, supplied trappers and prospectors, and performed workaday toil for Eskimo and Indian masters.

Explorers on skis found they could make long forays from base camps by "skijoring" behind a few fast sled dogs. Since the skis offered little friction, the dogs could tow a man at high speed all day and the skier could hold the traces with one hand for hours.

RICHARD HARRINGTON AND (ABOVE) BJØRN STAIB NORTH POLE EXPEDITION

Sometimes over, sometimes in: Lacking floes to ferry across, sled dogs swim the leads, or cracks, in the Arctic ice mantle with little fear of the frigid water. Dunked in brine that would quickly kill a man, one dog makes a crossing (above) during the Staib expedition; others await their turns or shake out their coats on the opposite side. Dogs survived immersions without harm if they were run briskly the next hour. Men wore skis as a precaution against dangerously thin ice.

Watery channel opens as spring nears in Canada's Northwest Territories (right). Eskimo catapults dogs across; sledge will bridge the gap for him. Drivers fit dogs with leather boots when ice becomes jagged.

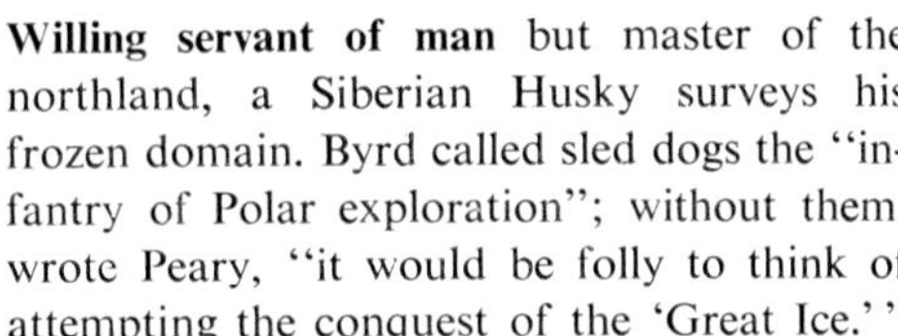

Willing servant of man but master of the northland, a Siberian Husky surveys his frozen domain. Byrd called sled dogs the "infantry of Polar exploration"; without them, wrote Peary, "it would be folly to think of attempting the conquest of the 'Great Ice.'"

Harnesses lack reins; drivers control teams by voice alone. Despite identical training, dogs may vary greatly, some straining at the first command, others lagging. Lead dog need not outfight others in the team; his eagerness and stamina inspire them to follow.

BAHNSEN, MONKMEYER

Aside from legendary feats in polar exploration, dog teams have made astonishing journeys. In the lifesaving relay of diphtheria serum from Nenana to Nome, Alaska, in 1925, sled dogs raced some 650 blizzard-swept miles in 5½ days, ordinarily a trip of 25 or 30 days. All of the teams made heroic runs and some of the Indian drivers with mongrel dogs made sprints of remarkable speed. But two lead dogs of Siberian strain gained lasting fame: Gunnar Kaasen's Balto sped 53 miles in 7½ hours, and Leonard Seppala's Togo covered 84 miles in one day.

The best known sled-dog headquarters in the United States is Chinook Kennels of Wonalancet, New Hampshire, on a pine-shaded slope spilling from the Sandwich Range. Here on winding forest trails hundreds of dogs have been trained for Antarctic expeditions and innumerable wartime search and rescue missions. Here, too, many GI's learned the knack of dog-sled driving.

"It's easier to train the dogs than the drivers," the owner of Chinook Kennels told me with a warm smile. Mrs. Milton Seeley has bred, trained, and raced sled dogs for more than 30 years. Training at Chinook Kennels is a matter of example. A puppy of about eight months is harnessed amid experienced dogs and learns from them. On snowless ground the dogs pull wheeled "gigs"—old cars stripped down to the chassis.

"At first he's playing, not pulling," said Mrs. Seeley. "But it doesn't take him long to get the idea." Educated in easy stages, most soon love their work. One out of ten displays the speed, obedience, and initiative of a first-rate lead dog. Some work well at the "point" positions, directly behind the lead dog; others prefer the "wheel" posts nearest the sled.

The driver directs his team entirely by voice, calling individual commands to each dog by name. Signals to turn go to the lead dog, who veers left or right in response. Rear dogs take the sled to the exact spot where their leader turned, then swing off to follow. The driver, riding behind on the sled runners, shifts his weight to help steer the sled.

The secret of a good team is the driver's knowledge of each dog's temperament and capacity. Under favorable conditions a 60- or 70-pound sled dog can pull about twice his own weight.

CHINOOK KENNELS' DOGS are descendants of Antarctic veterans. Among them are burly Malamutes, ideal for heavy freighting in rough terrain, and the lighter Siberian Huskies, speediest of all. Each has the "snowshoe foot," with thick fur between the toes, a plumed tail, and the heavy double coat that serves the arctic dog as a natural sleeping bag. Some strains of the Husky are born blue-eyed, which seems to immunize them against the sled dog's saddest malady, snow blindness.

No pampered pet's life awaits this brace of sled-dog pups, pride of Peter Sydney of Banks Island, Canada. Strictly draft animals, they will stay outside the Eskimo's house even in 50°-below-zero weather. When a relative dies, some Eskimos give a dog the name of the deceased.

WINFIELD PARKS, NATIONAL GEOGRAPHIC PHOTOGRAPHER

I was struck by the dogs' energy. A chill north wind, portending snow, inspired them to a ceaseless trot around their runs. They leaped on and off ice-glazed doghouse roofs, deliberately slanted to help develop their sure-footedness.

Among the 50-odd dogs I saw were blue-eyed Jerry, a beautiful Husky who showed great promise as a lead dog; gentle Ballerina, who spurned her food till each of her 10-week-old puppies' stomachs bulged; and massive, gray-coated Gripp. Six of his Malamute sons were at that very moment in Antarctica.

Today's lumbering tractor-trains and ski-shod airplanes haul most of the tonnage of polar expeditions, but the dependable dog team still serves. Some thirty dogs accompanied Operation Deep Freeze to Antarctica for rescue work in foul flying weather or through terrain otherwise impassable.

Bravo, a Malamute-Husky born on the white continent, became the mascot of the first group ever to spend the six-month winter night at the South Pole. A month after his first birthday, Bravo frolicked beside two of the expedition members as they ventured out of the shelters in weather colder than man or dog had ever felt before—102° below zero! While the two men snugged their fur hoods tighter and clumped along in boots frozen hard as iron, the dog bounded ahead in a bluish cloud of flying snow.

Copper sun burnishes a pewter world, turns man and dogs to ebony in a timeless frieze of the F

Dr. Paul A. Siple, scientific leader of the expedition, knew that Bravo would be good for the men psychologically. And during the long isolation, the small band of scientists and Navy technicians found in Bravo a welcome confidant, a much-needed safety valve for human emotions. He became so spoiled that, as one man put it, "he doesn't even know he's a dog."

Though sled dogs might seem the exclusive property of the extreme latitudes, they helped push back America's western frontier. Explorers like Lewis and Clark saw how the Indians put dogs to work pulling sleds. So it is not surprising that pioneers in Utah used not only handcarts and covered wagons but sleds drawn by dogs. In the Rockies and the Sierras, dog teams hauled freight, mail, and even occasional passengers. Drivers resting during runs in the Rockies dug holes in the snow; exhausted dogs and their blanketed masters moved in together to keep from freezing to death.

During gold rush days in California an enterprising company hitched Newfoundlands and St. Bernards to sleds and operated an "express" service across the mountains. And in Colorado one man even used a dog-drawn toboggan to carry mail and supplies to the early settlers.

Often the dogs used were not the familiar born-to-the-harness breeds. With

orth. Eskimo seeks water holes where seals breathe; one seal a week will feed his nine-dog team.

CLYDE HARE

a good sled dog bringing a price of some $70, drivers were inclined to hitch up any mongrel of passable size and make up for its shortcomings by their own lungpower. "To be a thorough expert in dog-training," wrote one observer in the 1870's, "a man must be able to imprecate freely and with considerable variety in at least three different languages . . . . curses delivered in French will get a train of dogs through or over any thing."

With many a heroic chapter behind them, the Siberian Husky, the Malamute, Eskimo, and Samoyed—another Siberian breed—have turned to a new vocation, the booming winter sport of dog-sled racing. A number of clubs have sprung up in North America; oldest in the United States is the New England Sled Dog Club, with several dozen teams and drivers from all walks of life. One of its members, Massachusetts veterinarian Dr. Roland Lombard, has repeatedly won two of the biggest races in Alaska, grueling three-day events in Fairbanks and Anchorage that demand top physical condition in both driver and dogs.

The pioneer New England club has also led the way, under the guiding hand of Mrs. Seeley, in organizing junior league racing to give young enthusiasts an early start in the sport. The youngsters, ranging in age up to 16 years, elect their own officers, judges, and timekeepers. Most important, each driver must train his own dogs.

Mrs. Seeley believes racing preserves the working qualities of northern breeds. "These dogs are born to work," she said as we sat in her pleasant rustic home. "Even if you merely harness one to a load of firewood, you give him an identity."

A few early writers, I recalled,

KATHLEEN REVIS

Dog-sled travelers lunch at a chalet high in the Rockies. Young Malamutes rest in foreground.

High country outing gives sled teams a new sporting role. Colorado's Toklat Kennels put lightweight Siberian Huskies in van, Eskimos in middle, heavy Malamutes "at wheel."

described the sled dog as unpredictably savage, perhaps due to maltreatment or crosses with arctic wolves. I was about to ask Mrs. Seeley's opinion when a furry pad gently touched my knee. In a moment another joined it. Ch. Alyeska's Suggen of Chinook was requesting permission to come aboard.

With 50 pounds of Siberian Husky on my lap, proffering a furry chest to be scratched, discussion of a sled dog's "ferocity" seemed inappropriate. The question never came up.

The sled dog's service to man for centuries is matched by that of other working dogs. Watchdogs like the ancient Molossian and the modern Mastiff

guarded Assyrian palace, Greek temple, and medieval manor. Romans and Greeks, Celts and Gauls clad courageous battle dogs in spiked collars or armor; in more recent conflict dogs have located the wounded and served as sentries, messengers, scouts, and sappers detecting mines. The clown's clever Tumbler of Elizabethan times furnished man with gentle entertainment, as does Lassie, our Collie television star—actually not a single dog but a series of them over the years—and innumerable canine troupes.

The turnspit was born to a treadmill life in the kitchens of Europe; others of his kind churned butter and turned water wheels. The lurcher hunted forbidden game in England's forests for his poaching master. Smugglers loaded pack dogs like the Great Pyrenees with contraband and sent them across frontiers. In colder climes, many a once-shaggy dog has shivered in silence as its master harvested its fur for mittens, boots, hats, and even upholstery stuffing.

Horseless until the Spaniards' arrival, North American Indians hitched their dogs—often hybrid wolves—to travois. One explorer reported more than 500 dogs used in a single pack train to move an entire Assiniboin village in southern

Ride in a two-dog-power cart delights Quebec youngsters. Draft dogs like this sturdy pair, a matched team of crossbred yellow Labradors belonging to a French Canadian family, are often seen today in Europe.

B. ANTHONY STEWART AND JOHN E. FLETCHER, NATIONAL GEOGRAPHIC PHOTOGRAPHERS

WILLARD R. CULVER

Milk cart rolls to creamery behind Bernese dairy woman and patient Schweizer Sennenhund. This Swiss type descends from dogs brought by Roman invaders some 2,000 years ago; today they herd, guard, and haul.

Canada. In Europe sturdy draft dogs still pull vendors' carts through cobbled streets and milk wagons down country lanes. The Portuguese Water Dog long retrieved tackle for the fishing fleets. And in Ponta Delgada in the Azores big shaggy dogs have been trained to carry a basket and a list to market and do the family shopping.

Coach dogs, often Great Danes, trotted beside the carriages of Europe; highwaymen thought twice before tangling with these four-footed escorts. The massive Newfoundland and St. Bernard have made heroic rescues at sea and in snow-choked mountain passes; the keen-nosed German Shepherd now detects illicit drugs and seeks out buried Alpine avalanche victims.

Dogs in England have been trained to sniff out bits of wreckage from airplane mishaps, to help experts pinpoint causes. One dog retrieved piece after piece from a downed helicopter, then barked up a tree until its handler arrived—and found a fragment embedded in the tree.

Even the odd truffle dog has done his part to serve his masters, sniffing out buried delicacies for the gourmet's table.

In such ways does the dog serve man today; tracking and trailing, herding and hauling, guiding and guarding. After watching them learning and performing

Fourteen awkward little Danes, all from a single litter, line up for a family portrait; they'll soon grow great in size and style. St. Bernard (below) appears unimpressed; his kind has been known to whelp 20 at a time. Old English Sheepdog (right) peers out at a hair-conditioned world—until a young friend lifts his veil: "He's in there, all right."

THOMAS WILKIE, PIX, AND (BELOW) FRANCIS ROUTT, WASHINGTON STAR. OPPOSITE: DENNIS STOCK, MAGNUM

their varied jobs, I cannot help agreeing with Doctor Caius:

"For if any be disposed to drawe the above named services into a table, what may more clearely, and with more vehemency of voyce giveth warning eyther of a wastefull beaste, or of a spoiling theefe than this? Who by his barcking (as good as a burning beacon) foreshoweth hassards at hand? What servant to his master more loving? What companion more trustie? What watchman more vigilant? What messinger more speedie? Finally what packhorse more patient?"

What creature, indeed, but the wagging, willing, working dog?

A Portfolio

Following are the working breeds, painted in full color for the National Geographic Magazine by Edward Herbert Miner and other artists.

Brace of Collies leads a hike. Smooth Collies once herded in England, Rough Collies in cooler Scotland.

WALTER A. WEBER, NATIONAL GEOGRAPHIC STAFF ARTIST

WALTER A. WEBER

Collie

IN THE FRONT RANKS of the working dogs of the world stands that lithe, alert aristocrat we call the Collie.

Three centuries ago and more, Scottish shepherds bred and trained canny, agile working dogs to tend the flocks that made their country's major industry. From them stemmed efficient "Coalie" or "Coaly" dogs —probably named either for the black-faced sheep they herded or for their own black color. Our modern Collie wears the abundant double coat that warmed these hard-working ancestors, but now in sable and white, blue merle, tri-color, or white.

Highland fastnesses could not forever conceal the virtues of this breed; dog fanciers admired it early in the 19th century. Then broader and shorter of head than now, it stood only about 14 inches at the shoulder.

The Collie made its British dog show debut in 1860, and Queen Victoria's admiration for the breed assured its rise to fashion. About 20 years later its United States popularity began. Selective breeding since has given us the larger, patrician-headed, show-type Collie so popular today.

Americans know this dog chiefly as a beautiful, intelligent companion, idealized by "Lassie," star of movies and television. But in the great sheep raising districts of Scotland, northern England, and Wales, he is still the shepherd's indispensable helper.

Not that the working Collie looks very much like the long-muzzled, beruffled, well-groomed specimens that grace the dog show benches. He stands as little chance of taking a beauty prize as a blue-ribbon winner has of defeating him in the great annual sheep dog trials of his native land. But the working type has the brains, courage, and stamina that keep Great Britain's sheep industry thriving. In the land of misty mountains one good dog does the work of a dozen men; no other animal could replace him.

Australian and New Zealand herders also swear by the working breed, and in America, where Colonial farmers probably first imported it, the Collie is the favorite farm dog today.

Some authorities believe that Rough and Smooth Collies originally were different breeds. But today their difference is confined to coat (Pointer-length in the Smooth), and both have appeared in the same litter. The smooth variety developed principally in Britain's county of Northumberland, as a cattle-drover's dog.

Rough or Smooth, the Collie is gentle and affectionate in nature, graceful in gait. Deep, moderately wide chest, sloping shoulders, and well-bent hocks hint at speed and strength. Light, tapering head and rounded muzzle, with slight "stop" between, lend an air of refinement. He is one of the most easily trained of dogs, but displays the Scot's common sense in occasional reluctance to repeat a trick he has just done well.

Above all, he shows a boundless sense of responsibility. Countless stories of a Collie herding a child from the path of an automobile echo a centuries-old heritage of faithful guardianship of whatever is committed to his charge.

Shoulder height 22–26 in. Weight 50–75 lbs.

WALTER A. WEBER, NATIONAL GEOGRAPHIC STAFF ARTIST

Double coat shields the Sheltie, like his Collie kin, from Shetland Islands storm and thistle spine.

Shetland Sheepdog

"LIKE A SCOTTISH COLLIE of the best kind seen through the wrong end of a telescope" —this is the nimble, quick-witted little beauty, the Shetland Sheepdog.

As rugged and charming as his weather-beaten native isles northeast of Scotland, the "Sheltie" doubtless sprang from the old Scottish working Collie crossed with small local dogs. Stern environment produced a working breed to match the islands' hardy Lilliputian livestock. Sound legs and feet, deep chest, strong-muscled back, and dense, Collie-colored coat fit him admirably for herding on rocky, stormswept pastures.

An 1840 engraving indicates that the Sheltie guarded the crofter's cottage and flock well over a century ago. Early efforts to fix the type introduced some spaniel blood, and that of Icelandic or Greenland dogs. Breeders later crossed in modern Collies to shape a refined show dog with basic working traits.

Long hidden from dog-fanciers' view, the breed went unrecognized by England's Kennel Club until 1909; it has been seen in the United States since 1911.

At times aloof toward strangers, the Sheltie is affectionate and responsive to his owner, usually scoring well in obedience trials. U.S. breeders seek the "ideal Collie in miniature"; the result is a bright farm helper, alert watchdog, and delightful companion all in one small package.

Shoulder height 13–16 in. Weight 15–20 lbs.

Bearlike Bobtails survey their flock through ha

Old English Sheepdog

AS HE COMES BOUNDING UP, long coat tossing like a huge floor mop, few can resist the charm of this good-natured bundle of dog. And as he peers out at you with those intelligent and friendly eyes, it seems to matter little whether his lineage is as old as his name implies.

Efforts to trace this shaggy dog's story falter back beyond the early 19th century, though a 1770 portrait by Gainsborough displays a fair specimen. His herd dog ancestry is said to include the Highland Collie and possibly the heavy-coated Russian Owtchar, brought to the British Isles aboard Baltic trading ships.

The Old English Sheepdog first appears in the west of England—Devon, Somerset, and Cornwall—where he was bred to drive sheep and cattle to fair or market. He barks with ringing authority and ambles after his charges with a peculiar rolling bearlike gait, though he can gallop fast when necessary.

EDWARD HERBERT MINER

urtains. Docked tail once signified tax-free status.

Tax-exempt as a drover's dog, the Old English Sheepdog customarily had his ornamental tail bobbed as a sign of his working status—hence his affectionate nickname Bobtail. Some puppies today are born tailless, but most have their tails docked at the first joint when three or four days old.

The breed first earned separate classification at a recognized British show in 1873, and reached the United States before 1890, where it since has gained in popularity.

Although the Bobtail has done a Collie's work in England and on the great sheep ranges of western Canada, he bears little likeness to the Collie-type farm dog; rather he resembles a great long-legged, round-headed, bounding terrier. His profuse outer coat surmounts an inner waterproof pile, and comes in gray, pigeon-blue, or blue merle, with or without white markings. Thickest on the rump, it is hard-textured and shaggy but free from curl.

This insulation fits him for almost any climate, hot, cold, or damp, but some potential owners express concern over its maintenance. Actually the Bobtail requires no greater care than any other long-haired breed. If his coat becomes matted, tangles should be gently teased out with the fingers. Otherwise periodic grooming with a stiff brush will suffice. (Like those of the snowy Samoyed, his combings furnish a first-class wool for knitters!)

The sturdy Bobtail stands tall, with squarish, compact body deep in the chest. He is agile for his size, with forelegs straight, strong, and full-boned; hindquarters rounded and muscular. Keen scent and hearing make up for vision commonly obscured by the hanging forelock. His skull—when it can be seen—appears square and roomy, befitting a dog of his intelligence.

Easy to train, the Old English Sheepdog makes a surprisingly good retriever, possessing a "soft mouth," an affinity for water, and an inclination to remain at his owner's heel. He serves well as sled dog and watchdog. At least one member of the breed submitted to a "G.I. haircut" and served honorably with U.S. forces in World War II.

This dog of character and charm is playful but never boisterous. He makes a fine companion for children, and his amiable, home-loving nature adapts to rural farmstead or city apartment.

The world looks at the Old English Sheepdog as a friendly, appealing curiosity of dogdom; the Bobtail peers back through his shaggy veil with the quiet dignity of one who knows his place in our affections is secure. *Shoulder height 22–28 in. Weight 50–70 lbs.*

Great Pyrenees

BRITISH CALL HIM the Pyrenean Mountain Dog; French, *Le Grand Chien des Montagnes*, or *Chien des Pyrenees*. In the United States he is the Great Pyrenees, aptly described as "an animated snowdrift."

This majestic dog takes his names from the mountains along the French-Spanish border where for centuries he has guarded shepherds' flocks and homes, carried packs, and pulled carts.

Like most members of the mastiff family, the Great Pyrenees has a proud and ancient history. His ancestors, probably migrants from Central Asia or Siberia, left identifiable remains in Bronze Age deposits more than 3,000 years ago. Even earlier, Babylonians pictured huge dogs resembling the breed.

In the snowy Pyrenees the breed developed in centuries of isolation as a shepherd's companion. Armored with spiked collar and long, thick coat, the huge and powerful dog patrolled high mountain pastures. Shepherds relied on him to battle wolves and bears, and often left him in sole charge of flocks. Their confidence was justified; early writers, struck by the breed's courage, sometimes called it the Pyrenean Wolfhound or Bearhound.

As predators declined, the Great Pyrenees took on general guard and draft work.

French nobility early saw the virtues of the mountain peasant's breed, and bands of these dogs guarded many large chateaux. Medieval sculptures of the royal coat of arms bear its likeness, and in the reign of Louis XIV the "White Furred Lords" became the fashion at court.

The Great Pyrenees apparently sailed aboard 17th century Basque fishing boats to Newfoundland, where colonists crossed it (possibly with the Curly-coated Retriever) to create, some say, the Newfoundland dog. Great Pyrenees blood is also said to run strong in the veins of today's St. Bernard.

The Great Pyrenees first reached the United States when General Lafayette gave a pair to an American friend in 1824, describing them as "of inestimable value to wool-growers in all regions exposed to the depredations of wolves and sheepkilling dogs." Few others were imported during the next century, and not until 1933 did the American Kennel Club recognize the breed.

The Great Pyrenees' herculean size and strength equip him admirably as a pack dog. Border smugglers so used him for many years between France and Spain. Some saw service in World War I, and the United States trained a few in World War II to carry machine guns, ammunition, and supplies.

Soundness weighs most heavily when judging this handsome breed. His broad, straight back and capacious chest evolved through centuries of arduous mountain work. His massive, wedge-shaped head curiously resembles that of the bear he once combated. Double dewclaws on each hind leg mark the typical specimen. His flat, snowy coat is sometimes marked with badger-gray or tan.

A fine, trustworthy dog with children, the Great Pyrenees guards his modern master's home with the loyalty and devotion he gave the mountain shepherd centuries ago. *Shoulder height 25–32 in. Weight 90–125 lbs.*

Huge and fearless, Great Pyrenees long protected flocks from wolves. In the United States he makes a fine watchdog and gentle companion.

WALTER A. WEBER, NATIONAL GEOGRAPHIC STAFF ARTIST

Woolly as the sheep he guards, Hungary's Komondor came from Asia with Magyars 1,000 years ago.

Komondor

IN WORKING GARB—a matted, rag-tag coat that sometimes sweeps the ground—the Komondor hardly looks an aristocrat. Yet Hungarian shepherds, who bred him for ten centuries or more, regard him as king of working dogs.

One of Europe's oldest breeds, this burly fellow is a formidable foe of the wolf. He stands guard against raiders, leaving the roundup to lesser breeds. His woolly armor shields against knifing winds of his native plains, as well as predator's fangs. This unkempt white coat, resembling that of the sheep he protects, lets him approach without alarming his flock.

When groomed for show, coat hanging in long cords, he seems a different dog—shaggily handsome, with deep, muscular chest, wide rump, and massive bone.

A Serb legend relates that the Komondor sprang from wolf cubs reared by 10th century shepherds. Expert opinion, however, holds that Magyar migrants brought him from the east, where he had descended from a powerful herd dog of the Russian steppes.

In Hungary today the breed is often seen in dog shows as well as on the plains. Police train some for guard work in the cities.

Still relatively rare in the United States, the Komondor won American Kennel Club recognition in 1937. The dog has proved intelligent and devoted to master and family, though somewhat suspicious of strangers. *Height 23½–34 in. Weight 80–140 lbs.*

Puli

A SHAGGY AND NIMBLE Hungarian shepherd dog, the Puli looks like a smaller, darker version of the Komondor, and his history is much the same.

But while the Komondor's bulk is better suited to guarding flocks, the agile, medium-sized Puli excels at herding. He sometimes controls the sheep by running across their backs. To stop a woolly runaway he may leap aboard and ride it like a broncobuster gentling a fractious horse. Shepherds sometimes fix a log or iron hoop to his collar to curb an occasional tendency to roam.

One authority attributes the Puli's ancestry to dogs of Iceland and Lapland, but general belief is that he came to Hungary with Asiatic invaders more than 1,000 years ago. A 1751 description of a "Hungarian Water Dog" fits today's Puli, indicating he may also have been used as a hunter.

The Puli's black, gray, or white coat of long, fine hair tends to mat or cord on his homeland plains. It grows profusely on his dome-shaped skull, hindquarters, and tail.

Still uncommon in the United States, the Puli joined American Kennel Club ranks in 1937. World War II halted experiments by the U.S. Department of Agriculture in crossing and training him for herding work in this country. Though often wary of strangers, he is by nature perky, inquisitive, and pleasant—entitling him to wider renown simply as an enjoyable companion.
Shoulder height 16–19 in. Weight 25–40 lbs.

Claws dug in, a Puli rides a runaway sheep to exhaustion, then gently herds it back to the flock.

WALTER A. WEBER, NATIONAL GEOGRAPHIC STAFF ARTIST, AND (LOWER) EDWARD HERBERT MINER

Welsh Corgis, Pembroke left, Cardigan right, chase cattle by nipping at their heels.

Rottweilers, descended from Roman cattle dogs, drove German butchers' herds.

Welsh Corgi (PEMBROKE AND CARDIGAN)

THE WELSH WORDS *cor* (dwarf) and *gi* (dog) give these droll-looking, delightful little dogs their name.

The Welsh ruler, Howel Dda, may have alluded to the Corgi when in the early 10th century he fixed the value of the "shepherd cur" at that of a prime ox. But everyone in Pembrokeshire and Cardiganshire has long known the value of these short-legged, long-bodied, fox-headed little farm dogs. Some call them "heelers" for the nimble way they drive a stubborn cow; they nip at a heel and drop flat to avoid the ensuing kick.

Not by chance do Pembroke and Cardigan Corgis resemble each other. Both have long performed the same task—herding cattle, sheep, swine; hunting rabbits, killing vermin. And they often were crossed before the Welsh Corgi caught dog exhibitors' fancy in 1925. But their early history was distinct.

The Cardigan Corgi migrated to the Welsh high country with warlike Celts more than 3,000 years ago. It stems from the same family as the Dachshund. Crosses with red and brindle herding dogs, and later with the Collie, produced its rather short and hard-textured coat (reddish, brindle, black-and-tan, black-and-white, or blue merle) and long and bushy tail.

A very short tail and a narrower muzzle mark the Pembroke Corgi. The breed's leading authority states it sprang from spitz-type dogs that Flemish weavers brought across the Channel A.D. 1107.

Britain's royal family has favored the Welsh Corgi since 1933, assuring its popularity. Thousands have found the Corgi as vigilant and good-humored in the home as he is useful on the farm.

Shoulder height 10–12 in. Weight 15–35 lbs.

Rottweiler

ROBUST, COURAGEOUS, calm, and efficient: these traits well suit the dogs that drove Roman legions' cattle over the Alps into central Europe. When the tide of conquest ebbed, some stayed behind in south Germany to flourish for 19 centuries as the breed we call the Rottweiler.

"Butcher's Dog of Rottweil" was the name he earned in a thriving market center in Württemberg. Livestock dealers setting out to buy cattle in the countryside thwarted thieves by tying their purses around his muscular neck; later he would drive their new-bought herds back to market. Merchants harnessed the sturdy dog to carts and posted him as guard.

A late 19th century German law banning cattle-driving with dogs almost spelled extinction for the Rottweiler; by 1905 few were to be found in the town whose name he bears.

Fortunately, the reawakened interest in working breeds which molded today's German Shepherd and Doberman Pinscher also saved the Rottweiler. His strong guardian instinct, obedience, and unexcitable nature equipped him splendidly for military and police duties. These same qualities, plus strong affection for his master, make the Rottweiler an ideal guard-companion dog.

Broad-skulled between his uncropped ears, he has a short, coarse, flat coat. Preferred color is black, with tan to rich mahogany markings on cheeks, muzzle, chest, and legs.

Recognized in the United States since 1935, the breed deserves wider renown.

Height 21¾–27 in. Weight 80–110 lbs.

Belgian Sheepdog

AMERICAN SOLDIERS of World War I marveled at the swift, intelligent dogs their Belgian allies used on the battlefield. Uncannily, the dogs located and aided wounded in no man's land, and raced with messages through fire few men could survive.

These were valiant Belgian sheepdogs, pressed into service from traditional pastoral pursuits. As with most dogs long bred as herdsmen's helpers, time obscures their background, though some relationship to the German Shepherd and other herding dogs of central Europe seems obvious.

Belgians differentiate at least six types of their sheepdogs. The American Kennel Club recognized three varieties until 1959 when it granted separate breed classification to the Groenendael, Tervuren, and Malinois. The Groenendael retained the official designation, Belgian Sheepdog.

This black beauty with the long smooth coat owes his beginning to a sheepdog breeder in the Belgian village of Groenendael, one Monsieur Rose. In 1885 he found in a litter a single long-haired black female puppy. Blacks were scarce then, and M. Rose searched for a year to find a similarly colored mate. The ebony strain they produced caught the public fancy when first shown at a Belgian show in 1898. Many entered the United States after World War I, and this breed remains the most popular of the Belgian sheepdogs here.

The Groenendael shows the countless generations of shrewd herders behind him in the way he often chooses to circle, rather than move on a straight course. Strongly muscled hindquarters spell a fast-gaited dog; indeed, the Belgian seems constantly and tirelessly in motion.

This son of Flanders has proved his courage in war, his intelligence in police work and obedience trials, and his spirited loyalty to his master in many emergencies.

Those who know him best say there is no more devoted companion, vigilant guardian, and willing worker.

Shoulder height 22–26 in. Weight 50–60 lbs.

Belgian Tervuren, Belgian Malinois

NEARLY identical in conformation and temperament, the three Belgian sheepdogs differ mainly in their coats.

Black-tipped fawn hair distinguishes the Tervuren and Malinois from the black Groenendael, though the lighter-hued breeds both wear black masks.

Like the Groenendael, with which he shares a common ancestor, the long-coated Tervuren is named for the town of his origin. Brought to the United States in the 1940's, he quickly won notice for his special aptitude in obedience work.

In addition to his talents as a patient and tireless herder, he exhibits a boundless curiosity, fearlessly investigating everything strange. He is a superb watchdog and a playful companion for children.

The Malinois, as intelligent and able as the Tervuren, developed as a type at the close of the 19th century around the town of Mechelen, or Malines, whence he gets his name. Because of his short coat, he is sometimes mistaken for a German Shepherd.

Shoulder height 22–26 in. Weight 50–60 lbs.

Intelligent Belgian sheepdogs served in wa and police work. Black Groenendael, black and-fawn Tervuren, and distant Malinois onc were varieties of the same breed.

JAMES GORDON IRVI

J.G.IRVING

WALTER A. WEBER

German Shepherd

NO WORKING BREED lays better claim to the title "Dog of all trades" than the amazingly versatile German Shepherd.

Thousands of persons doomed to blindness owe near-normal lives to his gentle and patient guidance. Police in Germany and Canada, in Baltimore's brick alleyways and London's mist-shrouded Hyde Park have found him a fearless law-enforcing ally. He guards a Chicago department store, a Kimberley diamond mine, a New York school system, an air base in the Pacific.

No one can calculate the number of lives the German Shepherd has saved in two World Wars, scenting out wounded, carrying medical supplies and messages, alerting jungle patrols against ambush, guarding coastlines from saboteurs, locating civilians buried in bomb debris. His mercy missions continue in peacetime: his unerring nose now leads rescuers to avalanche victims buried under snow in the Swiss Alps.

Today's handsome, intelligent German Shepherd is a highly refined composite of several herding types of centuries ago. These include a lithe, rather small dog of the north German plains and a sturdy, larger animal of mountain regions to the south.

As the 19th century waned, Germany's pastoral era waned with it. A few breeders, however, sought to preserve the splendid working qualities of their shepherding dogs. Most notable was a captain of cavalry, Max von Stephanitz, whose crusade to standardize the breed began in 1889 and culminated in one of the largest breed clubs in the world.

The German Shepherd's remarkable record on police patrol and World War I battlefield made worldwide attention inevitable. Millions of American moviegoers thrilled to the celluloid exploits of Strongheart and Rin Tin Tin, and it seemed for a time that every family wanted one of these rugged, attractive "police dogs."

Such popularity carried its price; careless breeding and "puppy factories" turned out many substandard specimens—shy, nervous, or snappish—and the breed plummeted as fast as it had risen. In the mid-twenties, every third dog registered in the United States was a German Shepherd; 1934 saw fewer than 800 registered. But its fanciers stood by their breed and nurtured its quality to the high level it enjoys today.

Too well known to need detailed description, the German Shepherd (more often called the Alsatian in England) displays an almost primitive beauty of form as he moves with smooth, free, long-trotting gait. His dense short coat ranges from black through wolf-gray, brindle, and brown to white, with the muzzle usually blackish. His expression speaks strength and nobility, courage without hostility.

Capt. Von Stephanitz and his associates sought a dog of "utility and intelligence." Their success seems remarkable.

Shoulder height 22–26 in. Weight 60–85 lbs.

Farmer-warriors of Belgium and France: t cattle-driving Bouvier des Flandres (rear) serv as messenger and first-aid dog in battle; bush browed sheepherder, the Briard (front), haul ammunition and put keen hearing to sentry us

Hard-working, dignified German Shepherd parents take time out to watch their youngsters have a ball.

WALTER A. WEBER, NATIONAL GEOGRAPHIC STAFF ARTIST

Briard

AN ACTIVE, ROBUST, weatherproof worker of the fields—this is the Briard, a popular French farmer's helper whose records date from the 12th century.

Named for his home district of Brie, the keen-eared and powerful breed also served with distinction as war and police dog.

The Briard easily shrugs rain and caked mud from his long and wavy coat (in all solid colors except white); shaggy brows shield his eyes from brush. A well-feathered tail hangs long and low with a sickle curve at its end. This dog's rather squarish conformation suggests a common ancestry with other European herders like the Owtchar, Highland Collie, and Old English Sheepdog.

The Briard's serious, quiet nature is endearing him to more and more American families; he returns the affection amply. *Height 22–27 in. Weight 60–80 lbs.*

EDWARD HERBERT MINER

Bouvier des Flandres

THIS "COWHERD OF FLANDERS" stems from hardy, centuries-old working stock, as likely as not whelped in cowshed or stable. These were the dogs of farmers, butchers, and cattle merchants in southwest Flanders and the northern hills of France.

Today's standardized Bouvier des Flandres loses none of the rugged appearance and qualities of his ancestors. Resembling the Giant Schnauzer, the compactly built Bouvier is deep in the brisket, with long, sloping shoulders and well-muscled hindquarters. He wears a tousled, wiry coat, ranging from fawn to black, pepper-and-salt, gray, and brindle. With cropped, triangular ears and docked tail, he carries no impedimenta; he is alert, vigorous, quick-moving.

The breed first appeared on the show bench at Brussels in 1910. Fanciers soon discerned its talents as watchdog, police dog, wartime messenger and ambulance dog. None earns a Belgian championship without first winning in working trials.

Restored from the ravages of World War I, the breed was recognized in the United States in the late 1930's. The Bouvier is now gaining the notice he warrants as a bright, responsible worker and fine companion. *Shoulder height $22\frac{3}{4}$–$27\frac{1}{2}$ in. Weight 80–105 lbs.*

Standard Schnauzer

BRIGHT AND FEARLESS, the terrierlike Schnauzer of Germany offers his many talents in three lively packages—large, medium, and small. Both extremes, Giant and Miniature, stem from the "middleweight" or Standard breed, now known simply as the Schnauzer.

The breed is probably at least 500 years old; Albrecht Dürer portrayed a Schnauzer-like dog in the 1490's. The breed seems to have originated in Württemberg and Bavaria from wire-haired Pinscher stock crossed with black German Poodle and a spitz-type dog. Some experts, however, indicate possible relationship with the Airedale, Irish, and Kerry Blue Terriers, as well as with rough-haired hounds of medieval Europe.

Whatever his antecedents, the Schnauzer has served for centuries as a master rat-catcher, yard and stable dog, and guard. His trademark—a luxuriant crop of whiskers—fringes a strong, blunt muzzle. His squarely built body is coated with dense, harsh hair, usually pepper-and-salt colored or black. The tail is docked to two inches or less, and high-set ears are usually cropped to stand erect.

The breed was first exhibited in Germany in 1879 as the Wire-haired Pinscher; from a prize-winning entry named Schnauzer (*Schnauze* is German for muzzle) came the breed name of today. Schnauzer clubs in Germany still test their dogs' ancient skill as vermin killers in ratting trials.

The Schnauzer was little known in the United States in the early 1900's but has since gained attention through obedience tests. In 1945 the American Kennel Club transferred the Standard from Terrier to Working Group, joining the Giant. (The Miniature remains with the Terriers.)

"A Schnauzer is not a 'pretty' dog," sums up one fancier of the breed. "His beauty is that of character, his devotion to home and family, and his service as the ideal companion and guardian."

Shoulder height 17–20 in. Weight 30–40 lbs.

Giant Schnauzer

LARGEST AND PERHAPS YOUNGEST of the three Schnauzer breeds, the Giant shares with the Standard and Miniature a vigorous yet eminently reliable temperament.

The Giant Schnauzer (once called the Münchener) was developed in Bavaria near Munich by cattlemen seeking a terrier type large and bold enough to move livestock to market. Early crosses of Standard Schnauzer with local herdsmen's dogs and later with the black Great Dane gave this stalwart dog his size and wiry salt-and-pepper or black coat. The similar Bouvier des Flandres is also said to be a relative.

When modern transportation supplanted cattle drives in Germany, the Giant Schnauzer remained as butcher's dog, stockyard helper, and brewery guard. He seldom was seen outside Bavaria until the early 1900's, when his career as police and military dog began. These have been his chief jobs since, though Norwegians sometimes harness him to a sled. A few of the rough-and-ready breed reached the United States in the 1920's but were overshadowed by the German Shepherd then at its peak of popularity.

Germany lost many fine Giant Schnauzers in World War II, and in its homeland the breed has been recovering slowly.

Height 21½–25½ in. Weight 80–100 lbs.

EDWIN MEGARGEE

Bewhiskered Schnauzers, Standard (top) and Giant, coolly survey an intruder through bushy brows.

powerful athlete, the Doberman Pinscher leaps to attack a "gunman." eel-trap jaws could snap an unpadded arm. Mixture of terrier agility d shepherd strength, Dobes also make docile guide dogs for the blind.

ERT E. LOUGHEED

Doberman Pinscher

NO ONE TODAY is certain of the ingredients, but Herr Louis Dobermann, a breeder and dogcatcher of Apolda, in Thüringia, Germany, set about in the 1870's to "brew" a truly remarkable dog.

He sought a breed built along the agile lines of a terrier, yet larger, with the shepherd's strength. It had to have speed, power, and intelligence, combined with temperamental fire and fearlessness.

We see the results of his experiments, refined and improved, in the lithe, steel-sinewed breed called the Doberman Pinscher.

In all likelihood the smooth-haired German Pinscher, the Rottweiler, and shepherd strains went into the Doberman's basic make-up. Many authorities believe the Manchester Terrier, the Greyhound, and possibly the Weimaraner later were added.

By 1890 Herr Dobermann had in rough form the dog he wanted. The early "Dobermann's dogs," as the breed once was called, were coarser bodied than today, shorter in the head, often longer haired. But they were "sharp"—totally without fear of man or beast. As one pioneer breeder confessed, "It required a good deal of courage to own one."

This original aggressiveness is now well controlled in the breed, although the Doberman can be a punishing fighter when necessary. Easily disciplined and quick to learn, he consistently ranks among the top breeds in obedience training. Many Dobermans serve as guides for the blind.

Originally designed as a watchdog and household guardian, the bold and inquisitive Doberman early proved himself a superb police and war dog. U.S. Marines in World War II adopted the breed as their official war dog. Dobermans were used, as German Shepherds were, to flush snipers from trees and caves, and to warn against enemy ambush in the Pacific. One named Andy saved a tank platoon stalled under heavy fire on Bougainville by spotting two concealed Japanese machine-gun nests.

The keen-nosed dogs have since made civilian careers of detecting nighttime prowlers in stores and warehouses and on estates.

For raw animal beauty the "Dobe" has few peers. He strides with the air of a superbly conditioned gymnast. From wedge-shaped head to docked tail he cuts a clean-lined, compactly muscled figure, and is often much heavier than he appears. Deep chest, tucked-up belly, straight forelegs, and strong, driving hindquarters provide his notable speed and endurance. Except where prohibited by law, the Doberman's ears are cropped to trim points. His smooth, hard coat is usually black and tan, but can be brown or blue.

Despite the breed's relatively recent origin, its popularity has gained rapidly throughout the United States since the Doberman Pinscher Club of America was formed in 1921. One fine specimen recently spurred the breed's fame by winning dogdom's highest American award—the Westminster Kennel Club's Best in Show—two years in a row.

Essentially a one-man dog, the Doberman Pinscher does not lavish affection on strangers; but when his respect and devotion are earned, he gives them for life.

Shoulder height 24–28 in. Weight 50–75 lbs.

Mastiff

"WHAT THE LION IS TO THE CAT, the Mastiff is to the dog, the noblest of the family"—so reads a 19th century opinion of this giant and fearless breed.

Originating in Asia, dogs of mastiff type adorn bas reliefs of Babylon and Assyria. Phoenicians probably brought them to Britain, where Caesar's legions admired their size and strength. Many were shipped to Rome to fight in the arena. Britons, too, pitted their Mastiffs against bulls and other animals.

"The force which is in them surmounteth all beleefe," reports an Elizabethan writer. "Three of them against a Beare, fowre against a Lyon are sufficient utterly to overmatch them." Tied during the day and loosed at night, the Mastiff for centuries was a terror to thieves and prowlers.

The modern breed is docile but still makes an impressive watchdog. An apricot, silver fawn, or dark fawn-brindle coat cloaks his massive and symmetrical form. Small, V-shaped ears and blunt muzzle are dark. A few decades ago fanciers counted only seven Mastiffs left in Britain, but imports from America have helped restore the breed there. *Height 27½–30 in. Weight 125–175 lbs.*

Bull Mastiff

POACHERS in 19th century England risked severe penalties; many would kill rather than face arrest. For protection, gamekeepers turned to the Bull Mastiff.

This "Gamekeeper's Night Dog" was bred specially to patrol Britain's vast estates and silently track down illegal hunters. The Mastiff, whose "awful looks the Traveller did Afright, the Vagabond by Day, the Thief by Night," had the size and courage for the job, but lacked speed and agility; the Bulldog of the fighting pit was over-fierce and too light. Crossing the two produced an ideal dog: fearless, big enough to pin a man to ground, yet controlled enough not to maul him.

In sporting contests, few men, even armed with clubs, could stay on their feet against a muzzled Bull Mastiff's battering lunges.

Though its ingredients are centuries old, the breed has gained prominence only since the 1880's. England's Kennel Club gave recognition in the 1920's, the American Kennel Club in the 1930's. Described as 60 per cent Mastiff and 40 per cent Bulldog, the Bull Mastiff is marked by a broad, square head and deep, wide chest. Black mask and ears accent a short, dense coat of fawn or brindle. Alert, powerful, and even-tempered, he trains well for police and guard duty. *Shoulder height 24–27 in. Weight 100–130 lbs.*

Britain's Mastiff (left) foug in Rome's arena; smal Bull Mastiff (right) patroll Victorian game preserves.

EDWARD HERBERT MINER

Great Dane ▶

THE "APOLLO OF DOGS," the Great Dane has been called; and so he is, with every line cleanly chiseled, coupling magnificent size and supple grace.

Despite its name, the breed as we know it today more likely was developed in Germany than in Denmark. The French unaccountably once called it the *Grand Danois* and this name has clung in English translation. Germans know it as the *Deutsche Dogge*, the latter word connoting a large mastiff type.

Some experts point to drawings on ancient Egyptian monuments and tombs as evidence that the Dane's ancestry stretches back 4,000 to 5,000 years. Others find a marked resemblance in the great Molossian dog of Greco-Roman times. A Greek coin dating about 39 B.C. depicts a huge dog thought by several to conform closely to the breed. But today's weight of opinion holds that our modern Dane results from a more recent mixture of Mastiff and Irish Wolfhound or Greyhound.

The Great Dane was originally bred to run down and fight the murderously tusked wild boar until hunters could dispatch it with swords or spears. This feat called for supreme courage, great strength of jaws, holding power, and agility. Sixteenth century etchings of hunting the wild boar show dogs of strictly Great Dane appearance.

Later the breed guarded German princes and accompanied English masters to the wars. The modern Dane has lost none of his forerunner's traits but the ferocity.

Few breeds can approach the majesty of the Great Dane, with his noble carriage, his massive head, and full, square jaw. Dark, lively eyes express great intelligence. A smooth, dense coat in brindle, fawn, blue, black, or harlequin covers his smoothly muscled body. Strong, sloping shoulders and powerful hindquarters drive him effortlessly in lithe and springy stride.

His elegant style made him a favorite coach dog of English nobility. 'No equipage can have arrived at the acme of grandeur," reports one 18th century observer, "until a couple of harlequin Danes precede the pomp."

Physically suited to spacious living, the "giant" dog nevertheless conducts himself with tact in many small apartments today, appearing to sense the havoc his size and strength might wreak. Though gentle and affectionate as a companion, he guards a home as alertly today as he did South African gold mines 60 years ago.

German Chancellor Bismarck's devotion to a Great Dane did much to spread the breed's fame; the death of his dog Tyras made news around the world. Danes have gained steadily in popularity since their appearance at British and American dog shows in the 1880's.

Freeman Lloyd, writing in the *National Geographic Magazine*, recalled that many years ago a trader commissioned him to select the best Great Dane available in South Africa for barter with Lobengula, a tribal ruler who had seen and admired one of the breed. The king had offered two wagonloads of ivory and more for such a dog.

Asked why he had taken such a fancy to the Great Dane, the monarch replied: "He is a king among dogs and suitable as a companion of Lobengula, King of the Matabele. As he followed at your heels, he kept his head high and did not take any notice of the barkings and yappings of my people's curs. He's a king among dogs."

Any Dane owner today would agree.

Shoulder height 28–32 in. Weight 100–150 lbs.

EDWIN MEGARGEE

Statuesque sentries, a brace of Great Danes guards the gates of a country estate. Their ancestors bayed wild boar in medieval German forests. Black-patched harlequin (left) once trotted as coach dog to wealthy British travelers.

Flop-eared Boxer pups play follow-the-leader up the porch step
Their breed has climbed popularity's heights in the United States i
the past 30 years. Undershot jaw reveals the Boxer's Bulldog bloo

ROBERT LOUGHE

Boxer

WHEN THE SEVEN-YEAR-OLD guest of honor walked to the head table at a New York testimonial banquet some years ago, more than 200 diners rose and cheered. The guest accepted the acclaim indifferently, concentrating his attention on a prime raw beefsteak placed before him.

The occasion was an unusual tribute to the handsome fawn-and-white Boxer dog, Ch. Bang Away of Sirrah Crest, on his retirement as the "winningest" contestant in American dog show history. In his lifetime he earned 121 Best in Show awards; his owner once refused $20,000 for him.

This dog and other fine show winners of his breed doubtless contributed to the great popularity the Boxer enjoys in the United States today. The upswing started in the 1930's when an imported champion won an impressive number of blue ribbons, bringing the breed to nationwide attention.

Bang Away, however, sitting through the laudatory speeches and presentations with dignified restraint, revealed the chief reason for the Boxer's high favor. It is the breed's nature to be self-assured yet modest; playful with his family but reserved toward strangers —in all, an admirable dog to have around the house.

The Boxer's origin is difficult to trace, but common belief is that his ancestors sprang from crosses between early forms of Great Dane and Bulldog, with perhaps terrier strains bred in. Flemish tapestries of the 16th and 17th centuries depict what appear to be his ancestral relatives hunting stag and boar. Endowed with great courage, agility, strength, and intelligence, this stub-tailed dog often was found in the bull pits, or fighting other dogs, until European laws forbade these sports in the 19th century.

Some believe the name Boxer was corrupted from the German word *Beiszer*, as in *Bullenbeiszer* (bull-biter or bull-baiter). Others think the now-extinct Brabanter, also called the *Boxl*, was an ancestor and gave the breed its name. A third opinion holds that it comes from the dog's fighting technique, in which he often appears to box with his front paws.

The Boxer joined the German Shepherd and the Doberman Pinscher as one of the dogs bred to a high point of development in the 1890's in Germany. His compact, squarely built figure was seen on the battlefields of both World Wars, and his alert, dependable nature fits him well for a peacetime vocation of leading the blind.

American breeders place special emphasis on the Boxer's unique head, seeking perfect proportion between slightly arched skull and powerful muzzle. Broad, curved thighs and straight forelegs give him a firm, elastic gait; he carries his cleanly muscled body with pride and nobility. A black mask contrasts with smooth, glossy coat of brindle or fawn; white markings often appear, but must not cover more than one-third of his body.

The energetic Boxer is ready to take his own part when necessary, yet is tractable. He displays great affection, loyalty, and protective feeling toward his master. One can ask no more of a fine canine companion.

Shoulder height 21–24 in. Weight 55–70 lbs.

WILLIAM H. BOND, NATIONAL GEOGRAPHIC STAFF ARTIST

Akita, dog of good fortune, today is protected in Japan as a "National Art Treasure."

Akita

NOBLE DOG OF JAPAN, the Akita traces his ancestry to the Nippon Inu, a large hunting dog kept by cave dwellers perhaps as early as 5,000 B.C. and whose likeness adorns tombs of some of that nation's earliest rulers.

Massive and well muscled, the Akita resembles a cross between a giant German Shepherd and the sled dogs that came to America with the Eskimos thousands of years ago. He takes his name from Akita prefecture on the island of Honshu.

Through much of history the Akita has been the dog of nobility, with special attendants to serve him. Handlers using "Dog Words" trained him to hunt boar, deer, and bear, and to retrieve wildfowl.

In more modern times he has come to symbolize health and happiness. Akita statues are presented as gifts to the newborn and as get-well tokens to the sick. Courageous, loyal, and intelligent, the Akita can guide a blind person, pull a sled, or guard a child—and suffer its teasing. Webbed feet make him a strong-swimming lifeguard.

Helen Keller brought the first Akitas to the United States in the 1930's, but it wasn't until after World War II that the breed became established here. Granted AKC recognition in 1973, the Akita has since skyrocketted in popularity. A clean pet, he washes himself like a cat. His medium-length coat varies in color from black to fawn, red, or white; his gait is brisk. *Height 25–27½ in. Weight 95–125 lbs.*

St. Bernard

MASSIVE AND MELANCHOLY-EYED, hero of hundreds of Alpine rescues, the St. Bernard bears a marked resemblance to Mastiff-like dogs graven on Assyrian reliefs 2,500 years ago. These, presumably, were ancestors of the "Molossian dogs" taken northward by the Caesars' legions and left behind in remote valleys when the Roman tide receded. From the latter stem today's lovable giants.

The breed's likeness appeared on Swiss coats-of-arms as early as 1350, but the hospice at Great St. Bernard Pass that gave the dogs their name probably acquired none until three centuries later. The monks used them first as watchdogs and pack dogs for milk and butter. About 1750, hospice guides began to train them for pathfinding and the rescue work that would bring world fame.

Disease, avalanches, and excessive inbreeding have threatened extinction from time to time, but crosses with the Great Pyrenees, Great Dane, Mastiff, and Swiss herding dogs helped the breed survive. The best-documented cross, with the Newfoundland about 1855, resulted in today's long-haired variety. The monks of St. Bernard, however, have always favored the short coat, which does not so easily cake with snow.

Breaking trail through Alpine drifts or dozing on the show bench, the St. Bernard cuts a striking figure, from wrinkled brow to thick, furred tail. Deep, arched chest, broad, straight back, and muscular hindquarters display tremendous power. Wide, close-set toes enable him to "swim" through snows often lying fifty feet deep in the pass that links Switzerland with Italy. His coat ranges from red to brindle with snowy markings that boldly blaze his chest, face, collar, feet, and tip of tail.

Despite his brute strength, the St. Bernard is usually gentle (one brought home young birds and rabbits unharmed!). This makes him a fine family pet—if the family is prepared to cope with an appetite matching the dog's Herculean stature.

Several years ago a North Dakota policeman pulled to safety a shivering 160-pound dog that had broken through ice on a river. Man finally had rescued a St. Bernard—token payment on a long-standing debt.

Height 25½–27½ in. Weight 125–175 lbs.

Deeds of valor are the heritage of the St. Bernard, savior of thousands of Alpine wayfarers.

EDWARD HERBERT MINER

Bernese Mountain Dog

TWENTY CENTURIES AGO Roman legions filed through the Great St. Bernard Pass on a trail of conquest into ancient Helvetia. They brought with them big Molossian- or Mastiff-like dogs to drive their cattle and guard their military outposts and trading stations. Some, wearing spiked collars, may have served in battle as well.

Living mementos of this northward push exist in Switzerland today; among them, four breeds loosely grouped as Swiss Mountain dogs. They include the Appenzell, Entlebuch, Large Swiss Mountain Dog, and the handsome, black-coated Bernese Mountain Dog. Through the centuries the first two have lost the stature of the ancient Molossian dog and today serve primarily as herders and drovers. But all four are known in their homeland as *Sennenhunde*—literally "cheesemaker's dogs"—for their common use pulling dairymen's carts.

Alone of the quartet the Bernese wears a long-haired coat, and he is outweighed only by the Large Swiss Mountain Dog. He takes his name from the Canton of Bern, where he traditionally hauled the wares of basket weavers to market. Once common in the Swiss valleys, the Bernese was eclipsed about 1840 by the St. Bernard (whose early history is similar) and imported breeds. Some 50 years later only a few Bernese dogs were to be found.

The breed owes its revival—perhaps even survival—chiefly to two Swiss dog experts. One, Franz Schertenlieb, in 1892 combed the countryside for breeding stock and discovered a few good specimens around the village of Dürrbach. As a result the dog since has often been called the *Dürrbachler*. Professor Albert Heim of Zürich made a careful study of all the mountain breeds and on his initiative a Bernese Mountain Dog club was formed in Switzerland in 1907.

Today the breed has regained its former popularity, though principally as a house pet and companion rather than as a cart dog. Found throughout Switzerland, the Bernese makes frequent appearances in that country's dog shows. Some introduced into Germany have been trained for police and rescue work. The British and American Kennel Clubs recognized the breed in the 1930's.

The Bernese dog's compact body marks him as one born to harness. About the size of a Collie, he is broad in the chest and rather short in the back, with straight, muscular forelegs, well-developed thighs, and round feet. His jet-black coat usually is blazed with white on chest, foreface, feet, and tail tip. Characteristic russet-brown or deep tan markings appear over the eyes and on the chest and feet.

A well-defined stop separates flat skull from strong, broad muzzle. Short, V-shaped ears lie close to his head; his fiery hazel eyes lend an alert expression.

Hardiness is built into the Bernese Mountain Dog; his long, wavy coat needs little grooming and warms him even in an unheated kennel. This legacy of imperial Rome finds little use as draft dog in the United States, but owners here prize him as a faithful guardian and companion.

Height 21–27½ in. Weight 65–85 lbs.

WALTER A. WEBER, NATIONAL GEOGRAPHIC STAFF ARTIST

Sleek, long coat distinguishes the Bernese from other Swiss mountain dogs. Sires of this noble animal toiled for the Romans 2,000 years ago.

Kuvasz

EDWARD HERBERT MINER

Once a palace guard, the snowy Kuvasz now serves as watchdog.

"ARMED GUARD of the nobility"; so means the word from which these big handsome dogs derive their name. For centuries they served faithfully as personal guardians to Hungary's aristocracy.

During the stormy 15th century reign of King Matthias I, when war and political intrigue racked the land, that monarch put more trust in his dogs than he did in the ambitious men about him. A Kuvasz accompanied him everywhere and stood sentry inside his door.

The king's kennels also bred the Kuvasz for the hunt. Gifts of pups were a sign of royal favor to loyal nobles and visiting dignitaries.

Many years later the noble breed joined two other fine Hungarian breeds, the Puli and the Komondor, as shepherd's helper. While the Puli served chiefly as herder, the Komondor and Kuvasz guarded against wolves and livestock thieves. The first two still ply their age-old trades on the lonely Hungarian plain; the Kuvasz is favored as a watchdog by farmers and townspeople.

The marked resemblance of the white-furred Kuvasz to the Great Pyrenees, which once guarded medieval French chateaux, suggests a common ancestry. The original home of the Kuvasz most likely was Tibet, and the Tibetan Mastiff his progenitor. The Turkish word *kawasz* from which the dog's name stems has led some to theorize that Ottoman Turks brought the breed into Europe from Asia. But others believe he was brought into Hungary along with the Puli and Komondor by invading Huns or Magyars more than 1,000 years ago.

Though sturdily built, the broad-backed Kuvasz is active and light-footed. His snowy coat is thick and slightly wavy. Ears lie close to his broad, flat skull; tail is carried low.

Still rare in the United States, some of the breed have found their way to western sheep ranges, where they have proved efficient herders. Others carry on their honored role as guardians of the household.

Shoulder height 24–28 in. Weight 70–90 lbs.

Through raging su

Newfoundland ▶

"A MAN IS NOT A GOOD MAN to me because he will feed me if I should be starving, or warm me if I should be freezing, or pull me out of a ditch if I should ever fall into one," wrote Thoreau in his *Walden*. "I can find you a Newfoundland dog that will do as much."

Many of these massive dogs have done far more, for this good-natured breed has a talent for saving human life. Tales are legion of Newfoundlands rescuing drowning children and adults. Many sailing vessels carried a Newfoundland as ship's dog—in effect a four-legged lifesaving apparatus.

One earned a medal as late as 1919 when a steamer ran aground off Newfoundland. Raging surf thwarted rescuers until a powerful Newfoundland dog carrying a light line plunged into the sea and linked ship with shore. A breeches buoy took off all 92 passengers safely, including an infant tucked in a mail bag.

Another Newfoundland may have altered history. The story has it that Napoleon, leaving his exile on Elba, slipped and fell into the sea. The night was dark and the Emperor could not swim. But for a crewman's Newfoundland there might have been no return to power for Napoleon, no Waterloo.

The Newfoundland's heroism beyond dispute, dog historians still debate his origin. Some theorize that Vikings carried his ancestors to North America in their black "bear dogs"; others, that the Great Pyrenees was his main progenitor. But more likely explorers' and codfishermen's retrievers produced bigger offspring in their Newfoundland home; when these black dogs were brought to Europe, they adopted the island's name.

The Landseer variety may well have begun with the Great Pyrenees that Basque fishermen of the 17th century took as ships' dogs to the Newfoundland Banks; presumably these great white dogs, crossed with the island's black dogs, produced the white-and-black type—named for Sir Edwin Landseer, whose paintings popularized the breed.

As heroic in proportion as in deed, the Newfoundland is deep-chested, broad in the back and head, with short, powerful muzzle. He has put his brawn to work hauling firewood and fish carts on his native island. He was trained as a pack dog in World War II.

His dense, flat, oily coat is dull jet-black, sometimes carrying white or bronze markings on toes, chest, or tail. Large webbed feet aid him as a tireless swimmer. As befits a water-loving dog, the Newfoundland makes a fine retriever. Two of the breed, shipwrecked off the Maryland coast in 1807, produced the Chesapeake Bay Retriever.

A dependable, deep-voiced protector of the home, the Newfoundland is nevertheless unusually mellow in disposition. He appoints himself as children's playmate and guardian, suffering the ear- and tail-tugging of small hands with saintly patience. Lord Byron's famous epitaph to his dog Boatswain well sums up the character of the breed:

"... beauty without vanity,
Strength without insolence,
Courage without ferocity,
And all the virtues of man without his
vices. . . ."

Shoulder height 26–28 in. Weight 110–150 lbs.

Newfoundland tows the life line of a sinking ship to shore. Landseer type wears a white-and-black coat. ▶

ROBERT E. LOUGHEED

R E LOUGHEED

Alaskan Malamute and his close relative, the Eskimo (left), are built for freighting, clothed for cold. Paws are big and well padded.

Alaskan Malamute

EARLY TRAVEL ACCOUNTS of *Alyeska*, as Alaska's Russian discoverers called it, mention the hard-working Malemiut Eskimos who inhabited the shores of Kotzebue Sound. Few of them fail to remark on the sturdy dogs these people used to haul their sleds.

Today's Alaskan Malamute bears the name of this tribe and is regarded as the oldest dog breed native to that land. His exact origin is shrouded in mystery. But heavy fur, prick ears, and plumed tail leave little doubt he is related to other sled dogs that probably migrated with their masters from eastern Asia long ago.

Garbed for temperatures reaching 60 to 70 degrees below zero, the Malamute grows guard hairs from three to six inches long, with a woolly undercoat up to two inches thick. Impregnated with natural oils, his waterproof coat is usually wolfish gray or black and white, with cap or mask markings on his head and muzzle.

Centuries of life in harness have developed a powerful, big-boned body with deep chest and muscular hindquarters capable of tremendous driving power. In a 1954 weight-pulling contest a 93-pound Malamute broke a dog-world's record by moving an incredible load of 2,103 pounds.

"A dog is only as good as his feet," say veterans of arctic treks. The Malamute is well equipped with large thick pads heavily protected with hair.

Similarly endowed is the Malamute's close relative, the Eskimo dog, a distinct breed that helped Admiral Peary conquer the North Pole. He paid these dogs well-deserved tribute: "Day after day they struggled back across that awful frozen desert, fighting for their lives and ours; day after day they worked till the last ounce of work was gone from them, and then fell dead in their tracks without a sound. . . ."

The burly, stout-hearted Eskimo, which has spread from Alaska to Labrador and Greenland, comes in nearly every known dog color. Once recognized by the American Kennel Club, he has been dropped for lack of registrations.

The Malamute, on the other hand, has regained the popularity he once enjoyed in Alaska's gold rush days. Sourdoughs prized him then for his ability to pull a sled, pack a 50-pound load, or hunt bear and lynx all day on a minimum of food.

During the heyday of Alaskan sled racing from 1909 to 1918 many drivers crossed the Arctic breeds, thus threatening the Malamute with mongrelization. Not until the 1920's did U.S. sportsmen take an interest in the breed, and with selected stock recapture and develop a pure strain.

Malamutes served with the Byrd Antarctic expeditions and have a remarkable record as rescue dogs with the Air Force. Parachuted with sled and driver into rugged arctic country, they have hauled hundreds of downed fliers to safety.

Despite the belief by some that he has wolf ancestry, the Malamute out of harness has won favor as a gentle pet. Toward humans he is docile and friendly, and is affectionate and patient with children.

Shoulder height 23–25 in. Weight 75–85 lbs.

Samoyed

THE VAST REACHES OF TUNDRA between the White Sea and the Yenisei River of Siberia are home to the Samoyed dog and the seminomadic people for whom he is named. Here a winter is considered mild unless even the hardy crows freeze to death. And here the breed developed pure through centuries of rigorous isolation as an all-round reindeer herder, sled dog, hunter, and companion.

Nature has outfitted the Samoyed well for his environment and tasks. Harsh, straight outer hairs and thick, soft undercoat shield him from bitter cold. Countless Arctic suns and snows have bleached his coat to a striking white, white-and-biscuit, or cream, although other colors sometimes occur. A broad back and deep chest give him strength and endurance in harness, and hair tufts between his toes serve as snowshoes.

Wedge-shaped head and thickly plumed tail complete the picture of this active, graceful, and intelligent dog, one of the most glamorous in today's show ring.

As sled dog of distinction, the Samoyed served Nansen, Shackleton, Scott, and other explorers in the Arctic and Antarctic.

The breed found its way to England some 90 years ago, and to the United States more recently. The owner of a "Sam" receives an unexpected bonus in the soft, white combings of his undercoat. Spun into yarn, they provide a fine-quality wool which Samoyed people have long used in making clothing.

Courageous yet gentle, the Samoyed seems always smiling. Centuries of close association with kindly masters have instilled a deep affection for humans. Owners of this splendid breed cannot help responding in kind. *Shoulder height 19–23½ in. Weight 36–67 lbs.*

Siberian Husky

A RUSSIAN TRADER entered a team of unusual-looking Siberian dogs in the 1909 All-Alaska Sweepstakes. They were generally smaller, lighter-boned, more foxlike in appearance than the native Alaskan dogs running in this famous sled dog race between Nome and Candle. The newcomers placed a surprising third over the grueling 408-mile course.

The following year a young Scot crossed the Bering Sea and brought back to Alaska a number of fine specimens of this Siberian breed. He entered three teams in the 1910 race. Two finished first and second.

Thus the speedy, handsome Siberian Husky claimed the widespread attention of North American dog drivers. He fast grew popular.

Swift Siberian Husky (left) is the s

This "new breed," of course, had been used beyond memory among the Chukchi people of northeastern Siberia. The Chukchi, like the Samoyeds, regarded dogs as among their most valuable possessions, breeding them true and keeping them inside their dwellings as companions, guards, and pets, besides working them in harness. The breed's gentle nature reflects centuries of affection and care by its masters.

Early explorers of North America referred to the Eskimo people they met as "Huskies." The term later came to mean any variety of Arctic sled dog; now it is part of the proper name of the Siberian Chukchi.

In the famous dash to diphtheria-stricken Nome in 1925, Siberian Huskies hauled lifesaving serum through gales at 50° below zero. Many served in Antarctic exploration; others pulled sleds in World War II.

In appearance, the medium-sized Siberian Husky is full-furred with a soft double coat, in contrast to the coarse and bearlike outercoats of the larger Malamute and Eskimo. His color runs a full range from white to black, often with striking cap and spectacle markings. His head is relatively narrow and finely chiseled, with strong jaws, high-set ears, and eyes of either brown or light blue—occasionally one of each color.

A moderately compact body, muscular shoulders and hindquarters, and straight, strong legs give him a swift and graceful gait. He has the same "snowshoe foot" and plumed tail that mark other Arctic breeds.

More and more dog owners have come to realize that the working Husky of the North can adapt himself comfortably and happily as an affectionate pet almost anywhere.
Shoulder height 20–23½ in. Weight 35–60 lbs.

og family's racer. Snowy, smiling Samoyed also herds reindeer. Both breeds hail from northern Asia.

EDWARD HERBERT MINER

CHAPTER SIX

The Heroic

As THE MAIL BUS wound up the slippery mountain road, taking me closer to the Great St. Bernard Pass, I marveled at the terrible whiteness of the glacial slopes and the dazzle of the canyons and ice walls ranging as far as the eye could see.

Since childhood I had been fascinated by tales of heroic St. Bernard dogs in the Swiss Alps. I had heard that these huge animals would lie in the snow next to an exhausted traveler and keep him warm, while others raced for help; that one named Lion had saved thirty-five people; and another, Barry, had saved forty, including an un-

Photographs by the author, from Three Lions

St. Bernard Today

conscious child he pulled from an icy ledge no man could reach. Now I was invited to visit and photograph the dogs at the famous hospice nestling 8,113 feet up in the strategic pass, one of the highest spots in Europe inhabited all year round. How would the present compare with the storied past?

Since the Middle Ages thousands of tradesmen, couriers, beggars, emperors, popes, and pilgrims bound for Rome had found shelter there as they struggled along the wintry road linking Italy and northern Europe. Over the years, I knew, the monks and their brave dogs had plucked hundreds from death's brink. But now people use highways that hug the valleys or burrow through nearby mountains in long tunnels; much Alpine rescue work, too, is done with aircraft. Did the monks still defy blizzards to search for lost travelers? And had their dogs ever really carried little casks of brandy around their necks?

I got off the bus in Bourg St. Pierre, a snowbound French-Swiss village. It was a bright January day, but the storekeeper warned me not to journey alone. The weather could change abruptly, he said. Precipices and deep fissures endangered even experienced climbers. Fortunately a hospice employee named Anselme was coming to fetch food for the monks. I could go up with him.

I had consolidated my camera equipment and clothing into a knapsack weighing about fifty pounds, and the storekeeper kindly lent me skis fitted with skins for uphill walking. Anselme, a short, wiry Italian, casually hoisted his huge bundle of purchases to his shoulder and we set out.

Six or eight houses from the village square the road disappeared under the snow; only a few ski tracks indicated the way to the pass. At first the crisp air was exhilarating and the slopes rose gently. But the footing became more difficult; breath came shorter as the air thinned; my load felt heavier all the time. I could hardly put one ski above the other when Anselme and I reached the small stone shed marking the climb's halfway point.

Stumbling into the next shelter, two-thirds of the way up, I fell exhausted, desperate for sleep. Anselme shook me and dragged me out into the fading light. I gasped for breath, thought I could not possibly go on. Then, mercifully, an enormous St. Bernard dog bounded up to me. He wore no cask of brandy, but after him came a monk with a canteen of hot tea and wine, which he made me drink. While the two men pulled me over the steepest places, the dog frisked ahead as if this were a summer stroll. The last 2,000 feet seemed straight up.

We reached the hospice well after dark, eight numbing hours after leaving the village. The snow crust was sheer ice now, the wind howling, when at last the lights of the hospice reached welcoming fingers to us across the snow. Above the bright doorway a great outline of buildings loomed in the cold starlight, as if part of this ice-cliffed landscape.

Downstairs in a cavernous kitchen, next to a great stove going full blast, I hungrily ate hot soup, bread, and cheese. Then a novice took me to my room, through echoing arched stone corridors dimly lit at long intervals.

"Tonight you are our only guest," he said. "Sleep well and God keep you."

AT BREAKFAST next morning I was welcomed by the prior, Father Quaglia, who introduced me to others in the hospice family of thirteen. Then we saw one of the canons off to visit the sick and conduct services in a snow-bound Italian village. We stood with him before the great outer door while the prior gave his blessing. In the kennel the dogs barked furiously, sensing an expedition.

"Isn't he taking a dog?" I asked one of the monks, as the canon skimmed down the mountainside, carrying prayer books and medicines.

"No, my friend. A dog can not keep up with a man on skis." He scanned the heavens and frowned. "It would be better if a dog could go with him, that is sure."

"Why?" I asked.

The young man looked grave. "We have learned that we can never trust the weather," he said. "On a day like this one November, Father Droz set out to guide six Italian mountaineers. The day was so favorable, and Father Droz knew the mountains so well, that he thought he wouldn't need any dogs.

"Soon we began to worry. The wind became stronger, but the air remained mild, and we recognized the foehn—a treacherous south wind, more fearful than a snowstorm. It plays havoc with the barometric pressure, and it loosens and melts masses of snow. Soon one of the Italians telephoned from a shelter. Father

A monk on skis greets Barry, his 150-pound friend. The breed is named for St. Bernard de Menthon, 11th century founder of a hospice that has sheltered thousands from Alpine blizzards.

Droz had been covered by an avalanche. He had walked ahead of the party to test the ground and was trapped in the sliding snow. It took us hours to dig him out. It was too late."

I asked how the dogs could have helped if they had been along in the first place.

"The dogs would have warned him. Some say they have a sort of sixth sense, but more likely it is their hearing. Several times they have pulled one of us out of the path of an avalanche before we could hear it coming. They are also trained to draw sleds with supplies. And if a canon has been in the hospital in Bourg St. Pierre, the dogs may bring him back to the hospice on a sled.

"But here is the keeper of the dogs, Father Emery. He will take you along to let the animals get a look at those cameras!"

I followed Father Emery to a long, low stone building about a hundred yards from the main hospice. Small rooms in the back are used for storing apples and other fruit. The front part houses the usual twelve to twenty St. Bernards.

As we approached this kennel by way of a long ramp, the dogs began barking. Father Emery

Alpine rescue tests monks and dogs. The sled-borne man, discovered in the snow by keen-nosed dogs, simulates an injured skier. For two centuries the booming barks of gentle St. Bernards have promised help for wayfarers imperiled by fog, avalanche, and storm in Great St. Bernard Pass between Switzerland and Italy.

PAUL POPPER

opened the door and quieted them with a word. We entered a large room, empty except for beds of straw near the walls. Here the dogs slept as Huskies do, huddled together for warmth. The cleared space gave them room for exercise.

Father Emery spoke again, and suddenly we were surrounded by the powerful beasts, yelping with delight at seeing their master. The dogs weigh from 140 to 160 pounds. Their dense white-and-fawn-colored coats make them look even bigger. In contrast to their puppylike exuberance, their mournful faces provide a comic effect. But this is offset by their great strength and friendliness. One can sense their dependability at once.

They regarded me soberly for a moment. Then the largest dog planted two great paws on my chest and licked my face.

"Well! You are honored!" Father Emery said. "This is Barry."

"Barry! Not the one that saved forty people? I thought he lived long ago."

"Forty-one people it was. You mean Barry the First, Barry 'the Lifesaver.' He served here about 150 years ago, and he was the bravest of them all."

I began snapping pictures. An attendant working with the dogs took one look at my cameras and ran off. He returned with a small cask and fastened it around Barry's neck. I glanced at Father Emery. He smiled. No, he said, the dogs had never carried casks on their missions, not once, as far as anyone at the hospice knew. This legend, he explained, probably owes its existence to an artist who drew the original Barry with a cask simply because he thought it would add interest, and the artist was right. The public loved the idea.

I couldn't resist and took pictures of a dog with a cask. Later at lunch I asked for details of the great Barry's exploits.

"There's a story that the forty-first man he found in the snow was a soldier," Father Emery said. "He was freezing and befuddled. When he saw Barry leap-

Brandy kegs were never carried in rescue work, according to monks at the hospice. But the dogs often pose with the traditional casks for the benefit of visitors.

Barry, rescue hero of half a century ago, stands watch over the stairs. Plunging into snow, he found a band of exhausted travelers; his barks summoned help. A fall into a gully cost his life in 1910. Taxidermy lost the breed's characteristic sagging jowls.

Barry is an honored name always given to the handsomest dog in the hospice kennels. The original Barry, about 150 years ago, rescued some 40 persons.

ing toward him, he thought he was a wolf and killed him with his sword. But as far as we know, Barry didn't really meet with such a sad end. He worked faithfully for twelve years, and when he seemed near the end of his strength the prior sent him to Bern. He was well cared for and lived another two years. He can still be seen mounted in a museum there."

I wondered about Barry's famous rescue of the little boy from the icy ledge. How had the dog managed to carry him down?

Father Emery's face lit up with enthusiasm. "Barry kept him warm and licked his face. That woke him up, and he threw his arms around Barry's neck. Barry began to drag him, but gently, you understand. The boy saw Barry needed his help, so he got on the animal's back and clasped his hands under his neck."

After lunch I returned to the kennels and watched the attendant feed the dogs their daily rations of horsemeat mixed with dog meal, in huge amounts.

"They're good eaters," he laughed. "So would you be if you raced about in the bitter cold as much as they do. Five pounds of food a day down every one of them, and they lick their chops for more. Their food comes up by car when the road is open in summer, and we store enough for the winter."

The feeding over, the dogs sniffed the air and milled about. The keeper said that after eating they usually went out for a run in the snow. Today, to show me what the dogs could do, the monks would enact a rescue. I waited near the hospice with the prior and the other canons while one of the novices skied away. He halted some distance from us and buried himself in the snow.

"Now," the prior said, "you are about to see the Great St. Bernard rescue dogs find a person trapped beneath an avalanche. Because of their fine sense

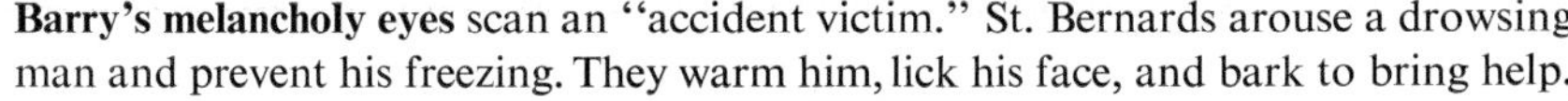

Barry's melancholy eyes scan an "accident victim." St. Bernards arouse a drowsing man and prevent his freezing. They warm him, lick his face, and bark to bring help.

Mail and supplies arrive at the hospice on skis; the dogs bark a welcome. Given Norwegian skis in 1878, St. Bernard fathers made extra pairs and introduced the sport to Switzerland.

of smell, they are marvelous at this job. They'll follow a scent that's hours old. And they can smell a man under a snowdrift, whether he's dead or alive.

"The dogs save precious time by discovering exactly where the person is buried. They begin to dig, and howl to direct us to the spot. The men help them, and together they get the victim out quickly. Watch, here come the dogs!"

The great animals poured out of the kennel and immediately fanned out, bounding through the snow. Sometimes they stayed on the top crust sniffing. Sometimes they sank and "swam" along, covering an amazing amount of ground without seeming to miss a single square foot. They worked in concert, as a pack, and in a very short time one of them had found the buried novice.

At once the dog dug the snow from the man and lay down, covering the body with his own. He began to bark and lick the man's face. The other dogs came and began barking too, setting up a dreadful din until the monks arrived with a

St. Bernard, in iron, points the way to his hospice, a welcome haven in the harsh November-to-May winter. The chain in his right hand binds a dragon at his feet that legend says he conquered in the pass.

mixture of hot tea and wine. They forced this down the throat of the "unconscious" man, then carried him to the hospice on a stretcher.

After dinner the monks told me of the hospice's beginnings. In ancient times, the prior said, many roads led over the mountains, but this was probably the most traveled one after the Romans improved it in the first century A.D. On the summit, not far from where the hospice now stands, they put a temple to Jupiter.

Tribesmen from the north captured the pass from the Romans. After them came the Huns, Vandals, and Saracens. Charlemagne passed through to be crowned in Rome. Priests established chapels along the route, but ruthless marauders looted and burned them as often as they were built. The pass became a haunt of thieves and robbers, who tortured and killed pilgrims and wayfaring tradesmen.

The prior continued: "Into these troubled times, so the legend goes, Bernard de Menthon was born in Savoy at the end of the 10th century, the son of the great feudal baron Richard de Menthon. He grew into a tall and strong young man, the pride of his parents. It was a calamity for his father when Bernard came back from his studies in Paris and announced that he intended to become a monk.

"His father arranged for him to marry an heiress and tried to force him to accept his position as a lord of Savoy. But on the night before the wedding Bernard tore the bars from his window and escaped.

"Bernard became an outstanding

churchman, a true Christian," the prior continued. "One night a handful of pilgrims stumbled into his church with a tale of horror. They had been attacked in the pass by the giant devil Procus, who worshiped at the statue of Jupiter. At once Bernard rallied the reluctant villagers and led them praying and singing through a terrible storm up to the Plain of Jupiter.

"Procus turned himself into a dragon and was about to swallow Bernard. But Bernard threw his stole around the devil's neck, and the stole became a chain, which held down the devil while Bernard killed him. The villagers demolished the images of Jupiter, and the pass was cleansed.

"Bernard told the villagers to build a hospice in the pass for travelers. There were many rocks on the plain; more rock was hauled great distances over icy trails. This was in the 11th century, but the hospice was not named for St. Bernard until about a hundred years later. First it was dedicated to St. Nicholas, the patron of children, sailors, captives, bankers, and pawnbrokers."

Napoleon crossed the Great St. Bernard Pass in the spring of 1800 with 40,000 soldiers, 5,000 horses, and 58 cannon on his way to crush the Austrians at Marengo. Each cannon was disassembled, enclosed in a hollow log, and dragged by scores of men. (Napoleon didn't ride a white charger, as depicted later, but a mule.) I was told that by Napoleon's time the monks of the hospice had been using dogs as lifesavers for about fifty years. It had not occurred to me that

It's mealtime; four-year-old Junon drowsily suckles her second litter. The usual brood numbers six; one dog whelped twelve. Pups are shipped as pets to the United States and elsewhere. Most are sold when two or three months old.

At the height of the breed's popularity, about 60 years ago, an English St. Bernard brought $6,500.

these big animals hadn't always been there, and I asked about their ancestors.

"No one knows for sure," explained Father Emery, "but probably they were the large short-haired mastiffs that appear in reliefs found in Assyria, dating from some 2,500 years ago. Wars and trade brought descendants of these animals from Asia to Greece and Rome. The Romans used them as watch dogs at their military posts.

"The Newfoundland was crossed in after Barry's time. Some say the Great Dane and the native sheep dog were too. Our St. Bernards combine the best traits of the mixture. Their hair is thick to protect against cold, and short to shed snow. They are tremendous fellows, strong as oxen, but gentle, affectionate, and wise."

I learned that the dogs first came to the pass toward the end of the 17th century. In those days the canons went about the countryside asking for gifts. Nobles in the neighboring valleys had been keeping dogs that looked much like today's St. Bernards—the head of one appears in a 14th century coat of arms—and they probably assumed that the monks would find them useful. They did, in the kitchen. With hungry travelers to be fed at all hours of day and night, meat was almost constantly roasting on a revolving spit. Prior Ballalu, who provided the first written mention of the dogs at the hospice, in 1708, credits Canon Vincent Camos with making "the wheel in which a dog is placed to turn the spit."

Before long the dogs also proved themselves valuable protection against dangerous guests. A band of robbers, having eaten and slept well, demanded that the prior guide them to the vault where valuables were kept. He took them to the dogs instead. They left at once, quietly.

JUST HOW USEFUL, I asked, are the dogs today? Many people think their heroic lifesaving days are over, that now they are kept only to please summer visitors. Father Emery replied after some thought. "It is true," he said, "the need for them is not so great now. But who can say that saving even one life is not a worthy thing? We believe that in the eyes of God service is service whether to the many or to the few. Having dogs here is an honored tradition, and most visitors wish to see them. But the dogs still do valuable work as well.

"In the frozen months there are generally a few skiers and still occasional pilgrims on foot. And of course, there are always smugglers of cigarettes and scarce foodstuffs. We care for everyone alike. We give help without condemnation, just as the storm makes no distinctions among its victims."

I had hoped to make the descent the following morning, but dawn came cloudy and cold. I spent the morning with Father Emery in the cobbler's shop, photographing a mother dog with her litter. It was hard to imagine her tiny wriggling puppies turning into huge furry beasts bounding over the snow. The rest of the day I relaxed in the company of the good men and their friendly animals.

Early the next morning I watched Anselme get ready to go into the village for provisions. We packed quickly, put on our skis, and were on our way in the

***"Allez-y!"* A keeper's command sends dogs avalanching down a powdery slop**

twilight before sunrise. Going down was much easier than coming up; scarcely three hours after leaving the hospice we skimmed into Bourg St. Pierre.

To my surprise, it was no longer a quiet little village. After my stay in the lonely, snowed-in pass, it seemed to me a large town, unbearably astir with every kind of noise except the cheerful barking of the St. Bernard dogs.

The Terrier Breeds

FOR LONG CENTURIES the noble hound was gentry's right. But as the chase swept by his wattle hut, the yeoman could turn to pat the wiry head of the little terrier who shared his lot. Pursuing not regal stag but fox and badger in burrow and cranny, this pint-sized packet of energy inspired the ballad's phrase: "Warriors of the fight are they, and every fight they win." Hearth not hunt is the terrier's focus today. Compact size and infectious good humor suit him well for town house and apartment role. The American Kennel Club's Arthur Frederick Jones fell under the terrier spell when a boy and has been their student and admirer ever since. Let him introduce you to the lovable warrior clan that has attained canine aristocracy the hard way—by earning it.

CHAPTER SEVEN

Down-to-earth Dogs, the Terriers

MY FIRST INTIMATE ACQUAINTANCE with the true terrier spirit goes back to my boyhood when we were given a dog called Joffre. Named appropriately for the great French marshal, he had a most commanding appearance and didn't know what quitting meant. But the donors neglected to give us his pedigree and it was some years before I realized that we had owned a Staffordshire Terrier. This was the breed that became famous in the pit fights—a vicious pastime requiring the utmost in courage.

With the family, Joffre pretended to be just a little lap dog. He liked all of us, and I shudder to think of what would have happened to anyone who tried to harm us. As a watchdog he was supreme; no stranger could come to the farm unannounced by his low growl. If we recognized friends, or the visitor looked reputable, it was only necessary to say "Okay, Joffre," and he would return to his watch post under a big tree.

If it was a tramp, Joffre would stalk forward, growling, the hair rising on his back. One man failed to take the hint and suddenly he saw a dog sailing through the air at him. Fortunately, he managed to tumble over the rail fence in time. Once an intruder was outside the yard Joffre was satisfied that his home and family were not in danger.

Joffre had several bad habits, but they simply proved his fire and ruggedness.

rier's merry fire glints through Miniature Schnauzer's alert eyes.

RT S. OAKES, NATIONAL GEOGRAPHIC PHOTOGRAPHER

For example, he liked to chase automobiles. Once he clamped his big jaws over the tire of a moving Model T and was carried right around the wheel, which passed over his neck. His heavy studded collar was ripped to pieces. The driver stopped, thinking that the dog was dead. He found Joffre back on his four sturdy feet, defying him to step out of the car.

Joffre also liked to tease horses by nipping them on the fetlocks. He usually got away with it, but one day Big Sam, a huge work horse, was ready. Sam pretended not to see Joffre sneaking up behind; suddenly, when the dog moved, so did the horse's hind leg. In the resulting explosion, Joffre soared 20 feet through the air and hit the side of a building.

Was Joffre hurt? Probably he was sore for a week but he never admitted it. However, he learned never again to fool around near horses' hind legs.

Then there was the time he and the family cat, Tommy, rode together in the big touring car stacked high with household effects. Joffre was tied to one side of the load; the cat lay confined in a basket on the opposite side. Somehow the cat worked free and probably taunted Joffre. The dog must have lunged, missed his footing, and fallen out of the noisy car. My father and brother noticed nothing wrong until people on the street began waving frantically. They stopped, to find Tommy riding atop the car and Joffre on the highway. How long he had been bumping alongside they did not know, but he bore no visible injuries and had just as much pep as ever. Joffre, we were certain, was the indestructible dog.

JOFFRE'S COURAGE and sturdiness, his devil-may-care demeanor runs with minor individual variations throughout the terrier clan. Dog show judges consider a terrier's fire essential. That is why the smart terrier handler in the show ring often brings his specimen face to face with another terrier; usually both dogs declare war immediately. But don't confuse willingness to fight with general bad temperament. Terriers like people much more than dogs—especially other terriers.

Terriers enjoy a good scrap, but sometimes they will surprise you. When our family's pet was an Airedale named Danny, several others of his breed lived near us. Neighbors had warned me to avoid one of these, regarded as a "toughie." A police-trained German Shepherd had once challenged him, I learned later, and had come off second best. One day we rounded a corner and there stood this very Airedale, probably an inch higher at the shoulder than my dog and many pounds heavier. Before I could tighten the lead, Danny had bounced forward and touched his nose to the other Airedale's. Both tails began wagging like mad. The other dog's owner shook his head. "Now I've seen everything," he said in awe. After that we encouraged meetings of the two Airedales and they never tired of seeing each other.

Few dispute the Airedale's title as "King of the Terriers." Those who know the breed find it justified not only in size but in little unexpected tributes. Theodore Roosevelt, who seldom identified the breeds he used in hunting, wrote in

KATHLEEN REVIS, NATIONAL GEOGRAPHIC PHOTOGRAPHER

Terrier roots run deep in Britain's rural life; these spirited pets play on a Worcester village green.

African Game Trails: "The Hills had a large Airedale Terrier, an energetic dog of much courage. Not long before our visit this dog put up a hyena from a bushy ravine in broad daylight, ran after it, overtook it, and flew at it. The hyena made no effective fight, although the dog—not a third its weight—bit it severely and delayed its flight so that it was killed."

Terriers in earlier times got hardly any written mention at all—and for good reason. When a peasant family sat down to enjoy a repast whose "meat course" legally should not have been there, it was not exactly shouted from the treetops of Sherwood Forest; the poaching the terriers did was enough to throw their masters into jail. But when a renowned hunter and trencherman like Henry VIII fell to a sizzling haunch of venison in his banquet hall, he might well regale the ladies with the story of the stag hunt and the part his hounds played in it, and a

TERRIER *and* FOX.

scrivener would dutifully record it. You may read of Norwegian Elkhounds, found buried with Viking chieftains, or of Salukis and Afghan Hounds, whose pictures adorn the tombs of Egypt's Pharaohs. The sporting dogs of royalty gained early and lasting fame.

But peruse a thousand dog books and you find no mention that a visiting monarch was presented with a brace of terriers. The terrier usually was the dog of the common man, sharing his master's anonymity, helping to hunt his food and protect his crops and livestock from foxes and other predators.

TERRIERS TAKE THEIR NAME from the Latin word for earth, *terra*, for the zeal they display in wriggling down into burrows to turn scrappy fur bearers out of house and home. They originated in the British Isles, but time obscures their early history. Perhaps the first mention of terriers occurs in the *Natural History* of Pliny the Elder, during the first century. When Romans invaded Britain in 55 B.C., he records, they found ". . . much to their surprise, small dogs that would follow their quarry to ground."

Dr. Johannes Caius, the famous Elizabethan dog authority, indicates that the terrier's job already was well defined in the 16th century. His *Of Englishe Dogges*, adapted by a student from the original Latin, reads in part:

"Another sorte there is which hunteth the Foxe and the Badger or Greye onely, whom we call Terrars, because they . . . creepe into the grounde, and by that means make afrayde, nyppe, and byte the Foxe and Badger in such sort, that eyther they teare them in pieces with theyr teeth beying in the bosome of the earth, or else hayle and pull them perforce out of their lurking angles, darke dongeons, and close caves . . . ."

Europe long regarded hunting with dogs as a sport of nobility. Reasoning that a shortened tail rendered a dog unsuitable for hunting (since a long tail should enable him to change direction quickly without falling flat on his muzzle), royalty decreed that owners of long-tailed dogs must pay an exorbitant tax. That's how most terriers wound up with docked tails. But owners soon discovered that such amputation did not prove the handicap expected. In fact, after digging down to a terrier in an underground passage, they found the sturdy, docked tail made a fine handle with which to yank the dog out into the open.

Inevitably, even the jaded court circles of London and Paris took note of these courageous little farm terriers. The stag, long the favorite quarry of the noble hunters, had been killed off or driven far from the cities. The fox became a substitute, but even its numbers declined. It became important to get the fox

Harried fox, driven to earth, faces terrier foe in early 19th century scene (left). Small size permits these fearless dogs to wriggle down through rocky passages to battle their quarry underground. Terriers below eagerly pursue a poultry-raiding polecat, which flees its covert.

FROM A PAINTING BY PHILIP REINAGLE, 1803, AND (LEFT) THE REV. WILLIAM BARKER DANIEL'S "RURAL SPORTS," 1805

"Billy" dispatches a rodent horde as bettors cheer in London's candlelit Westminster Pit. Rat killing furnished "poor man's" sport in the 1820's, as bearbaiting did for the wealthy. The winning terrier was the one that killed the most rats in the shortest time; famed Billy once slew 100 in 5½ minutes.

that hounds had run to ground, rather than depend on finding another. After all, no hunt was a success unless the coveted "brush" (tail of the fox) could be presented to some charming lady or to an especially daring rider.

Oddly, although the fox hunt is usually regarded as British in origin, Louis XIII of France maintained the first pack of exclusively fox-hunting hounds in the early 17th century—complete with terriers and digging tools. By 1690 throughout England terriers commonly accompanied the hound packs, to draw the fox from his hole at a hunt's conclusion.

Terrier men even today are justly proud of the heedless, flaming courage with which their favorites plunge into a dark tunnel after their quarry. Here the badger or fox, facing the light, usually has all the initial advantage. And once close-in fighting begins, the terrier often cannot drag his foe all the way to the surface. That is why those who hunt with terriers go equipped with picks and shovels. The digging is an accepted part of the sport; as is the first-aid kit to repair torn ears, ripped paws, and sometimes gouged eyes. The damage may be great, but terriers are not whimperers.

The Fox Terrier which evolved from Britain's traditional sport followed the Union Jack all over the world. Military officers at colonial outposts organized hunt clubs and dog clubs at which they held shows of their favorites.

After England's first all-breed dog show at Newcastle in 1859, breeders began to improve the appearance of all dogs, terriers included. The Fox Terrier, both Smooth and Wire, grew much more stylish—longer of head and leg. Some huntsmen and masters of hounds, concerned over this trend, began to try out other terrier breeds long noted in various localities for going to ground after foxes. Prominent among these old-timers were the Borders, the Lakelands, and the Welsh. One of the best, however, was "manufactured" from various English, Irish, and Scottish breeds. The pint-sized, full-of-spunk dog that resulted is today's Norwich Terrier. Two strains exist, the prick-eared and the drop-eared. It is said that pound for pound no other terrier can match the Norwich.

"PIERCE EGAN'S ANECDOTES," LONDON, 1827

Not all terriers ready and willing to tangle with Mr. Reynard knew the pageantry of pink coats, silky-coated horseflesh, the bell tones of the hounds, and stirring notes of the hunting horn. One denied this glamour is the Bedlington. He looks like a lamb—but fights like a demon. Actually he *is* lamblike with his human family and friends, but he seldom can resist the impulse to fly at another dog. This is simply an old heritage. His ancestors provided the sporting pastimes of dogfighting, rat killing, and racing for Northumberland coal miners. The Bedlington is sturdily built beneath his soft coat, and his reflexes are lightning fast. His roached back gives him the same kind of reach that one finds in the Greyhound and the Whippet. Possibly he carries some Greyhound blood from centuries ago.

I first came to know the breed in the 1920's, when early efforts were made to popularize it here. The United States was not ready then for such a different-looking terrier. Fortunately, a smart style of trimming has made it into one of the most easily recognized of breeds. With many Best in Show wins to its credit here, the Bedlington is now a familiar sight in American cities.

ONE FINDS a wide range of sharply defined characters among the terriers; each displays its own philosophy of life. Some eagerly seek your attention; others take the opposite approach. Probably no dog is more faithful to his master than the Scottish Terrier,

B. ANTHONY STEWART AND (RIGHT) ROBERT F. SISSON, NATIONAL GEOGRAPHIC PHOTOGRAPHERS

Cairn Terrier (above), tiniest of Scotland's earth dogs, won his name for his ability to wriggle into rock piles for foxes.

Scottish Terrier (left), fearless vermin killer, begs a treat in famed northern Scotland locale.

but even with the person a Scottie loves best he cannot always break down his reserve.

Traces of the Scottie's dour manner appear in Scotland's other terrier breeds. They are all related. Indeed, when first exhibited at 19th century English shows, all were lumped into one classification. Today we distinguish them as the Cairn, the West Highland White, the Skye, and the Scottie. All evolved in the west of Scotland, where life was hard for man and beast alike. A man's dog was his close companion, at times his only one. Each could read the other's thoughts; both were suspicious of strangers. Thus the dogs, even today, have a character of their own. You'll find them wasting nothing, from porridge to greetings. But underneath—if you're lucky enough to dig so deep—you'll find a warm heart.

People, it has been said, grow to resemble their dogs. Likewise, dog breeds often reflect the people of their native countries. Whereas some Scottish breeds are dour, the Irish breeds are carefree and happy, with seemingly no thought for the morrow. You will find this quality in both the red-coated Irish Terrier and the Kerry Blue, relatives far back, some authorities believe. The quick-moving Irish is alert to all that goes on about him. As a boy I thought the breed was a bit noisy, for our neighbors' Irish seemed always to be barking. But it was exuberant barking, a fact I did not understand until many years later.

Kerries are a trifle more reserved, but in friendly company they love to romp. I doubt if a Kerry ever dodged combat with another dog, yet he fights not from meanness but for the pure Irish joy of it.

The one outlander of the terrier clan is Germany's bewhiskered Miniature Schnauzer. This frisky breed may never have gone to ground like others of his group, but undoubtedly he was a ratter and he has the terrier's characteristic quick spirit. A friend of mine recently acquired a Miniature, and I have been hearing much about his charm. This is a dog that

DAVID S. BOYER, NATIONAL GEOGRAPHIC STAFF

A Border Terrier teams with Foxhounds in England's traditional sport. Farmers of the Cheviot Hills bred him with legs long enough to follow a horse, body small enough to follow a fox to earth.

WALTER CHANDOHA AND (BELOW) G. D. KELLER

"But I'm all ready to go!" A Fox Terrier pleads to join a shopping trip. Button-nosed Irish Terrier pups below share his charm.

lives for the family alone, and especially for one member of that family. He may resent the intrusion of strangers, but when with his own people his personality shines. Few breeds show more natural obedience. These little dogs do what they are told because they want so much to please.

Of all the terriers that have worked courageously for their masters, particularly their peasant masters of the Middle Ages, perhaps the one that came closest to gaining royal recognition was the Skye. Apparently he at least made his way into the castle during the last of the Tudor family's reign. Dr. Caius tells us of a dog ". . . brought out of the barbarous borders fro' the uttermost countryes northward . . . Which by reason of the length of heare, makes showe neither of face nor of body." This, certainly, is the Skye. Even the toy that was bred down from the Skye, the Yorkshire Terrier, is not so well hidden; the Yorkie's bright little face is there for all to admire. Skye fanciers contend that their dog is as easily kept as many of the other breeds, but perhaps they forget those muddy spring days.

Since World War II many of the terriers have declined in popularity, chiefly because of a shortage of kennel help. About half the terrier breeds must be stripped and trimmed by experts to look their best. Amateurs can learn the art of "putting down" a terrier, but first attempts are usually discouraging. However, some terriers take only tidying up to look presentable.

One is the Manchester Terrier. Among the oldest of the entire group, he has probably contributed more to other breeds than any other terrier. His hard, smooth black coat, marked in tan, and his trim, athletic build appear in younger terrier breeds as well as other types of purebred dog. Like the Bedlington, the Manchester was a poor man's breed, developed in England for inexpensive sport. His quick-moving ancestors were renowned as rat killers.

Long ago, when the breed was known as the Black and Tan, its fanciers began to reproduce it in smaller sizes. A range of terriers resulted weighing from about

Terrier tug helps ships moor in Le Havre's busy harbor. Self-appointed dock hand Pete, a wire-haired Fox Terrier, tows a line ashore to a U. S. Coast Guardsman at left. Outpowered but undaunted, he tussles at right with a visiting cutter until a human seadog makes it fast.

U. S. COAST GUARD

ORLANDO, THREE LIONS

Bred for pluck, barbered for beauty, a Sealyham basks under frequent grooming. The Sealy's first breeder a century ago rejected any dog that failed to fight a full-grown polecat to the death. Today this charming terrier endears himself through his bubbling sense of humor.

20 to as little as two-and-a-half pounds. I remember years ago my grandmother owned one of these in-between specimens, weighing about 10 pounds. He would tackle any rodent that moved, with true terrier instinct. He was an affectionate extrovert, inquisitive and adventurous. His curiosity, sadly, brought about his demise. One day, trying to catch what was being said on a lower floor, he leaned out too far over the stairwell and slipped. We were all disconsolate.

Terrier breeders, like some cooks, have taken delight for centuries in adding a dash of this and a spot of that, and then testing, adding something different, and testing again. Such was the case about 1850 with Capt. John Edwardes of Haverfordwest, in Wales, who developed the Sealyham Terrier. After many experiments he got what he wanted, a dog with the courage to face the worst that the badger and otter could deal out. But the Sealyham, for all his hunting ferocity, never lost the qualities that endear him as a pet.

Visiting a kennel of Sealyhams when I first began writing about dogs, I was amazed at their friendliness and captivated by their sense of comedy. Sealies like to be handled; they have a way of looking out of the corners of their eyes that shows they want your attention every second. The Sealy is not a large dog, but he has a big and enjoyable spirit.

Perhaps he gets it from one of the breeds that helped fashion him, the Dandie Dinmont Terrier, a favorite in the Scottish-English border country for many centuries. My first close contact with this delightful breed, years ago, left me chuckling with appreciation. I was visiting the home of one of the leading breeders of Dandie Dinmonts. Suddenly a tiny, tousled figure appeared in the doorway. I thought little of it, for whenever one enters a home the house pets invariably come to see what's going on.

But strangely, this little terrier made no effort to approach us. He remained in the doorway and began to strike absurd poses. He sat up straight and cocked his fuzzy, topknotted head to one side. He flattened out his front paws and placed his muzzle down but left his rear end aloft; all the while his long tail swayed as rhythmically as a metronome. He continued these outlandish poses until his owner finally said, "Okay, we see you. Come on over and get acquainted with our visitor." She then turned to me and explained: "My friend here has a delightful sense of humor. He's a born clown. Life never grows boring when you have a Dandie Dinmont Terrier in the house."

I reflected later that she might well have been speaking of the whole terrier tribe. Every one of these irresistible breeds has the appealing nature, the gallantry of spirit, and the capacity for affection that banishes boredom from any household. Few persons who have once owned terriers ever want to be without them again. They are heart-stealers for sure.

A Portfolio

Following are the terrier breeds, painted in full color for the National Geographic Magazine by Staff Artist Walter A. Weber and others.

Scottish Terrier

AS PROUD AS A KILTIE parading to the skirl of bagpipes, the Scottish Terrier is the most independent of all the brave little earth dogs that have come out of Scotland.

In his native Highlands, the Scottie gained fame hunting down vermin on the estates of tartaned nobles. With reckless courage he pursued fox or badger into hole or cairn. Large, strong toenails fitted him to dig out his quarry; powerful teeth enabled him to dispatch it efficiently. So noted was the Scottie or his 16th century ancestor that King James I of England sent six such terriers to France as gifts.

Until 1882 at least three north-of-the-Tweed terrier breeds bore the name "Scottish." But in that year, after hot debate, today's sturdy die-hard gained exclusive right to the title. Immediately thereafter, he made his United States debut.

JAMES GORDON IRVING

Wiry-coated Scottie and silky-haired Skye won fame as varmint hunters in Scotland.

The little Scottish spitfire made a strong impression on Americans because of his spirit. At first he was as rough and ragged as the Highlands that produced him, but gradually exhibitors worked out the style of trimming he carries today. The Scottie's enormous popularity, however, stemmed largely from the work of commercial artists, who fell in love with the alert little breed. Soon Scotties peered wistfully from greeting cards and billboards the nation over. The Scottie placed among the ten most popular breeds from 1929 to 1944.

Franklin D. Roosevelt's Scottie Fala became a national celebrity. The President's constant companion (Fala now sleeps at his feet in Hyde Park, New York) was even the subject of a key political address during one presidential campaign.

Originally called the Aberdeen Terrier, the Scottie is a puzzle to his historians. Some admirers recognize him in a 16th century description of an "earth dog used in hunting the fox and the brocke," but skeptics see only a forerunner. Certain authorities go so far as to hail the Scottie as the oldest canine variety indigenous to Britain.

But under any name and with any history, the bewhiskered Scottie embodies every virtue of the ground dog. His wide-set, almond-shaped eyes bespeak an intelligence that responds readily to training. He is equally at home in apartment or farmhouse. Dignified and aloof, he rarely bestows his affection beyond the family circle.

The Scottie's coat is hard and wiry, with a dense undercoat; colors are black, gray, wheaten, or brindle. His forelegs are short and his hindquarters powerful. This combined with a broad, deep chest determines his unique rolling gait; for as they reach out, the Scottie's forelegs turn in. A gaily carried tail gives him a jaunty air.

The hardy little Highlander, dour but lovable, is a lot of dog in a compact package.
Shoulder height 10 in. Weight 18–22 lbs.

Skye Terrier

OF ALL THE TERRIERS that have helped to write the pages of Scotland's history, no other can claim the Skye's distinctions.

Little changed through four centuries, this peppery Gaelic hunter has found favor with king and commoner alike. Ready to battle varmint or predator at a moment's notice, the Skye has a softer side he seldom shows to the stranger. His capacity for love and loyalty was shaped on his native Isle of Skye; there among lonely Hebridean crags master and dog often provided each other's sole companionship.

In Edinburgh a memorial commemorates a famous Skye, Greyfriars Bobby, reputed to have stood guard for ten years at his master's grave.

Among the Skye's many fanciers was Queen Victoria of England. Her Majesty kept both the prick-eared (shown here) and the drop-eared varieties, and these Skyes were always along when the Queen strolled in her flower gardens at Windsor, Osborne, or Balmoral. So ancient is the breed's lineage that Victoria's Skyes were mirror images of those prized by her predecessor, Queen Elizabeth I.

The Skye's straight-haired coat, ranging in color from cream to black, is so profuse it covers his eyes, so long it sweeps the ground. It protected him from the teeth of wild animals as well as the cutting winds of his island home. A massive head, exceptionally long body, long tail, and short legs also mark the breed.

The Skye is an alert guard for the home, living up to the motto of the Skye Club of Scotland—"Wha daur meddle wi' me."

Nearly two-thirds of the breeds in America are more popular than the Skye, but his adherents are just as happy to have it that way. They love him as he is.
Shoulder height 8½–11 in. Weight 18–25 lbs.

Cairn Terrier

SMALLEST OF SCOTLAND'S TERRIERS, the Cairn specializes in pursuing game into tiny crevices. His very name stems from his uncanny ability to squeeze between the rocks of Scottish cairns. These memorials to departed clansmen offered peerless refuge to foxes and smaller vermin—until the little ground dog struck like fury.

While the Cairn's lineage extends far back into the mists of Highland history, he and the breed we now know as the West Highland White did not go their separate ways until early in the 20th century.

The Cairn retained the original colors. His double coat, ranging through sandy, red, gray, and brindle to nearly black, blends with heather and bracken and once provided useful camouflage. Nor have centuries altered the agility, hardiness, and courage that marked his vermin-hunting ancestors.

A broad head with a pointed muzzle and strong jaws fits the Cairn well for the terrier trade. He has a mischievous, foxy expression, and keen dark eyes and erect ears give him an air of constant alertness.

The Cairn first came to America in 1913. In popularity he now stands about a fourth of the way from the top of the American Kennel Club's registered breeds.

Despite his outdoor heritage, the Cairn—who tends to be a one-man dog—is happy any place with his master, including the confines of an apartment. His eagerness to please makes him an unending delight; he will even forego his shrill bark to avoid disturbing neighbors. Also he is easy to care for; the Cairn never requires more than a cursory tidying-up at home or in the show ring.

Shoulder height 9½–10 in. Weight 13–14 lbs.

Sealyham Terrier

THAT INIMITABLE CLOWN, the Sealyham Terrier, has retained his gay sense of humor despite all efforts to make him a single-minded vermin destroyer.

Capt. John Edwardes, who developed the breed in the 1850's to run with the hounds at Sealyham, his Pembrokeshire estate, preserved only the fiercest fighting strains. He disposed of any dog that flinched, and the stocky little hunter he produced wreaked havoc among the otters, badgers, and foxes of Wales.

But balancing the Sealyham's pluck and determination is a lovable comic streak. This may come from the Dandie Dinmont, an adorable wit whose blood mingles with that of other terriers in the Sealy's veins.

First recognized as a separate breed in Great Britain in 1911, the Sealy made his American bow in the same year, winning instant popularity. With trim wire-haired coat, short legs, bushy beard, and exclamation-point tail, he has a stylish look. Usually all white, he sometimes has head and ear markings of lemon, tan, or badger.

An even temper adapts him admirably to life in the home. He not only learns tricks with ease but loves to perform them.

Despite his poise in the parlor, the modern Sealy can still go to ground. His admirers in the United States sponsor terrier digs to keep his working instincts alive.

Shoulder height 10–12 in. Weight 18–25 lbs.

Fashionable white Sealyham is everybody friend; puckish little Cairn is a one-man pe Sealies were bred to hunt otter in Wales; t Cairn has long been foe of the Highland fo

EDWARD HERBERT MIN

MINER

England's sturdy Lakeland casts eyes across the bord

Lakeland Terrier

POMP AND CIRCUMSTANCE may be the birthright of certain breeds, but the long-legged Lakeland Terrier seldom saw hunting pink or heard the call of the sportsman's horn until long after he had made his reputation as a practical exterminator of the raiding fox.

In England's celebrated Lake District farmers hunted out of necessity. Accompanied by a brace of hounds and a terrier or two, they'd tramp the steep, wild fells tracking foxes that threatened their flocks. They bred a terrier to a size, weight, and temper that fitted him to go to earth after a fox.

Then known as the Patterdale Terrier, the breed ranged in color from white to the shades we know in the Lakeland today—blue and tan or black and tan. The whites were generally used to hunt the otter, for this reason: younger hounds occasionally mistook the darker terriers for otters in the muddy waters and mauled them severely.

The fame of the Lakeland spread, and soon he gained entry to the hunt clubs, where his perseverance became legendary. In 1871, one of Lord Lonsdale's Lakelands is said to have crawled 23 feet under rock in pursuit of an otter. It took three days of blasting to free the terrier. Other Lakelands have survived 10 to 12 days underground.

A thick wire coat protects this hardy hunter from underbrush. Fanciers trim his front legs to keep the hair from becoming shaggy and to provide a symmetrical look. *Shoulder height 13–15 in. Weight 15–17 lbs.*

JAMES GORDON IRVING

a fun-loving little Highlander, the Westie, bred for hard and dangerous work as a vermin destroyer.

West Highland White Terrier

COCKY AND TOUGH, the West Highland White Terrier is Scottish to the core. Indeed, if he could speak, his burr would be as thick as his snowy coat and only a fellow Highlander could ken him.

Less dour than his cousin the Scottie, the Westie loves to romp and play. This endears him to his owners, but makes him short of ideal as a watchdog. Nonetheless, he tempers his funmaking with dignity.

The baby-faced little dog originated on the estate of the Malcolms of Poltalloch in Argyllshire. Here in the fastness of the western Highlands was developed the splendid white coat that sets him apart from the Cairn Terrier, whose ancestry he shares.

Some authorities maintain that the Westie derives directly from white puppies produced in Cairn litters. Since Scottish lairds preferred their earth dogs to blend with the heather, whites were regarded with disfavor —except at Poltalloch.

The West Highland White came to the United States in the early 1900's but was initially exhibited as the Roseneath Terrier, a name stemming from the estate of the Duke of Argyll, where the American importer had first seen the breed.

Although to some extent a one-man dog, the Westie's good temper makes him an engaging family pet. He looks much like the Scottie, except that he is pure white with a coal-black nose.

Shoulder height 10–11 in. Weight 14–18 lbs.

J.G.I

Buoyant spirits mark the Smooth and Wire-haired Fox Terriers, which once battled Reynard in his den. This sprightly earth dog makes a superb companion thanks to his cheerful nature and inborn sense of loyalty.
JAMES GORDON IRVING

Fox Terrier

LIKE SUNSHINE AND DANCING, the irrepressibly gay Fox Terrier has brought joy to his friends in many lands. He is an exceptionally alert fellow with an inquisitive, mischievous nature. He wants to be part of everything that's happening, and usually manages to shoulder his way in.

This compulsion for activity made the Fox Terrier a prime favorite of those who rode to hounds in his native England with a brace of terriers carried in baskets by a servant. The master knew that when the fox sought sanctuary in a drain or scampered into his den, the Fox Terriers would unhesitatingly go to earth and drag him out or battle him beneath the ground.

The Fox Terrier owes his present good looks to a curious circumstance. As a working terrier, he was more courageous than handsome. But when dog shows started in England, breeders began to pattern him after a horse—the Hunter!

In successive generations they lengthened the terrier's head and legs, and even made his gait approximate that of his equine partner. The little dogs always were close companions of the horse used in the hunt. Many a Fox Terrier spent his nights curled up in the straw, sharing a box stall with his particular friend.

Though structurally identical, the wire-haired and smooth varieties of the Fox Terrier may have stemmed from widely different stock. One student of the breed believes that the Smooth emerged mainly from various crosses of the Greyhound, the Beagle, the Bull Terrier, and the old smooth-coated black-and-tan, and that the Wire sprang from the rough-coated black-and-tan working terrier common to Durham, Derbyshire, and Wales.

In the early days of breeding, Smooths were crossed with Wires to give the latter cleaner lines and the white color that predominates—with black or tan markings—in both varieties today. This interbreeding has largely been discontinued.

Bright, deep-set eyes and pointed ears turned forward give the Fox Terrier a lively, questioning look. Powerful jaws are shaped for combat with his hereditary foe; gaily carried tail mirrors his jaunty disposition.

The Fox Terrier arrived in the United States in 1875. For almost forty years the Smooths far outnumbered the Wires. When Westminster first began selecting a Best in Show in 1907, a Smooth took the ribbon, repeating the feat the next two years. The fourth year saw another Fox Terrier with the same smooth coat go to the top.

In 1915, the Wires took over, and they have since hit the jackpot at Madison Square Garden no fewer than twelve times. Fox Terriers have won this coveted award, Best in Show, more than any other breed.

They ranked among the American Kennel Club's ten most popular breeds for 23 years, and are still in the top third.

Though still responsive to the sound of the hunter's horn, the current edition of the cheerful, sociable, and lavishly affectionate Fox Terrier makes an ideal pet in town or country.

Height 13–15½ in. Weight 15–18 lbs.

Bull Terrier

LIKE A GLADIATOR OF OLD, the Bull Terrier is a professional battler. Shrewd 19th century breeders, with an eye on the fighting pit, molded him into the most efficient canine fighting machine the world had ever seen. He would sooner fight than eat.

Generations of Bull Terriers took on all comers in the pit, bore without whimpering the cruelest punishment, and died rather than save themselves with a show of cowardice.

Many a young blood of the day gloried in the courage and stamina of his Bull Terrier and let no occasion slip by where he could have his dog prove him a keen judge of dogflesh. This heritage of valor, along with his glistening white coat, won for the Bull Terrier a prized name—"the White Cavalier."

Pit fighting may be forgotten history for most of the breed today. But its shadow falls across every specimen of the fearless dog

WALTER A. WEBER, NATIONAL GEOGRAPHIC STAFF ARTIST

Sleek white Bull Terrier once fought for a living; Dandie Dinmont got his name from a book.

that brought the only touch of nobility to this brutal "sport"; steel-like muscles and driving courage are still built-in equipment for the Bull Terrier.

He traces his ancestry to the Bull-and-terrier, crossbred from the hard-bitten Bulldogs of the bull- and bearbaiting era and the elegant, and now extinct, white English Terrier. A dash of Spanish Pointer blood helped increase the size.

Incredibly, in view of his history, the Bull Terrier has an even, dependable disposition. He delights in human companionship, returns affection with interest, and makes a marvelous pet. In fact, the years have so modified his belligerence that Bull Terriers even compete in obedience trials, where the cardinal sin is fighting another dog.

Some recalcitrant owners, however, flatly refuse to train their Bulls for obedience on the theory that it vitiates their traditional character.

The long-accepted Bull Terrier type is pure white with a black nose. In 1936 the colored variety—which may be any color but white—was admitted to dog show competition. Both are handsome, symmetrical dogs with splendid physiques, powerful jaws, and triangular eyes full of fire.

Shoulder height 15–18 in. Weight 30–60 lbs.

Dandie Dinmont Terrier

FUZZY LIGHT HAIR spilling over his face, the Dandie Dinmont Terrier looks at you with the wide-eyed, almost blank stare of a circus clown. But, like the clown, he is gauging your mood. And at the psychologically precise moment he will delight you with some whimsical antic.

Dignified but droll, the Dandie Dinmont is made up for the role. His fluffy topknot imparts an air of buoyant good humor. His forelegs are shorter than his hindlegs, and he carries his slightly curved tail at a jaunty 45-degree angle.

Seeing this low-slung terrier at play, you may reasonably question the tales of his hunting prowess against fox, badger, and otter. One lady brought a Dandie home from Europe for the express purpose of ridding her farm of rats. Enroute she began to have doubts; no dog so affectionate and funloving as the Dandie Dinmont could face those ferocious rodents.

But once the wise little terrier sized up the situation on the farm, the lady's troubles were over. Swinging into furious action, he solved her rat problem swiftly and finally.

As early as 1700 the Dandie had made a formidable reputation as a vermin exterminator. Few farmers along the English-Scottish border were without a terrier of this breed. But it required a century and a literary masterpiece for the Dandie to come by his name.

Sir Walter Scott introduced in his novel *Guy Mannering* a character named Dandie Dinmont who kept six of the terriers. Wrote Sir Walter of Dandie's dogs: "They fear naething that ever cam' wi' a hairy skin on't." So apt was the description that the name of the fictional master became the name of the breed.

The Dandie's rough double coat is composed of both hard and soft hair; as a result it is crisp rather than wiry to the touch. His colors are mustard (any shade from dark ocher to cream) and pepper (from blue gray to silver).

The Dandie's quick intelligence makes him a fine watchdog. He adapts well to city life and is protectively fond of children. Were this terrier's delightful nature more widely known, no doubt he would soon be one of America's most popular dogs.

Shoulder height 8–11 in. Weight 18–24 lbs.

WILLIAM H. BOND, NATIONAL GEOGRAPHIC STAFF ARTIST

Soft-coated Wheaten Terrier: an Irish charmer.

Soft-coated Wheaten Terrier

GENTLE DOG of Ireland's fields and fens, the Soft-coated Wheaten Terrier combines characteristics unusual among terrier breeds: He displays little of their scrappiness, he is not a "yapper," and his softly curling coat does not shed or give off doggy odors. These, combined with courage, hardiness, and an amiable disposition tinged with flashes of pixyish humor, make him an ideal companion for young and old alike.

Although the Wheaten's origins are obscure, authorities believe he descends from the old English Black and Tan Terrier and that he may be the oldest of the native Irish terriers. Accounts of the 1800's mention him as a familiar sight around farmyards of Tipperary, Cork, Kerry, and other southern counties. Because he obeyed silent visual signals, poachers used him to hunt game—a calling that earned him a reputation as "the poor man's Irish Wolfhound." During the famine of the 1840's he frequently stood guard over stocks of potatoes.

Wheatens have been in the United States for several decades, but they were not shown or registered until the late 1940's, and it was not until a decade later that interest in them burgeoned. They won full AKC recognition in 1973 and already rank about midway in popularity among fellow terriers.

Wheaten pups, usually dark at birth, grow into the distinctive wheat-colored coats that give them their name at about 18 months. *Shoulder height 18–19 in. Weight 35–45 lbs.*

Locked in combat, a Border Terrier grapples with a snarling fox.

WALTER A. WEBER, NATIONAL GEOGRAPHIC STAFF ARTIST

Border Terrier

RUGGED AS THE REGION that gave him his name, the Border Terrier hails from the Cheviot Hills, which form a natural barrier between England and Scotland.

The gnarled terrain of the hills provided abundant cover for the big native foxes that preyed on sheep, poultry, and even calves. Local farmers soon discovered that short-legged terriers, though willing enough to tangle with the foxes, couldn't always keep up with them.

The solution was to breed a dog with legs long enough to keep pace with a mounted hunter, yet short enough to go to ground after a fox. The plucky, tireless Border Terrier not only met this norm, but showed himself to be one of the bravest and most powerful of his gallant tribe. He'd bolt or beat his fox every time. He has been known to kill a full-grown badger in single combat.

A wiry coat, dense underneath and reddish or wheaten in color, shields him from hostile teeth and the rains and mists of his native hills. His short, broad, otterlike head is equipped with powerful jaws.

The Border is a dog of many accomplishments. He has herded sheep and cattle, and he makes an alert watchdog. At the same time, he is a gentle companion to children, and even gets on well with cats.

In the popularity sweepstakes, the Border is a late starter. England recognized him as a breed only in 1920 and he is still little known in the United States. But with his abilities and personality his future is assured.
Height 10-12 in. Weight 11½–15½ lbs.

American Staffordshire Terrier

BULLDOG AND TERRIER BLOOD in almost equal proportions courses through the veins of the stocky, courageous Staffordshire Terrier.

Here is the direct descendant of the Bull-and-terrier or Pit Bullterrier that wrote so brave and sordid a chapter of canine history in England's fighting pits of the early 19th century. From this basic stock the white Bull Terrier later derived.

The Staffordshire is named for the miners of Staffordshire, England, who continued to breed pit dogs for clandestine sport long after dogfights were declared illegal.

The United States first came to know the Staffordshire in 1870; initially he was called Yankee Terrier or American Bull Terrier. Breeders on this side of the Atlantic have stressed size and conformation, with the result that the American dog now outweighs his English counterpart, the Staffordshire Bull Terrier, by some ten pounds.

His short, smooth coat may be any color, although brindle is the most common. Ears are generally cropped for show.

Thanks to his pit-fighting heritage, the Staffordshire is more than able to take care of himself in a scrap. As a watchdog, he has a gift for distinguishing harmless strangers from those with evil intent, and has the means to discourage the latter.

But the modern dog is no brawler. He has become a thorough gentleman, reliable and well-controlled. Some are noted obedience winners. As a pet there is no more devoted and charming companion than the Staffordshire. He'd gladly give his life for you.
Shoulder height 17–19 in. Weight 35–50 lbs.

Ex-fighters let off steam in play. The stur Staffordshire, originally bred from pit-fighti stock, is today a keen and lively household p He loves to frolic with children.

WALTER A. WEBER, NATIONAL GEOGRAPHIC STAFF AR

WALTER A. WEBER

WALTER A. WEBER, NATIONAL GEOGRAPHIC STAFF ARTIST

The unknown holds no terror for the dynamic little Norwich; each new situation is a challenge.

Norwich Terrier

BIG DOGS, LIKE BIG PEOPLE, can rely on size to gain their ends. But the small human and the small canine seldom relax.

The observation is exemplified in the feverish activity of the Norwich Terrier, a tiny dynamo who seizes every opportunity to tackle the seemingly impossible. A natural ratter and spunky hunter of fox and badger, he displays courage so awesome that "honorable scars from fair wear and tear shall not count against" him in the show ring.

British sportsmen developed the breed around 1880, probably from a cross between the Irish, Scottish, and English terriers.

The Norwich has variously been called the Cantab, after Cambridge University where he enjoyed his first vogue; the Trumpington, after the home town of an early breeder; and the Jones, after a Norwich huntsman who helped introduce the short-legged battler into the United States after World War I.

The Norwich's success in the field is largely due to maternal training. The little dams take great care in coaching their puppies in terrier skills. The mothers are fiercely protective, making it unwise to reach into a Norwich nest to touch a puppy.

The Norwich may have either erect or drop ears. His hard, wiry coat, usually red though sometimes black and tan or grizzle, collects no dirt and requires no trimming, characteristics that make this one-man dog an ideal house pet.
Shoulder height 10 in. Weight 11–12 lbs.

Australian Terrier

HOMESTEADERS on the Australian frontier in the early 1800's found a valuable ally against marauders and trespassers in a small rough-coated terrier. Imported from England, this scrapper with blue coat and tan legs and face had an almost infallible instinct for detecting the distant approach of strangers. Extremely hard to acquire, he was guarded by his master as diligently as he guarded his master's household.

Australians developed various strains of this alert little sentinel, introducing different bloodlines as immigrants arrived with other dogs. By the turn of the century a distinctive breed with a long, low-set body had emerged—the Australian Terrier.

Most experts agree on his composition because of familiar characteristics seen in his makeup: the Scottie's harsh weatherproof coat; the Yorkshire's blue-and-tan color; the Cairn's erect ears; the Skye's long back; the Dandie Dinmont's soft-haired topknot. The Irish and perhaps Manchester terriers may have contributed to the color of the red and sandy coated varieties.

Through the years this rugged mite has won fame as a hunter of rats and snakes, yet he has also tended sheep and guarded mines.

Only recently popularized in the United States, the friendly Aussie gained admittance to American Kennel Club registry in 1960. Quiet for a terrier and requiring little grooming, he makes an ideal pet.
Shoulder height 10 in. Weight 12–14 lbs.

Rugged, all-purpose dog of the outback, the Australian Terrier was death to rats and snakes.

JAMES GORDON IRVING

Alike in loyalty if not in looks are the lamblike Bedlington, tall Airedale, and fiery Irish Terrier.

Bedlington

A LIONLIKE HEART beats beneath the lamblike exterior of the Bedlington Terrier. This most distinctive of earth dogs was the pride and joy of coal miners around Bedlington in Northumberland, England. After a day in the bowels of the earth, the miners took keen delight in this game little terrier with coat of blue as enticing as the sky.

Dog racing was one of the miners' favorite sports, and the Bedlington's speed was so dazzling that he became known as the "miner's racehorse." And when rain ruined the racing, a barn or shed could always be found for a dogfight or a rat-killing contest. Many a wager was won—and lost—on a Bedlington's skill in the pits.

His roached back and lightninglike movement stem from Whippet ancestors; his vermin-killing proficiency, blue coloring, and white topknot reflect kinship with the Dandie Dinmont Terrier. The Bedlington's soft, linty coat may also be liver or sandy with traces of tan.

First shown in England in the mid-1800's, the breed reached the United States around 1900. Winner of highest honors at dog shows, tractable and devoted, the stout-hearted Bedlington makes a loving and lovable pet. *Shoulder height 15–16 in. Weight 22–24 lbs.*

EDWARD HERBERT MINER

The Airedale's terrier blood as well as his black and tan coloring come from the Broken-haired or Old English Terrier. But his winsome character probably stems from his other forebear, the lovable Otterhound.

Developed in the mid-19th century as an all-around hunter, the Airedale was known as the Working, Waterside, and Bingley Terrier. His present name caught on after he was exhibited at the Airedale Agricultural Society's 1879 show in Yorkshire, England.

Arriving in the United States at the turn of the century, the Airedale so captured the public fancy that, in the 1920's, to call someone a "regular Airedale" was to stamp him as a gay blade indeed.

Shoulder height 21–23 in. Weight 40–60 lbs.

Airedale Terrier

ANYONE WHO has ever owned an Airedale believes that this big terrier could win the heart of a statue. Largest member of the earth dog family, he is versatility personified.

During World War I his valor made him a dependable battlefield messenger, while his intelligence made him a sentry that brooked no nonsense.

His strength and trainability fit him well for police work, and several European police forces have found him an effective way to put teeth into the law. He also possesses the terrier flair for the hunt, and is afraid of nothing that walks or crawls. Mountain lions, wolves, and bears have felt the clamp of his viselike jaws.

Despite his ferocity in the field, the big fellow remains a puppy at heart and enjoys being pampered. As a pet, he is a thoughtful companion to every member of the family and is particularly patient with children.

Irish Terrier

A FIGHTING IRISHMAN to the core, this terrier has few equals for reckless courage. During an African hunt some years ago, a lion was brought to bay in dense bush. The hunters loosed their dog pack—including an Irish Terrier—in an attempt to dislodge the lion, but without success.

Then suddenly the king of beasts bolted from cover. As he dashed into the open, his tail streamed straight out behind. And there, teeth locked on the end of it, was the little Irish Terrier!

Though his parent stock, the wire-haired Black and Tan Terrier, flourished throughout the British Isles, the Irishman found a place in the hearts and homes of the Emerald Isle as the poor man's sentinel, farmer's friend, and gentleman's favorite.

His fame as a hunter and vermin destroyer spread, and by the 1880's the breed was well established in England and the United States.

Playful with children and a zealous family guardian, the Irish Terrier is at home in country or city. As he attains years, this daredevil with the red or wheaten coat takes on a dignity unusual in a dog his size.

Shoulder height 16–18 in. Weight 22–30 lbs.

Manchester Terrier

AS CLEAN OF LINE as a Greyhound, the Manchester Terrier is a portrait of sleek canine beauty. Lean power is suggested in his distinctive build. His long, wedge-shaped head is a study in tapered keenness. Mahogany markings point up the richness of his glossy black coat.

The Manchester's ancestry goes back to the famous old Black and Tan Terrier, a coarse-coated earth dog that once terrorized the rodent world. The Black and Tan's prowess as a ratter is legendary; in the less-than-sanitary Middle Ages he was almost as effective as a modern wonder drug in battling rat-caused epidemics.

The Manchester has preserved this family specialty. Indeed, the modern dog—lightning-fast in his reflexes and with a constant urge to action against his hereditary enemy—is often called the Rat Terrier.

Spirit and vigor characterize both the sleek Manchester, trained for England's rat pits, and Ireland

The present-day breed was developed in Manchester, England, where rat killing and rabbit coursing were popular pastimes. One breeder, seeking a dog skilled in both pursuits, crossed a Whippet with the old rat killer. The result was the handsome Manchester: trim, fast, and lethal to vermin.

After proving themselves in the rat pits and fields, the new terriers became popular throughout their homeland. Late in the last century the name Manchester was dropped and the dog was called the Black and Tan Terrier after his distinguished forefather.

At the turn of the century, the breed slipped into decline in England when a law which forbade ear-cropping was passed and breeders despaired of producing an attractive dog with button ears. But the breed had already established a beachhead in the United States, where both cropped and uncropped ears are seen.

Recent years have seen interest rise in the graceful little gamester, whose original name was restored in 1923 when the Manchester Terrier Club of America was formed.

A one-man dog, the Manchester is unstinting in devotion to his master. His short coat appeals to housekeepers who might shy away from his rougher-coated cousins.
Shoulder height 10–14 in. Weight 12–22 lbs.

porting Kerry Blue Terrier.

EDWARD HERBERT MINER

Kerry Blue Terrier

AS IRISH AS A SHAMROCK, the Kerry Blue is a jack of all canine trades and a master of most. He goes to earth, trails, hunts, and retrieves. In the hills of his County Kerry home he still herds sheep and drives cattle. The English have used him successfully in police work.

Developed early in the 19th century, the Kerry probably represents a cross between a now-extinct Irish herding breed and the Irish Wolfhound. In texture, profusion, and color the well-knit terrier's coat indicates that his herding ancestor might have been related to the Old English Sheepdog.

Dark at birth, the Kerry's coat "clears" to a characteristic blue-gray at maturity. The dog's long head terminates in deep, muscular jaws; these serve him well, for he is a formidable fighter when aroused.

In Ireland, where he is known as the Irish Blue, the Kerry retains his reputation as a working terrier. No trimming of any kind is permitted in the ring, and none may win a show award without first proving his mettle in a field trial.

In America and England, where the bushy-browed dog made his debut in 1922, the situation is different. Every hair of his neatly trimmed coat is combed into place before he steps into the show ring, and he is a companion more than a worker. Easily trained, he adapts well to city or country, and has few equals as a watchdog. He is affectionate with his human family but has a particularly deep well of devotion for his master.
Shoulder height 17½–19½ in. Weight 30–40 lbs.

"Come on, let's play!" The lively Welshman invi

Welsh Terrier

OLD SPORTING PRINTS disclose that the Welsh Terrier belongs to the canine family once known to fox hunters as "kennel terriers."

These small, hard-coated dogs lived with the hounds in their kennels, ran with the packs in the hunt, and climaxed the chase by going underground after the fox.

Actually, the black and tan coat of the Welsh Terrier has been definite for so long that this breed is regarded as one of the oldest in the British Isles. Certain authorities even maintain that the Welsh is identical to the famous old Black and Tan which sired so many terrier breeds.

His strong, compact frame, intelligent expression, and the color and texture of his coat make the Welshie look like an Airedale

EDWARD HERBERT MINER

s bewhiskered little Schnauzer friend to romp.

Miniature Schnauzer

THE HEAVY BEARD that all but hides the muzzle of the Miniature Schnauzer provides him with a comic opera mask behind which he can plan his endearing mischief undetected. This playful little dog loves to be with people. He'll shun his own kind anytime for a chance to consort with and tease his human friends.

Derived from his larger cousin, the Standard Schnauzer, by way of a cross with a toy breed, the Affenpinscher, the Miniature does not share the blood and inheritance of the British terriers. However, his efficiency as a vermin killer more than qualifies him for the title of terrier. In his native Germany, he maintains a proud reputation as a ratter.

Although the Miniature Schnauzer is peace-loving by nature, long, powerful jaws and a strongly muscled body equip him to take care of himself in a scrap. His harsh, wiry coat is a characteristic pepper and salt color.

Bred in the United States since 1925, the little Schnauzer makes a sensible watchdog, intelligent and alert. But his fondness for human companionship makes the role of pet the one he loves best.
Shoulder height 12–14 in. Weight 12–18 lbs.

in miniature. But his personality is uniquely his own. Calmest and best mannered of the terriers, the Welshie has a gift for winning friends. At the same time, the forthright little dog is eager to give a good account of himself. Going to ground or rounding up livestock, he will discharge his duties satisfactorily or die in the attempt.

Though his lineage is long, his breed was not classified in Britain until about 1885. First seen in the United States several years later, he did not gain much notice until after the turn of the century.

In this country the Welsh Terrier has little opportunity to display the sporting skills he still employs in his native land. Here his role is watchdog and companion in the home. But he adapts readily to his environment and makes a smart, affectionate family pet.
Shoulder height 14–15 in. Weight 19–21 lbs.

The Non-sporting Breeds

SOME READ INTO THIS GROUP'S NAME a faintly disparaging note.
But could these cosmopolitan canines speak in their own defense
Monsieur Poodle might shrug an impeccably barbered shoulder and say:
Did your forefathers brave wintry waters to fetch ducks as mine once did?
Mister Bulldog would cock a leathery eyebrow and snort:
Non-sporting, sir? No member of my breed ever turned tail to a bull!
The Dalmatian could rightly ask: *What sportsman knows more about horses than I?*
The Chow Chow, hunting comrade of emperors, the Keeshond, and the Boston Terrier
would also rally to the challenge. Non-sporting dogs we call them, but
companion dogs they are, standing confident and ready for our appraisal.
With National Geographic editor Merle Severy
let us meet them, one by one.

MERLE SEVERY

Bright-eyed, heads-up look of the Poodle has hypnotized an army of admirers. His warmth, intelligence, and devotion make him a blue-ribbon pet even when he doesn't measure up to the show ring.
WALTER CHANDOHA

CHAPTER EIGHT

The Companion Dogs

And what would monsieur like? A suede jacket with roll collar? White storm boots? A Foreign Intrigue trench coat? Of course, a vented back—we don't want to interfere with the happy wagging tail, do we?

What Monsieur Poodle really wants is to be a dog, not a clotheshorse. But he goes along with this frilly treatment because, like all non-sporting dogs, his principal aim is to please his master. And more and more Poodles are pleasing more and more masters. Ranked 18th in American Kennel Club registrations in 1951, the Poodle rocketed in popularity after Best in Show wins at Westminster in 1956, 1958, and 1959. Record registrations in 1960 shot him into first place among all breeds—and there he stayed. In 1969 the AKC registered 274,000 Poodles, nearly 200,000 more than the highest mark set by the Cocker Spaniel during that breed's 17-year reign as America's top dog.

Caught up in the Poodle craze, some owners dye him pink or blue, paint his toenails, spray him with perfume, fit him with rhinestone collars and jeweled berets, and insist that he wear booties and wraps. Kennel shops in larger cities provide an astounding array: mink stoles and cashmere sweaters, snowsuits and silk negligees.

One New York specialty shop outfitted a white Miniature Poodle and her black escort to go to a costume ball as "Night and Day." The lady wore a

FPG

H. ARMSTRONG ROBERTS AND (BELOW) ALPHA PHOTO ASSOCIATES

Poodles *à la mode* get the full treatment from toe to topknot—nail polish, rhinestone collars, jeweled cloaks, even pink hair rinses. Chic French actress (opposite) reflects the love millions of her countrymen feel for the *caniche*, or Poodle.

yellow velvet coat. Over her head like a halo hovered a golden sun, secured to her collar. He wore a black velvet coat and leggings, spangled with stars. A moon hung over his head. It was enough to break a St. Bernard's heart.

And at a Massachusetts pet shop a woman bought several coats with matching collars for her Poodle. At the door she stopped and said, "Oh, I almost forgot what I really came in for. He has to go to a Christmas party and is supposed to take a present."

JUSTIN LOCKE

One privileged Poodle, who shares her mistress's bedroom, rides down a special chute when it's time for a servant to take her for her morning walk.

Coddled canines inclined to paunchiness can turn to exercise machines and low-calorie foods. Horoscopes tell Phideau when he'll have his day, hairdos bolster his ego, tranquilizers soothe his nerves. And if the going gets really rough, he may even see a psychologist.

Several factors may account for the Poodle's amazing rise to favor. He has no doggy odor and never sheds. He comes in a wide range of solid colors and in three convenient sizes—Standard, Miniature, and Toy. He can be trimmed, or clipped, in a variety of styles—though only three are acceptable in the show ring. Gentle, affectionate, cooperative, he has natural appeal. And he is extremely intelligent.

Freeman Lloyd recalled in the *National Geographic Magazine* a dog he bought with some misgiving in London many years ago. It was a white Poodle, rather bedraggled-looking and no longer young, but there was a look in his eye Lloyd could not resist. The first surprise came when he took the Poodle to his apartment and fed him. When finished, the dog daintily picked up the plate and, sitting up, held it out for seconds.

That evening friends dropped in. Lloyd offered them beer and gave the dog water, which he declined. Someone suggested the dog might like beer too, so they offered him some. Down it went with slurping relish. Then and there the Poodle got his name: Boozer.

The real surprise came when Lloyd took Boozer backstage at a music hall which featured a dog act. Boozer no sooner saw the props than he hopped on

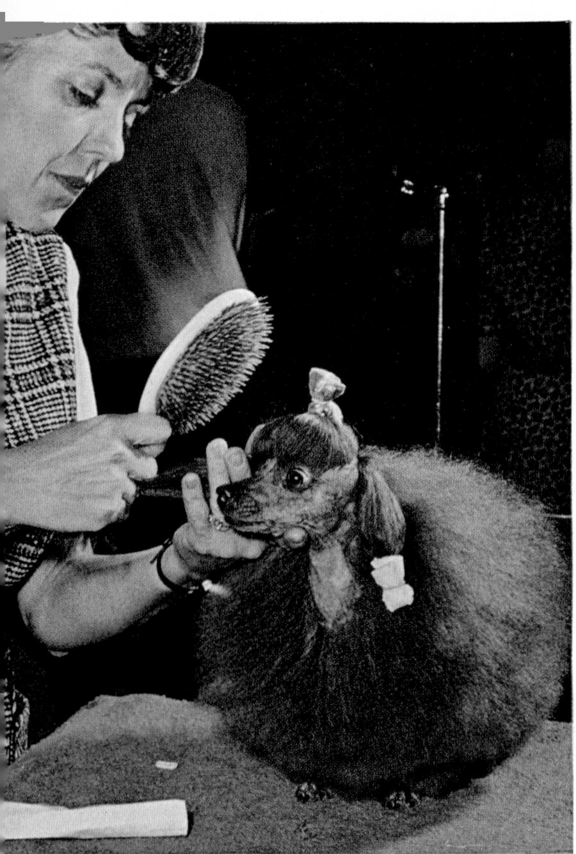

Show time! Off with the glittering froufrou; here the Poodle competes *au naturel.* But before the big moment the glamor dog must endure a ritual of grooming that matches any movie queen's.

First a bath and shampoo. Dry thoroughly; an electric hair dryer helps. Trim the coat and clip the nails. Carefully clean the insides of the ears. Then tie them (right) or wrap them in paper (left) to keep them out of the dog's mouth. Tie the topknot, too, to avoid a tangle. Now brush, stroke after stroke, hour after hour—but lightly, else the hair may break or pull out. Finally, untie ears and topknot, brush a bit more, and on with the show!

a bright-colored keg and rolled it with perfect poise across the stage. He was obviously an old vaudeville trouper, so Lloyd reluctantly sold him to the theater man.

The Poodle's heritage as a performer runs back to the 17th and 18th centuries when dancing Poodles amused ladies of the court. Later, troupes of Poodles barnstormed the provinces. In one act they mimicked a battle, even firing guns. One Poodle did card tricks. But a Poodle anecdote I particularly like concerns another solo performer on a bridge across the River Seine in Paris.

A British officer crossing the Pont Neuf was startled by a black Poodle that pounced on his glistening boots with muddy paws. Annoyed, the proud Britisher walked on and was relieved to find a bootblack at the end of the bridge. Next day the jaunty dog repeated the muddy assault. On the third day, the officer stopped to investigate. He watched the Poodle shuttle from mud puddle to passer-by, planting sloppy paws on the shoes of each. The Poodle was drumming up business for his master the bootblack!

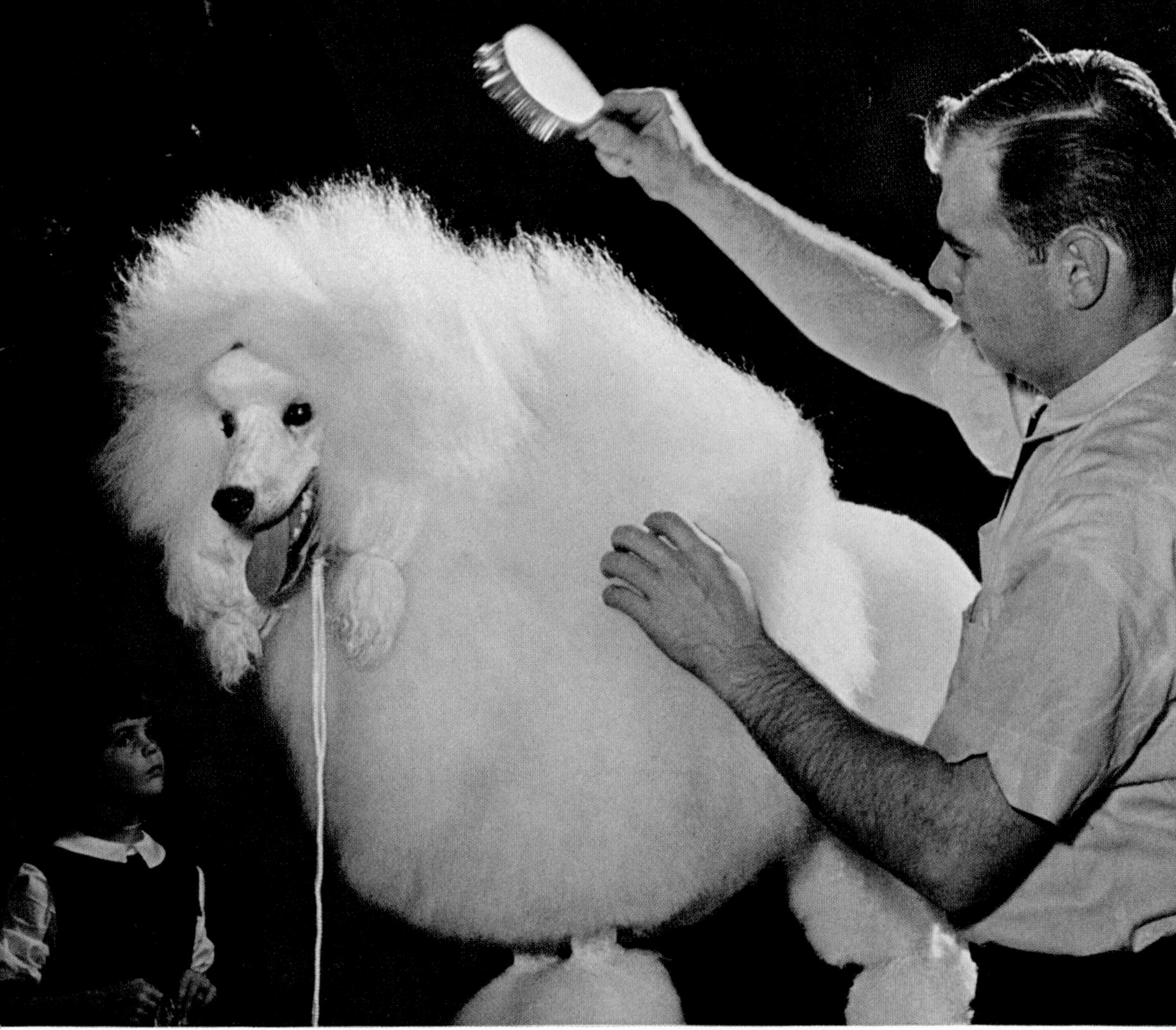

ROBERT S. OAKES, NATIONAL GEOGRAPHIC STAFF

THE NON-SPORTING BREEDS come from many lands: from China and Tibet, from Europe and America. They stem from regal ancestors, and from dogs of humbler caste. But they have one thing in common: they all make fine companions. If admirers of sporting breeds tend to lift an eyebrow at the non-sporting type, let them bear in mind that almost every dog once filled a useful role. That some are no longer productively employed is no reflection on the dogs; it means their masters' habits have changed.

In days when meat on the table depended on the hunt's success, the Poodle was a hard-working "water dogge" who retrieved game for his country master. But urban society placed higher premium on his intelligence and responsive nature, and today his is a companion role. The Dalmatian, once a coach dog that challenged highwaymen and cleared the way for his master's carriage, now rides in an air-conditioned car. And what would an 18th century bullbaiting fan say at calling a Bulldog non-sporting? "Sir, there is no gamer dog!"

Bulldog grip, bulldog courage, bulldog determination are not idle phrases. The Bulldog, symbol of Britain as the Poodle is of France, displayed these qualities to an almost incredible degree when bullbaiting and dogfights were

B. ANTHONY STEWART, NATIONAL GEOGRAPHIC PHOTOGRAPHER

Dalmatians and horses, longtime friends, pause under the oaks at St. Simons Island, Georgia.

popular amusements in his native England. He was called upon to lick many times his weight in maddened bulls.

From animal fights in Rome's Colosseum down through the 18th century, gory contests like these were accepted custom. Royalty and commoner found "pleasant sport" in seeing dogs "wearie a bull dead at the stake."

Queen Elizabeth avidly fancied baiting sports. In 1559 she entertained the French ambassador with music and a splendid dinner, after which English dogs baited bulls and bears. Again, we read that in 1600 she "commanded the beares, the bull, and the ape, to be baited in the Tilt-yard."

In London Thursday was baiting day. In 1591 the Privy Council forbade the showing of stage plays that day lest attendance suffer at the more respectable contests between dog and bull or bear. A drawing of the city in Shakespeare's time shows "The Bear Garden" to be as prominent as the Globe Theater.

Baiting bulls may have begun with medieval butchers, who brought in cattle for slaughter with the help of dogs. Setting dogs at the bull was long believed to make its meat more tender. The Mastiff, "huge, stubborne, ouglie, eger, burthenous of bodie . . . terrible and fearfull to behold," was a natural choice for this work. And perhaps as naturally in those rude and less humane times, villagers and townspeople would make sport of this clash between dog and bull.

Later dogs were bred especially for baiting. Desired features were agility, a squat body difficult to hook with a horn, and a powerful, undershot jaw and receding nose to enable the dog to breathe while pinning his bull. Certainly he was less bulky, longer in leg, and faster than today's Bulldog.

In the barbarous baiting spectacle, the bull, tethered to a stake at the end of several yards of stout rope, was goaded to a frenzy with sharp sticks and the cries of the boisterous crowd. A Bulldog, loosed at the enraged beast "whose cruel hornes do threat desperate danger," charged in to seize the bull by the tender nose and bring him to his knees.

Ideal pal for a boy, the hardy Dalmatian can keep pace with the most energetic youngster.

WALTER CHANDOHA

Repeated efforts were made to prohibit bullbaiting, but to no avail. The court held that the sport was "a sweet and comfortable recreation fitted for the solace and comfort of a peaceable people." When the Puritans tried to abolish it during the Commonwealth, scoffers said they were motivated more by a desire to inhibit the spectators' pleasure than by compassion for the bull. Finally, under mounting critical fire, baiting lost ground, and in 1835 was prohibited by act of Parliament.

DOGFIGHTING, outlawed in Great Britain at the same time, went undercover and, as a result of the abolition of bull- and bearbaiting, became even more popular for years. Sad to say, these clandestine contests persist sporadically to this day. Let Freeman Lloyd tell of such a fight:

"I once saw a professional dogfight in a foul-smelling, secret hall in the East End of London—an evil place known as Dog Thieves' Kitchen.

"In a canvas-floored pit two heavy Bull-and-terrier dogs fought to the death, each straining to fasten its teeth in the 'neck hole' of its rival, while two degraded men urged the gladiators to greater fury.

"When the dogs got grips on each other, the handlers kneeled beside them, striking the canvas to induce them to bite harder. The sickening spectacle ended as soon as one of the dogs was declared dead."

Dogfights flourished in England long after Parliament banned them and bullbaiting in 1835. Motley crowds of watermen, coachmen, lamplighters, and swells wagered noisily on cruel contests that sometimes lasted two hours. Bulldogs and terriers sired these gladiators of the candlelit pits.

ROSENWALD COLLECTION, NATIONAL GALLERY OF ART, WASHINGTON, D.C.

One up—five to go! Spanish artist Francisco de Goya captured the fury of a bull beset by dogs. Bullbaitings like this entertained the Elizabethan court. One eyewitness reported dogs tossed 30 feet into the air. England's fearless, tenacious Bulldog was bred just for this sport.

From fighting stock like this came one of America's most lovable pets, the Boston Terrier. Parents of this friendly dog were bred down in weight from brindle and white Bull-and-terriers, whose background centered on the fighting pit. Such was the ancestry of the Massachusetts dog known as Barnard's Tom, pillar of the Boston Terrier studbook. First called Round Head and American Bull Terrier and exhibited with the Bull Terriers, the breed received its present name in 1891. The little Bostonian has earned great popularity in his native America, and in England is sometimes nicknamed Black Satin Gentleman.

The French Bulldog, small and compact, has bat ears and a pert Gallic expression that distinguish him from his dour English cousin. Introduced into Britain and America in the late 1800's, the *bouledogue français* was warmly received and has many avid fanciers today.

Another Continental is the spectacled Keeshond. Long the favorite of Dutch bargemen, he got his name during the widespread political unrest preceding the French Revolution. Holland was divided into two camps: the middle-class Patriots and the upper-class partisans of the Prince of Orange. Though the leader of the popular party, Cornelis van Gyselaer, made little impression on history's course, his dog gained undying fame. Kees (a nickname for Cornelis) gave his name to his entire breed. *Hond* means dog in Dutch.

This "dog of the people" became the mascot of the Patriots, who scorned the nobility's Pug. Unfortunately for the Keeshond, the "war of the dogs" ended with the Prince of Orange's party on top. People with Keeshonden quietly disposed of their pets and the dog faded from view. Rediscovered a century and a half later, he has risen to new popularity.

Across the border in Belgium, the sprightly Schipperke is the traditional barge dog. His heavy coat is usually black and he is often born without a tail. Whether descended from curl-tailed spitz, as some maintain, or a black Belgian sheepdog, he is a delight to have around—bright, alert, and loyal.

From the Orient comes a regal pair. Raised in the shadow of the world's loftiest peaks, Tibet's "Lion Dog," the Lhasa Apso, has long been a favorite in lamaseries and noble Tibetan homes. Consort of China's "Celestial Emperors," the Chow Chow is so blue-blooded it shows in his blue-black tongue. During his 2,000-year history he has served both as hunter and as "chow": Chinese considered a tender, rice-fattened Chow a choice meat dish.

Bushed Bulldog snoozes away. The breed, no longer vicious, retains its legendary courage.

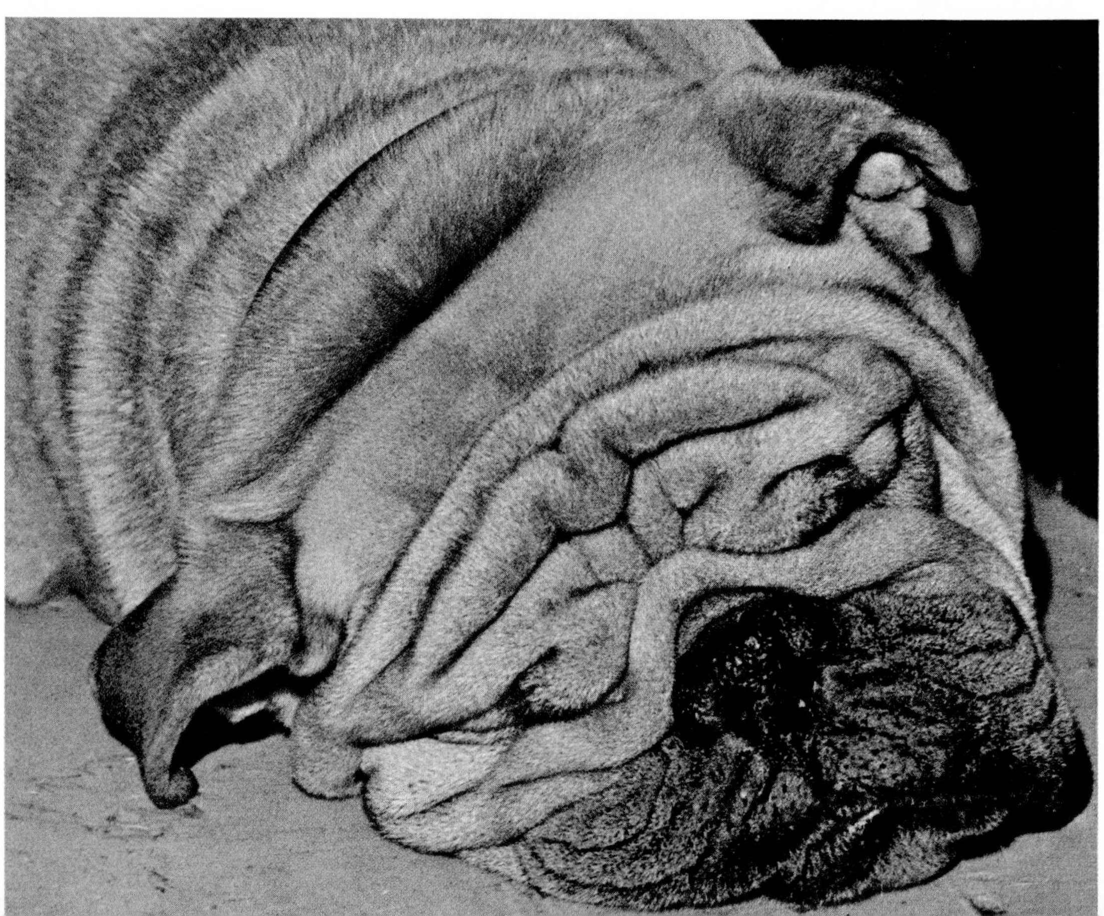

Gruff countenance of brindle Bulldog (left) belies an amiable disposition. Saucy Boston Terrier (above) prefers a gentler life than his ancestors' fighting pit.

WALTER CHANDOHA AND (RIGHT) H. ARMSTRONG ROBERTS. OPPOSITE: JERRY COOKE, PHOTO RESEARCHERS

Though the companion dog may be unemployed, his paw has never lost its skill. Just try him. A Poodle can still retrieve a downed duck, as some sportsmen have discovered; a Keeshond will guard a car as well as a barge; the Bulldog will pin a prowler as neatly as he did a bull; a Dalmatian will be as solicitous of your child as he was of his friend the horse; and I suppose you could still fatten and eat a Chow Chow, though I'd hardly recommend it. Just be his friend. Like the others of his group he'll love you in return.

A Portfolio

Following are the non-sporting breeds, painted in full color for the National Geographic Magazine by Staff Artist Walter A. Weber and Robert Lougheed.

Fun-loving Poodles forget their show-ring coiffures in a live romp. Apricot Standard sports English saddle trim, white Standar wears continental clip, and black Miniature prances in a puppy cu

ROBERT LOUGHE

Poodle

THE ELEGANT AND VERSATILE POODLE stars in many dog acts. He takes directions like a trouper and rarely yields to bursts of temperament. His understanding makes him seem almost human.

Though the theater is in his blood, the Poodle might well scorn such undignified tricks as jumping through hoops. Fashionable ladies have lionized him since the days of Louis XVI. Duchesses fondle his floppy ears and pompon tail; countesses plant adoring kisses on his refined brow. Powdered, perfumed, and beribboned, the Poodle accepts this homage with courtly dignity.

But the truth must out! This canine aristocrat is probably just a rough-and-tumble water dog that has crashed high society. Even his French ancestry may be suspect, although he is often regarded as the national dog of France. He became known as the French Poodle because ladies liked to get their dogs as well as their clothes from France. But the word Poodle itself comes from the German *pudeln* (meaning to splash about in water); other lands claim him too.

Dog historians note that an unclipped Poodle strongly resembles England's old rough-haired water dog and the Irish Water Spaniel. The Portuguese Water Dog might also be mistaken for a large Poodle. This working dog is clipped from ribs to stern to facilitate movement in the water; warm fur protects heart and lungs. Ancient Roman art shows dogs with the same leonine cut.

Though his ancestry can only be guessed, today's Poodle traces back to the 16th century with little change except for slightly longer legs, head, and muzzle. The French still call him *caniche* (from *chien canne*, duck dog), which echoes his early renown as retriever.

Many people today regret clipping styles that make the Poodle look like a sissy. With a muffler around neck and shoulders, ruffles about his ankles, and gay ribbons tied to head and tail, he reminds one of a little girl going to a party. They feel it an affront to his dignity when his mistress marches him off to a canine beauty parlor for shampoo, hair styling, manicure—"the works." But this barbering is not just affectation. Untended, the Poodle's coat becomes a corded mass that sweeps the ground.

Poodles in the United States come in three official varieties: Standard, Miniature, and Toy. All are identical except for size, and come in a number of solid colors. Black and white are the most common.

Champion Poodles may sell for thousands of dollars. Some hire out to model the latest Beau Brummel canine wear. One that modeled the poodle haircut for women earned a reported $11,000 in modeling and stud fees in a single year.

Despite all, the Poodle remains unspoiled. One champion proved his mettle in a spaniel field trial in Connecticut, swimming in fine style as he brought in his duck. Enthusiasts look to the day when the Poodle is a recognized retriever. Until then he remains a companionable, obedient pet that enjoys tricks as keenly as his owner.

Standard: *Above 15 in. Weight 40–65 lbs.*
Miniature: *10–15 in. Weight 15–25 lbs.*
Toy: *See page 350.*

THE
NEWS

Dalmatian

WHO COULD CONFUSE the dapper Dalmatian with any other member of the canine family? Black spots on a clean white coat, classic features, splendid gait—his appearance is as distinctive today as it was in an era of broughams, coaches, and rutted dirt roads.

No one knows were the Dalmatian came from—only that it probably was not from the Adriatic coast region that gave him his name. His first mention in England may be this entry from an Elizabethan journal: "There is also at this day among us a newe kinde of dogge brought out of Fraunce . . . . speckled all over with white and black . . . ."

With his English masters the Dalmatian would achieve fame as a coach dog, protecting goods and travelers from brigands and clearing the roadways of wandering animals. Versatile, he also showed skill as a shepherd, pointer, retriever, and ratter.

In the Gay Nineties, horse-drawn fire companies in America adopted the swift and hardy coach dog as their mascot, a tradition that continues to this day. As a household companion, he remains ever popular. His coin-size spots, scattered on him at random, merge only at his ears. Pups are born all white; spots appear in about five weeks.

An alert mind and quiet reserve make the Dalmatian a dependable family pet, playful but courteous, friendly but protective.
Shoulder height 19–23 in. Weight 35–50 lbs.

Canine footmen in smart black-and-white livery, Dalmatians tirelessly attend their master's carriag

WALTER A. WEBER, NATIONAL GEOGRAPHIC STAFF ARTI

WILLIAM H. BOND, NATIONAL GEOGRAPHIC STAFF ARTIST

Saucy eyes twinkle from clouds of fur to reveal the appealing nature of the Bichon Frisé.

Bichon Frisé

HIS NAME IN FRENCH means, roughly, "cute and curly," and during the Renaissance aristocratic owners so pampered him that the verb *bichonner*, to caress, was coined. But whatever called or however gussied, this small dog with a big-dog temperament basks again in the glow of returning popularity.

Native to the Mediterranean, the Bichon Frisé descends from the Barbet, or Water Spaniel. Mariners of antiquity, captivated by the breed's sunny, easygoing manner, took it from port to port, eventually establishing the dogs in the Canary Islands. Here Venetian sailors rediscovered them in the 14th century and returned them to the Continent, where they soon found favor among nobles and wealthy merchants.

Bichons reached France in the 1500's and became such favorites with Henry III that the king and his court are said to have carried their pets in beribboned baskets suspended from the neck. But in the late 1800's Bichons fell from favor. Thereafter they lived in obscurity as just another street dog, leading the blind and accompanying organ grinders until French fanciers again revived the breed in the years after World War I.

The little dog with soulful, shoe-button eyes came to the United States in 1956. He has since won a rapidly growing circle of admirers, despite a snow-white coat that requires frequent grooming to look its best. Granted AKC recognition in 1973, Bichons already rank in the top half of the nation's most popular registered breeds. *Shoulder height 8–12 in. Weight 12–17 lbs.*

Bulldog

COURAGE AND TENACITY mark the Bulldog, symbol of his native England and mascot of Yale University and the United States Marines. But don't let his fierce looks frighten you. All the viciousness has been bred out of this old gladiator that once gloried in fights to the death. He is as docile as a lamb, and far more affectionate.

Time obscures the Bulldog's origin, but most likely he stems from ancient Mastiff stock, known in medieval England and France as the Alaunt and in Elizabethan times as the Mastiffe or Bandogge. The brutal pastime from which he takes his name may have begun with this incident described in *The Survey of Stamford:* "William Earl Warren, Lord of this town in the reign of King John (1209), standing upon the walls of his castle at Stamford, saw two bulls fighting for a cow in the castle meadow, till all the butchers' dogs pursued one of the bulls . . . This so pleased the Earl that he gave the castle meadow . . . to the butchers . . . on condition that they should find a 'mad bull' on a day six weeks before Christmas for the continuance of that sport for ever."

Bullbaiting soon acquired "refinements": the bull was tethered and the dog was trained to seize its sensitive nose or ear and hang on until he brought the beast to its knees.

Ferocious countenance and a bloody history in the fighting rings of England belie the modern Bulldog's gentle, loving nature.

WALTER A. WEBER, NATIONAL GEOGRAPHIC STAFF ARTIST

By Henry VIII's day bullbaiting had become the diversion of all levels of society. During the reign of his daughter Queen Elizabeth, London's chief baiting events began to be held at the Bankside Bear Gardens in Southwark, said to seat 1,000 spectators. James I regaled his guests with baitings, as did his successor, Charles I.

These early Bulldogs little resembled the squat, barrel-shaped breed we know today. Taller and sturdier, they weighed 100 pounds or more. Then, 150 years ago, the pit fighters were bred lighter in bone and faster. They resembled the Staffordshire Terrier, rather long-legged, with thin, straight tail, and coat mostly of white. Terrier and Greyhound blood probably had been added to the basic Mastiff strain. Over the years, perhaps helped by crosses with the Pug, breeders developed the undershot jaw and pushed-in nose that enabled the dog to hang onto the bull and still breathe.

When baitings and dogfights were outlawed in 1835, there seemed little more use for the old warrior. At one time it was said that only three true Bulldogs remained in England. But with typical tenacity, the Bulldog hung on. Fanciers organized to save him. The growing popularity of dog shows gave them an incentive to restore and perpetuate the unforgettable dog.

England's Bulldog club was founded in 1875, America's in 1890. Breeders eliminated his ferocity and made him one of the gentlest of creatures.

Today's ideal Bulldog is of medium size, with thick-set, low-slung body, massive, short-faced head, wide shoulders, and sturdy limbs. Preferred colors in his smooth coat are red or other brindle, solid white, red, fawn, or fallow, and piebald. His bearing suggests stability, vigor, and strength. Courageous but never aggressive, he is kind, peaceful, and dignified. His homely smile would melt a heart of stone.

A loose-jointed, shuffling, sideways gait gives the Bulldog his characteristic roll. Thick, broad flews overhang his jaw, and heavy wrinkles cover head and face. His massive jaws are broad and square, the lower jaw thrust forward of the upper, and turned up. The short tail is straight or screw.

Some critics call today's Bulldog a grotesque deformity—short-legged, short-winded, short-lived, barely able to reproduce his kind. (Sterility often occurs in bitches, and many require Caesarean sections when whelping.) But everyone admits that no dog show would be complete without the presence of this good-hearted plug-ugly who has long since lived down the stigma of the "sport" that made him what he is.

Shoulder height 10–15 in. Weight 30–70 lbs.

Tibetan Terrier

FROM THE CRAGGY mountains of Tibet comes a small, shaggy dog noted for his loyalty, affection, and amiable disposition. Although called a terrier because of his size, he does not act like one at all. He lacks the aggressive, peppery temper; his stance and bearing are decidedly un-terrierlike.

A dog of ancient lineage, the Tibetan Terrier has flourished nearly unchanged for 2,000 years. His forebears accompanied Mongol armies into Europe more than a millennium ago and may have established that nimble Hungarian sheep dog, the Puli.

For centuries lamas have raised these dogs as companions to share the solitude of remote monasteries. The monks referred to them as "little people" and treated them as such. Highly esteemed, the dogs were never sold but were given as tokens of luck or as expressions of profound gratitude.

The first Tibetan Terriers to reach the Western World in modern times did so in the 1930's—as gifts to an English medical missionary who had saved the life of a Tibetan woman. They first came to the United States in the mid-1950's and were granted full AKC status as a non-sporting breed in 1973.

Blocky and sturdy of build, Tibetan Terriers make superb family pets. They enjoy travel and are extremely sensitive to human moods. Their thick, tousled coats, like human hair in texture, are virtually non-allergenic and come in many colors.

Shoulder height 14–16 in. Weight 18–30 lbs.

Tibetan Terrier, holy dog of the Himalayas, peers at his world through a curtain of hair that protects his eyes from wind and glare.

WILLIAM H. BOND, NATIONAL GEOGRAPHIC STAFF ARTIST

WALTER A. WEBER, NATIONAL GEOGRAPHIC STAFF ARTIST

Pint-sized playboys, Frenchies are homebodies at heart. Bat ears characterize the friendly breed.

French Bulldog

THIS BLITHE SPIRIT, bat-eared and brindle, beckons one to play at every glance. Diminutive, short-coated, and sweet-tempered, the frisky French Bulldog was bred for genial companionship. Never was bull baited by this Continental gentleman!

His story begins only about 100 years ago when French breeders began to work with Toy Bulldogs from England. Some authorities maintain that crosses with small, short-faced dogs from Spain and other Mediterranean lands also went into making the gnomelike *bouledogue français*.

He lacked the dour countenance of his English uncle and has never shared his national acclaim. But he captured the fancy of fashionable Parisiennes who sought a *petit divertissement*, a companionable, easy-to-care-for dog for city life.

At first the Frenchie lacked the uniformity of type that would insure his perpetuation. But American fanciers formed a club in his name (the first anywhere) and standardized him: large bat ears, rounded forehead, wide dark eyes, coat of brindle, brindle and white, fawn, or white, and short tapered tail, either straight or screw.

He's been an *enfant favori* with apartment dwellers ever since.

Shoulder height 10–14 in. Weight 19–28 lbs.

Dignity tussles with the urge to chase in the keen mind of a proper Bostonian. This top favori

Boston Terrier

THE HISTORIC TEA PARTY that helped to bring fame to Boston, Massachusetts, preceded by almost a century the smart little dog that was to take the city's name. But this fellow represents his home town well.

Like early New England stock, his forebears were English. But he was bred away from rough-and-tumble pit-fighter traits and jacketed in conservative black with spotless white shirtfront. He became as refined and proper a Bostonian as ever walked Beacon Street. Should he bark with a Brahmin accent, breeders would likely consider their work complete.

The Boston Terrier's history, more easily traced than most, began right after the Civil War, when dogfights were still popular. Bulldog and terrier crosses were often brought to America from England. Some were like our Bull Terriers or Staffordshires. Most were hardy, vicious mongrels.

Robert C. Hooper of Boston bought one

WALTER A. WEBER, NATIONAL GEOGRAPHIC STAFF ARTIST

…vas bred in America from pit-fighting stock.

such Bull-and-terrier that had come to America with a seaman. Mating it with a similar dog of undetermined ancestry, Hooper produced the Adam of what was to become one of America's all-time favorite breeds.

Fanciers of the Boston like to relate his genealogy, coupling the dogs' names to their owners': Hooper's Judge was mated to Burnett's Gyp to produce Wells's Eph, which, mated to Tobin's Kate, produced Barnard's Tom, pillar of the new breed.

Hooper-bred dogs—smaller and quite different from the standard Bull Terriers—were shown in Boston in 1878 and made an instant hit. In a little more than ten years, about thirty Boston fanciers, exhibiting their dogs as Round Heads or American Bull Terriers, organized a breed club.

Bull Terrier backers heatedly opposed the upstart breed and the American Kennel Club refused recognition. In 1891 the fanciers changed the name of their increasingly popular breed to Boston Terrier, and two years later it made the canine social register—admittance to AKC rolls.

The new name was an apt choice. To many Indian tribes, a "Boston" was any citizen of the United States, and this dog is indeed all-American.

In those early years the dogs varied greatly in conformation, size, and color, and only after much debate and work by the breeders did the Boston Terrier achieve his present elegant standard.

The Boston Terrier ranked among America's top ten favorites from 1900 to 1963 and captivated millions of fanciers the world over. He appears keen and alert, determined, even-tempered, and kind. He has replaced ancestral fighting instincts with courtesy and irresistible charm.

Looking more terrier than Bulldog, the Boston Bull, as he is sometimes called, is the most scrupulous terrier in the world. His hair is short, smooth, and lustrous. The cut of his sedate coat, more often brindle than black, reveals his snow-white "shirt." This handsome white blaze on the face, collar, breast, forelegs, and hind legs below the hocks is the trade-mark of the breed.

The Boston's big dark eyes are set wide apart, and his face is free from the wrinkled brow and loose flews of the Bulldog. His batlike ears, from early French Bulldog crosses, may be cropped. The low-carried tail is short, straight, and tapered, or is the typical Bulldog screwtail.

Bred for city life, this small, neat, affectionate apartment dweller is justifiably popular everywhere.

Shoulder height 8–14 in. Weight 12–25 lbs.

Warmly dressed Chow Chows show off their blue-black tongues.

Chow Chow

THE ALMOND-EYED CHOW CHOW boasts one of dogdom's proudest heritages. He lounged on Chinese palace grounds centuries before many breeds existed. A Han dynasty bas-relief establishes him as hunting dog more than 2,000 years ago.

A Tang emperor around the seventh century A.D. reportedly kenneled 2,500 braces of Chow-type "hounds"; to accompany this canine contingent he employed 10,000 huntsmen. Despite this royal role and his services as guard, sled dog, and pet, the Chow often ended his days as a tasty dish of meat.

The Chinese call him "wolf dog," "bear dog," "black-tongued dog"—anything but Chow Chow, which is pidgin English for Oriental briç-a-brac. Sailing masters in the late 1700's found it easier to write "chow chow" than to detail the cargo, dogs included.

Queen Victoria spurred interest in the breed when she imported a pair in 1880. Shown in the United States 10 years later, the Chow became the rage in the 1920's.

Blue-black tongue and mouth and stilted gait mark the Chow. Deep, solid-colored fur, doubtless from arctic ancestors, forms a leonine ruff. Plumed tail curls gracefully. Ears stand stiffly erect.

Aloof, lordly, and independent, the bear-like breed warns off strangers with his apparent scowl. He is playful with his master and patient with his master's children, but shows scant interest in others.

Shoulder height 18–20 in. Weight 40–65 lbs.

Keeshond

LONG AN INNOCENT VICTIM of politics, the wolf-gray Keeshond of Holland has surged back to popularity. Centuries ago the Dutch employed him to guard their barges and catch rats. He won their hearts with his loyalty and companionship, and during their struggle with the nobility the people chose him as their mascot.

Following this involvement in turbulent 18th century politics, the Keeshond fell from favor. But around 1920 the Baroness van Hardencroek, tracing the breed, found many surviving on barges and farms. Some owners had even kept stud books. Under her aegis, the bright, prick-eared dog swept back into fashion in his homeland and made a hit abroad. Surprisingly, he had changed little during his long eclipse, judging from paintings by Jan Steen and other artists.

The Husky-like Keeshond is a member of the spitz family. A luxuriant ruff sets off his alert, foxlike face, lined as though he were wearing spectacles. His standoff coat looks neat with little grooming. *Shoulder height 17–18 in. Weight 35–45 lbs.*

As Dutch as wooden shoes, a Keeshond smartly carries his master's paper.

WALTER A. WEBER, NATIONAL GEOGRAPHIC STAFF ARTIST

WALTER A. WEBER, NATIONAL GEOGRAPHIC STAFF ARTIST

The "Little Captain," ever alert, guards his master's boat. The Schipperke hails from Belgium.

Schipperke

HIS NAME IN FLEMISH means "little captain" and reflects this lively dog's long service on Belgian waterways. Taking little room in cramped quarters, he guarded barge and cargo, hustled tow horses, and kept down rats. In town he was shoemaker's companion and rode guard on tradesmen's vans.

In 1690, when Brussels workmen held a show of the solid-black breed, he was known as "Little Spitz," which suggests his ancestry. But some authorities maintain that one of Belgium's black sheepdogs sired him.

Queen Marie Henriette of Belgium launched the commoner's dog in society when she acquired one in 1885. The Little Captain soon came to America, but attracted only sporadic interest until about 1930. Admirers praise his gentle way with children, his watchfulness, and his loyalty.

The docked-tail Schip has a sharp, foxy look and plenty of energy. His abundant, rough coat needs little care. Many reach the age of 15 or 16. One in Scotland lived to 21. *Shoulder height 9–12 in. Weight 12–18 lbs.*

Lhasa Apso

FROM BEYOND THE LOFTY HIMALAYAS comes this exotic little breed, raised in Buddhist monasteries and villages around the sacred city of Lhasa in Tibet.

Wearing enough hair to clothe many a larger dog, this animated Santa Claus beard lives in snug comfort among the icy peaks of his homeland, where he is called *Abso Seng Kye*—"Bark Lion Sentinel Dog." For eight centuries he has used sharp hearing and instinct to tell friend from foe. The burly Tibetan Mastiff is chained outside the house; this mop of a dog mounts guard inside.

The Dalai Lama presented Lhasa Apsos to Manchu emperors and other notables. The Chinese considered it a great honor to own one, reputed to bring good luck. Their artists often used him as model for a lion!

Long famed in the Orient, the breed has but recently come to the attention of dog fanciers in the West. First called the Talisman Dog or the Lhasa Terrier in England, he received his present name in 1934. In 1955, the American Kennel Club switched him from Terrier to Non-sporting group.

The Lhasa Apso's dense coat is straight and hard, not woolly or silky. Golden or lionlike colors are preferred because of his "lion dog" name. His tail curls over his back.

Assured of increasing popularity as a companion, this little dog loyally serves those he has learned to trust. Dark eyes shine appealingly as he awaits a sign of appreciation for his zealous guarding of the family and home.

Shoulder height 9½–11 in. Weight 15–20 lbs.

A cascade of hair screens the wary Lhasa Apso from the world about him; keen senses tune him in.

LIVING
OF

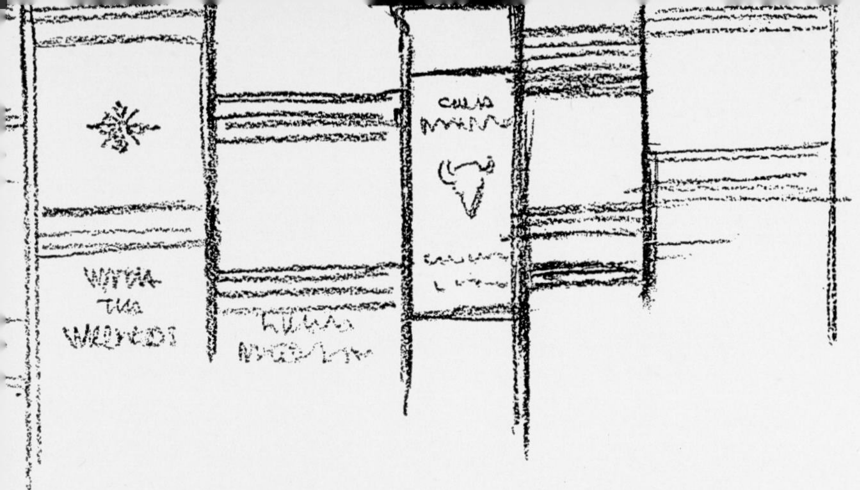

The Toy Breeds

SCARCELY BIGGER THAN A BOOK END, the little dog of luxury plays an outsized role. He furnishes the lap with cheering warmth, signals with soprano bark the deliveryman's approach, accepts with grateful wriggle the pampering his mistress bestows. Weighty obligations these, but the toy has never shirked them in long centuries as pet. The Chihuahua, Aztec legend says, gave his life to guide his noble master's soul to the hereafter; the King Charles served as "Spaniell Gentle, or the comforter," to England's ladies. The proud Pekingese escorted Chinese emperors, and what duchess of Hogarth's day could feel correct without a Pug to complete her retinue? Arthur Frederick Jones has followed the fortunes of these tiny breeds for decades. With him as guide we now visit Dogs in Toyland.

NATIONAL GALLERY OF ART, WASHINGTON, D.C.

Favorite of 18th century nobility, a jaunty Pug frisks in the park with the Marquesa de Pontejos: a Goya masterpiece. Napoleon's Josephine also prized the Pug as a pet.

CHAPTER NINE

Toy Dogs, Pets of Kings and Commoners

TRY GIVING A TOY DOG A STRENUOUS JOB—chasing a fox or retrieving a duck—and his size will make him a washout. He just isn't built for heavy work. But enter him in an obedience trial and he may show his larger competitors what discipline is all about. Give him a bit of your heart and a share of your home and he'll repay you with affection and courage that almost pop the seams of his little body. Small wonder that these small wonders we call Toy Dogs have been perennial favorites of man.

Their loyalty is legendary. A Toy Spaniel shared the last days of Mary Queen of Scots and followed her to the scaffold. Even as the headsman's ax fell, the small dog stood vigil by her side. And Parisians swore they saw Marie Antoinette's Papillon riding in the tumbrel with the French queen as she was taken to the guillotine.

The snowy little Maltese was already an ancient breed when Publius, Roman governor of Malta, had a picture painted of his beloved pet Issa, so that he might never lose her image. Italian Greyhounds, high-strung miniatures of the big racing dogs, were popular pets when Pompeii was destroyed. And Grecian urns dating to 400 B.C. show children romping with small pets that match in appearance today's Pomeranian.

Toy-sized dogs have long enjoyed special favor in royal households. Henry

VIII, though fond of hunting dogs, became so annoyed at them loping in and out of his palace rooms that he finally ordered all dogs kept outside "except some small spanyells for ladies or others." Dr. Johannes Caius, physician to the hearty monarch's children, might have preferred no exceptions at all. These ladies' dogs, wrote Doctor Caius, were "instruments of folly for them to play and dally withall, to tryfle away the treasure of time, to withdraw their mindes from more commendable exercise, and to content their corrupted concupiscences with vaine disport."

In his treatise on "Englishe Dogges," the good doctor gave much space to the "Spaniell Gentle, or the comforter," known today as the English Toy Spaniel. Why "comforter?" These warm little dogs were used "to asswage the sicknesse of the stomacke"; they were the forerunners of the hot-water bottle!

But the "comforter" was not always the "Spaniell Gentle." A female Toy Spaniel was the constant companion of the Earl of Wiltshire, whom Henry VIII sent to Rome to petition the Pope for a marriage annulment. An audience with the pontiff ended, so the tale goes, when the Earl's peppery pet bit the Pope's toe. Perhaps the cause would have failed anyway, but the course of history might have been different if the Earl had left his pet at home.

This same breed was a darling of the monarchs of France. Louis XIII carried a Toy Spaniel in a basket hung from his shoulder and played with the dog even when courtiers addressed him. Though they were not certain he was listening, the more astute blended pleas for favors with compliments to the tiny pet.

Toy Dogs have even gone to war. An Italian Greyhound went into battle in the saddlebag of Frederick the Great of Prussia. And at the end of the last century, Lobengula, warrior king of the Matabele in South Africa, took such a fancy to a prancing Italian Greyhound owned by a theatrical manager that he traded 200 cattle for it!

DOWN THROUGH THE CENTURIES, dog breeders have given the ladies small versions of the hunting dogs of their men. Perhaps the most popular sporting dog of the Middle Ages was the Spaniel, an affectionate hunter that dismayed the ladies by the mud it accumulated afield. Enterprising breeders set about to produce a toy version that could cuddle on a gentlewoman's lap or doze under a drawing-room chair. The result was the "dwarf spaniel," known today as the Papillon. Originally drop-eared, this famous toy was later bred for the erect, butterfly-shaped ears that inspired its French name.

In Elizabethan England, when the terriers of Scotland were just becoming known outside the borders of their rocky homeland, a perky, long-haired working terrier from the windswept Isle of Skye caught the Queen's fancy. Over the next two centuries the Skye Terrier attracted a keen following of sportsmen. Hearing them extol its virtues, their ladies thought it would make an ideal pet, "if only it were small." A group of Scottish weavers in Lancashire and Yorkshire thought so too. Persistent selective breeding plus a few judicious crosses resulted, about the middle of the 19th century, in a little fellow eight inches high at the shoulder and weighing about five pounds. His coat was steel blue, turning to golden tan on his head and legs. It took generations before the new breed, now called the Yorkshire Terrier, could maintain type.

Today's Yorkie is not the dog for the harried housewife. Let him out in a muddy back yard without special preparation and in short order his silky, ground-sweeping coat needs hours of grooming. Yet his popularity continues to grow. In one decade American Kennel Club registrations for this breed multiplied more than ten times—a meteoric climb comparable to that of the Chihuahua. This south-of-the-border mite owes its rise to Xavier Cugat, the "rhumba king," who kept one or two with him constantly on his weekly television show. Millions watched "Cugie" hold his pets while he led his band, and the demand for both smooth and long-haired Chihuahuas soared.

Yorkshires seldom appear on television, and they come in only one coat style: beautiful but bothersome. What then makes the Yorkie popular? Old terrier men say it's his spirit. The Yorkie may be small, but he has a stiff-backed dignity that brooks no

NEAL P. DAVIS

"No more elegant dog exists," wrote a Victorian fancier of the Italian Greyhound, an ancient toy breed possessing "a refinement of form and a grace in every movement."

He thought them too delicate for the "rough touch of masculine hands . . . a tender handling alone is light enough to save from effacement the peach bloom that seems to adorn them."

Pug pups look like urchins with dirty faces. But dark muzzles win only praise for these popular toys; in fact, the blacker, the better.

Vest-pocket Chihuahua puppy already shows the telltale apple-round head; large, flaring ears come later. Mouse-sized at birth, Chihuahuas seldom grow to six pounds.

Button-eyed brace of young Papillons makes a snug fit in a handbag. Some say their family tree includes early specimens of Chihuahuas brought to Spain by Cortez.

WALTER CHANDOHA AND (TOP) MARY ELEANOR BROWNING, PHOTO TRENDS

Proud Pekingese looks back on a regal career already ancient in the Tang dynasty of the eighth century. Brought a captive from China in 1860, the haughty mite has since conquered the Western world's fancy. Disdaining the role of lap dog, the Peke wears an expression suggesting courage and boldness rather than daintiness or delicacy.

interference. Despite his bearing, he unbends with those he loves and takes great delight in attention.

One of dogdom's greatest showmen was a Yorkie, Ch. Star Twilight of Clu-Mor. Twice I watched him take Best in Group at Westminster. After the second win he went on to top the toy group at the International Kennel Club Show in Chicago, and then took Best in Show at the Harbor Cities Kennel Club event in Long Beach, California. His show career began when the breed had fewer than 200 registrations a year; by the time he passed from the scene, yearly registrations were in the thousands.

One of the daintiest and handsomest of toys is the Pomeranian, a member of the wolf-spitz family of dogs found throughout Europe, Asia, and Africa. The colors of its luxuriant standoff coat almost run the canine spectrum. Exhibitors place great stress on the long-haired tail that lies over the back, spread like a fan. A Pom without this gorgeous spray has little chance in the show ring. Some years ago when the American Kennel Club awarded yearly prizes to American-bred dogs that had won most in their respective groups, the woman who owned the top toy, a Pomeranian, brought him to AKC headquarters to receive the award in front of photographers and newsreel cameramen. While technicians bustled over cables and cameras, she watched from a doorway with her little champion in the crook of her elbow. At that moment a Wire-haired Fox Terrier and his handler approached the room. The handler, holding

Pop-eyed Chihuahua, looking as if he'd seen a ghost, gets a shampoo and rubdown in a kitchen beauty parlor. But his young mistress (right) loves him muddy or clean. This wee Mexican doglet ranks high in the toy popularity poll in the United States.

the dog on a loose lead, was talking to someone. The terrier leaped, and dropped to the floor with the lovely plume of the Pom's tail in his teeth! More sparks flew than if someone had crossed a couple of the electrical cables. Fortunately, the Pom was old enough to have been retired anyway. He never appeared in competition again.

Every summer during my boyhood I visited a family who owned a dozen Poms. At the age of ten I believed all dogs were as easy-going as our own Cocker Spaniel. But on my first visit I swung my feet out of bed and found a group of Pomeranians circling them, ready to nip the toe that made a false move. Ever dutiful, they had discovered a stranger in one of their master's beds and were holding him until help arrived. Gradually the Poms and I grew to understand each other, and later stays were more amicable.

The elfin member of the Poodle trio, shaven and shorn, cavorted about the courts of France and Spain during the 18th century and may well reign as America's favorite toy today. His leadership cannot be verified; all three sizes of the breed are registered simply as "Poodles" since they can be interbred. Standard, Miniature, or Toy, the Poodle has a rollicking personality that dominates any gathering. He is a born clown and loves applause.

Toy dogs often suffer unwarranted attacks. Elizabethan lords and ladies, complained Doctor Caius, "not onely lull them in theyr lappes, but kysse them with their lippes, and make them their prettie playfellowes." Times changed;

ORLANDO, THREE LIONS

some toy breeds pranced into the limelight while others padded into the shadows of obscurity. But the barbs continued.

It wasn't the Pug's fault that he became the overweight, wheezy companion of similar dowagers in the horse-and-buggy era. Yet as the era faded, so did the Pug's popularity. From top toy he slipped rapidly to near-extinction in the United States. But he still had a friend: Mrs. Sarah Given Waller of Libertyville, Illinois. And Mrs. Waller had a plan.

When Sarah Given was a small child she wanted to keep a dog, but her parents objected. Instead of refusing to have one around the house, her father said yes, she could have a dog—so long as it was a Pug dog. He knew that his youngster would find it nearly impossible to buy such an extremely rare breed.

Then in 1928 the daughter who yearned for a dog started Sigvale Kennels and set out to bring back the Pug, vanishing victim of humorists who for decades had pictured him as an indolent, silk-cushioned, grunting little muncher of bonbons, as outdated as the open barouche in which he once rode. I used to see such pampered Pugs during boyhood summers in Southampton, Long Island, and the picture painted by the critics was, sadly, an accurate one.

But Mrs. Waller soon rediscovered the merits of the cobby little Pug: an unusually clean pet, a spirited funster, an affectionate companion, a courageous and vigilant guardian. To introduce others to these forgotten virtues, she began placing her best show specimens with new kennels all over the country—and taking dog trade-ins in exchange! She got a grand Russian Wolfhound, several good Cocker Spaniels, and a lot of just plain dogs, but the unique plan worked well. Since 1957 the Pug has ranked among the top third of AKC-registered breeds. And many of today's champions trace their lineage to Sigvale.

When the Pekingese took over as the most popular toy it also was maligned by many. At first discounted by Best in Show judges, Pekes now get full consideration and often make it to the top. Indeed, the all-time record for Best in Show triumphs was racked up a few years ago by a Pekingese with 126 awards, including highest honors at Westminster. This perky Peke could walk away with the hearts of even the severest critics of his breed. Watch him now as the judge names him Best in Show: his handler, a woman of American Indian descent, breaks into an Indian dance right in the show ring with the wee winner

FRANCIS ROUTT, WASHINGTON STAR, AND (OPPOSITE) PAUL J. DENNEHY

Admiration shining in her Toy Poodle eyes, Gregoire's Davey Dumpling gazes demurely at her Bulldog hero, Champion Morris's Blockbuster. "My, what a big mouth you have," her look might seem to say.

"What'll it be? One at a time or both of you?" flashes the Pekingese to the scowling Boxer.

at her heels. Suddenly she ends the dance, spreads her arms wide, and Champion Chik T'Sun of Caversham—scion of the sacred dogs of China—gathers his little legs under him and bounds into her embrace!

This mixture of playfulness and devotion has won for toy breeds not only a seat at the right hand of royalty but also a warm spot by many a humble hearth. Today they still rank as true aristocrats. Saucy but poised, they grant us an audience on the following pages. Let's not keep them waiting!

A Portfolio

Following are the toy breeds, photographed in color for the National Geographic Magazine by Walter Chandoha and others.

FPG AND (OPPOSITE) WALTER CHANDOHA

Plume-tailed Pomeranian, sled dogs' tiny descendant, banquets on a few spoonfuls of food a day.

Toy Poodle

ASKED WHY HER TOY POODLE didn't talk, a St. Louis lady explained:

"Louie's too smart to talk. If he did, people would want him to recite nursery rhymes all the time. It would make life dreadfully boring for him and he knows it."

That this lady considered her Toy Poodle not only a member of the family but a person as well will raise few eyebrows among fanciers of the breed. They are already convinced Poodles are people—very special people—and act toward them accordingly.

And the Poodles themselves seem to prefer people to other dogs. Often they live in lavish luxury, hobnobbing with society matrons, statesmen, famous personalities.

Identical with the larger Poodles in every way except size, and no doubt bred down from them, Toy Poodles appear in 16th century drawings by the German artist Albrecht Dürer. By the late 1700's, Spain had enthroned the Toy as its special favorite, and Goya was painting them. They became the rage at Versailles.

Eighteenth century England fell in love with a sleeve dog known as the White Cuban, thought to have been a cross between a Poodle and a Maltese.

The Toy Poodle has rarely done a lick of work in his entire career. But breeding him with a terrier produced a dog for one of the world's oddest occupations: hunting truffles. Epicures prize these hard-to-find edible fungi growing just under the surface of the ground. Keen-nosed truffle dogs scent them out and their masters dig them up.

Toy Poodles, as eager to please as their bigger brethren, come in almost any solid color their fanciers favor: white, black, brown, silver, gray, cream, apricot (right). Equable in temperament, highly intelligent, and smart in appearance, they are adored by children as well as grownups.

Shoulder height to 10 in. Weight 8–12 lbs.

English saddle clip adds glamor to a little dog with big appeal, the Toy Pood

Pomeranian

BRIGHT-EYED AND BUSHY-TAILED, the perky Pomeranian of today looks very much like the frisky little dogs that appear on Greek gems and jars from ancient times.

But northern Europe rather than the sunny Mediterranean was more likely his ancestral home. The Pom gets his deep fur from distant sled dog forebears in Iceland and Lapland; spitz heritage shows in every feature.

His name represents a later chapter: it was probably in the old Prussian province of Pomerania that breeders shrank him from sheepdog size to toy. But he kept the sheepdog's cunning and, in obedience tests, sometimes emerges top dog.

Queen Victoria's partiality to the Pom popularized this mincing ball of fluff in England. Making his American debut in the 1890's, he has since become one of the most popular of the toys. So small are Poms at birth that three can be held in one hand. *Shoulder height 5–7 in. Weight 3–7 lbs.*

MARY ELEANOR BROWNING, PHOTO TRENDS, AND (BELOW) SALLY ANNE THOMPSON, PHOTO RESEARCHERS

Elegant Papillon descends from dwarf spaniels that won the hearts of Europe's courtiers. Titian, Rubens, and Boucher painted Papillons into their portraits of noble ladies. A late comer to America, the little dog ranks high with fanciers today. Ground color of the breed is white with black, sable, or red markings.

Oriental women carried the dainty, plume-tailed Japanese Spaniel in their kimono sleeves. Spry and alert, this stylish little aristocrat forgets neither friend nor foe. His popularity in America led to dog rustling in Japan.

Papillon

MARIE ANTOINETTE, so the legend goes, noticed one day that the ears of her dwarf spaniel looked like the wings of a butterfly.

"*Ah, mon petit papillon!*" she exclaimed in delight. "Oh, my little butterfly!"

So dearly did she love her "butterfly" that when she was trundled off to the guillotine during the French Revolution, she took him with her. Witnesses to her last hours are said to have seen his telltale ears protruding from the folds of her skirt.

The butterfly ears account for the dog's present name, but some Papillons still have drop ears like other spaniels. This type is known as Epagneul Nain, meaning "dwarf spaniel" in French. The two varieties are judged in the same class at shows.

Just how the drooping ears of some toy spaniels became erect is a matter for speculation, but Spain and Italy first bred dwarf spaniels in large numbers. In 1545 one was sold to a lady who later became queen of Poland. A century later a man named Filipponi of Bologna sold many to the court of Louis XIV, and the dogs traveled on muleback to their homes in France.

Madame de Pompadour, mistress of Louis XV, cherished two, Mimi and Inez.

Still popular in France today, the breed did not reach England in any strength until about 1900. A Papillon club was formed in the United States in 1935 and the breed is enjoying increasing success in America.

The Papillon is hardy. He needs no coddling in winter and suffers little in summer heat. He even makes a fair mouser.

An excellent dog for children, the lively little "butterfly" owes his success to good looks and an appealing personality. As one fancier put it, a Papillon "pulls at your heartstrings."

Shoulder height 9½–11½ in. Weight 8–12 lbs.

Japanese Spaniel

WHEN COMMODORE PERRY opened Japan to Western trade in 1853, his hosts presented him with several little Japanese Spaniels as tokens of esteem.

A pair given to Queen Victoria made the breed known in England. Queen Alexandra in turn took a lively interest in them. During the Russo-Japanese War she stressed Britain's neutrality by posing with a Japanese Spaniel under her left arm and a Russian Wolfhound (Borzoi) at her right side.

Following Perry's voyage, American demand for the dogs reached such a peak that dognaping became rife in Japan. Departing ships took on contingents of dogs. But interest slackened when the Pekingese caught the public eye. Even Japanese fanciers turned to other dogs. Breeders in Europe and America have nevertheless maintained the quality of this high-stepping toy.

Though long associated with Japan, the Japanese Spaniel may have originated in China. Similar dogs appear on old Chinese temples, pottery, and embroidery. China's emperors may have made gifts of these dogs to the Mikados. Sometimes called the Japanese Chin or Chin Chin, the fine-boned breed looks like a tall, slim version of his relative, the Pekingese. But his coat, usually black and white, is silkier.

He views strangers with disdain and may meet advances with a snarl, but makes a smart, lively companion for those he likes.

Shoulder height 8–10 in. Weight 6–9 lbs.

Pekingese

SALLY ANNE THOMPSON, PHOTO RESEARCHERS, AND (OPPOSITE) WALTER CHANDOHA

Once the sacred dog of China, the bold and regal Pekingese sports a black mask and spectacles, and a feathered tail.

BLACK KNIGHT was his name. He dined on turtle soup and drank the finest sherry. He attended Lord Mayor's banquets in London and was presented at Buckingham Palace.

Oblivious of the fact that he was less than a foot tall, Black Knight led the gay life of aristocratic London. This dog-about-town sipped champagne, and at the race track barked tips on the horses as his mistress read him the entries.

Made a freeman of the City of London at a dinner in the ancient Guildhall, he was given "the right to feed goats on the Thames Embankment, enter all public buildings, and hunt polecats in the precincts of St. Paul's"—so he recalled in his "autobiography," *The Diary of a Freeman.* When he died in 1955, obituaries recounted his exploits. But this canine celebrity was not the first Pekingese to receive such adulation.

Ancient ancestors of the Peke were honored dogs of the imperial palace in Peking. To the Chinese they were sacred symbols of the protector of their faith, the Buddha lion. At ceremonies, two of these Lion Dogs preceded the emperor, two followed, bearing the corners of his robe. They shared the emperor's couch and food, and the theft of one was punishable by death.

When British forces stormed Peking in 1860 the Chinese killed their sacred dogs lest they fall into the hands of the "foreign devils." But several live dogs were found behind the palace draperies. One was presented to Queen Victoria, who named him Looty. Admiral John Hay bred the other dogs; more subsequently found their way to England.

Toward the end of the 19th century the Dowager Empress Tzu Hsi favored Alice Roosevelt and J. P. Morgan with Pekes as gifts, but most of America's breeding stock came from England. The exotic canine quickly caught on and has remained one of the most popular dogs in the United States.

As quaint as Ming porcelain, the Peke has dignity that verges on arrogance. Fearing nothing on earth, he merely condescends to strangers. But he is not above enjoying a good romp with his master.

Empress Tzu Hsi once handed down a decree concerning the breed: "Let its color be that of the lion, a golden sable, to be carried in the sleeve of a yellow robe; or the color of a red bear, or striped like a dragon, so that there may be dogs appropriate to each of the imperial robes." Today at dog shows all colors are appropriate in the Peke's long, straight coat, with its luxuriant mane. *Shoulder height 5–7 in. Weight 7–14 lbs.*

Maltese

FOR MORE THAN 28 CENTURIES "ye ancient dogge of Malta" has wooed and won the hearts of ladies. This dainty, snow-white dwarf is said to have supped on the rarest of foods served by queens in vessels of gold.

One of the oldest of breeds, the Maltese spent his early days on the Mediterranean island of Malta, made famous for its wealth by the seagoing Phoenicians.

So devoted was Publius, Roman governor of Malta in the first century A.D., to his Maltese, Issa, that the poet Martial treated the pair in one of his famous epigrams:

"Issa is more frolicsome than Catulla's sparrow. Issa is purer than a dove's kiss. Issa is gentler than a maiden. Issa is more precious than Indian gems. . . . Lest the last days that she sees light should snatch her from him forever, Publius has had her picture painted."

To keep the pups portable in size, tradition says the ancients dosed them with spirits and kenneled them in canisters. In Elizabethan England they were considered "meete playfellowes for minsing mistrisses to beare in their bosoms."

The breed was exhibited at one of England's first bench shows in 1862. Britain and the United States recognize only wholly white specimens, although fawn-colored "Lion Dogs of Malta," clipped like Poodles, occasionally appear at shows on the Continent.

Earlier known as the Maltese Terrier, the dog is probably more spaniel than terrier. One authority even suggests sheepdog ancestry, reporting that Maltese will mount guard for hours, tend ducks, even attempt to herd cattle! Despite these heroic feats, owners sometimes keep their pets in glass cases for fear a draft will chill them.

Amiable and intelligent, the silky-haired Maltese makes an affectionate pet, but he does require much attention.

Shoulder height 5–7 in. Weight 4–6 lbs.

Moplike Maltese charmed ancient Greeks and Romans; these make a lovable lapful.

WALTER CHANDOHA

Upturned noses mirror the proud ancestry of these English Toy Spaniels, shown in three of the breed's four color varieties: the tricolored Prince Charles (left), the Ruby, and the half-grown red-and-white Blenheim.

English Toy Spaniel

TASSEL-EARED TOY SPANIELS won the heart of Mary Stuart during her childhood in France. They shared her triumph when she went to Scotland as queen and, unlike many human friends, shared her fall with equal loyalty. A Toy Spaniel followed her to the scaffold.

In those perilous times when a king's own kin might plot against him, the Toy Spaniel set an example of faithfulness and affection. British monarchs from Henry VIII on were fond of him. Even austere Elizabeth I rejoiced in the company of the "delicate, neate, and pretty kind of dogges called the Spaniell Gentle, or the comforter."

Charles II cherished the black-and-tan toy so much that dogs of this color today are known as King Charles Spaniels.

Red-and-white Toy Spaniels soon won the interest of John Churchill, first Duke of Marlborough. Dogs he and his successors bred at Blenheim Palace showed true spaniel heritage in their skill at hunting woodcock.

Though named the English Toy Spaniel, the breed probably first appeared in Spain. Dogs from China and Japan were later bred in, some authorities say. Paintings by Titian and Veronese show these little spaniels with Renaissance ladies of rank. Louis XIV and his family are portrayed with one. Toy Spaniels of Staffordshire china were "Guardians of the Hearth" in many a Victorian home.

Today the Toy Spaniel breed is seen in four color varieties. The Blenheim is white and red; the King Charles, black and tan; the Prince Charles, white, black, and tan; the Ruby, chestnut red.

A Toy Spaniel's ears are so long they nearly touch the ground. The long silky coat is soft and wavy, with a profuse mane in front. Dome of the head overhangs the large, dark eyes and almost meets the upturned nose. *Shoulder height 7–9 in. Weight 9–12 lbs.*

Pug

WHEN LADIES WORE BUSTLES and men sported handle-bar mustaches, this Mastiff in miniature basked in favor. Then half a century ago he fell from eminence before Pekingese and Pomeranian rivals. He retired to obscurity and only a few admirers sought him out. But he endured his humble station with equanimity, for he has borne many changes in fashion and always come back.

His latest return to vogue, starting in the 1930's, by the 1960's had placed him 16th among American Kennel Club breeds.

Perhaps the oldest of the small, short-faced dogs, the Pug probably hails from China. He traveled to Europe in the 17th century with traders of the Dutch East India Company and quickly became the darling of Dutch, French, and Italian nobility.

He reached England about the time William and Mary ascended the throne in 1689. A half century later, he had conquered British aristocracy. Few ladies of fashion wanted to be seen without him. Perhaps his wizened face made theirs seem more beautiful.

The black Pug made his appearance after the fawn-colored Willoughby variety. He arose perhaps from an infusion of blood from the Japanese Pug, a breed similar to the Toy Spaniels. Today Pugs of different colors are often bred together. Silver, apricot-fawn, or black are all acceptable at shows.

The Pug has remained truer to type than most other breeds; the coil-tailed, stiff-legged Pug of today is like that of the Georgian period. He looks out of big dark eyes set in a round, black-muzzled head. Small, thin ears are button- or rose-shaped, body is compact and square. Requiring little care, Pugs make neat, obedient, companionable pets. *Shoulder height 7–9 in. Weight 14–18 lbs.*

Pugnacious look masks the gentle nature of this cobby little dog; Pug's ears are like black velvet.

Perky terrier ways and a long, glossy coat give the rugged little Silky (above) a winsome look. Descendant of Buddhist holy dogs, American Kennel Club newcomer Shih Tzu (right) sports white blaze on forehead, symbolizing one of the superior marks of Buddha. Tiniest of toys but giants in popularity, Chihuahuas (below) come in either short or long coats.

MARILJAC KENNELS AND (LEFT) VICTOR BALDWIN. BELOW: WALTER CHANDOHA

Silky Terrier

THE HAIRY little dog, not more than ten inches high at the shoulder, sized up the big Dalmatian, then lunged. His master pulled him away. "Silkies," the man explained, "have no conception of how small they are."

This indomitable spirit marks the Silky Terrier, a breed developed around 1900 from a cross between the Australian and Yorkshire Terriers. Originally known as the Sydney Silky for the city of his origin, he was later called the Australian Silky Terrier.

From his Yorkshire stock the Silky acquired the soft coat with hair five or six inches long. Black and tan at birth, it changes with maturity. The tan remains on head and legs but the black turns blue.

First exhibited in Australia in 1907, the Silky spread to Britain, then to the United States. In 1959 the American Kennel Club granted him recognition.

A born watchdog, he regards strangers warily. But with friends he is affectionate and remains a puppy at heart all his life.
Shoulder height 9–10 in. Weight 8–10 lbs.

Shih Tzu

SHAGGY TYKE of sacred lineage, the Shih Tzu shares with the look-alike Lhasa Apso a common history—and a common ancestor, a holy dog of the East. Until 1950 the American Kennel Club registered the Shih Tzu (pronounced shid zoo) as a Lhasa Apso but in 1969 granted it full recognition.

Fanciers claim this hardy little fellow displays the courage of a lion—but then, he's only living up to his name, which means "lion" in Chinese. The breed was known in Tibet as early as the seventh century.

By 1750 it had died out there but lived on in China, where it had been introduced centuries before as tribute from the Dalai Lama. The emperors carefully nurtured the breed in the imperial palace at Peking along with the Pekingese.

The Shih Tzu, though often mistaken for the Lhasa Apso, has a broader head, a shorter nose with a stop, or angle, at the forehead, and wears a beard and mustache. His long wavy coat, which needs daily combing, comes in all colors. Loyal, loving, and alert, he remains playful in old age.
Shoulder height 8–11 in. Weight 9–18 lbs.

Chihuahua

THE WORLD'S SMALLEST DOG, the Chihuahua may tip the scales at little more than a pound. But despite his size, he descends from dogs charged with a cruel burden by the Aztecs.

When an Aztec noble died, his people are said to have sacrificed one of these dogs and burned the two bodies together in the belief that the man's sins would be transferred to the dog. The dog's soul would then guide the human soul to heaven.

The Chihuahua is thought to be the product of a small Asiatic hairless dog, brought by migrating Indian tribes, and the long-coated Techichi, known in Mexico as early as the ninth century. The first specimens of the modern breed were found about 1850 in the Mexican state of Chihuahua.

Today's Chihuahua is graceful and compact and wears a saucy expression. His wide public prefers him in solid colors. It also favors the glossy, smooth-coated variety to the long-haired one, whose soft and silky hair resembles that of the Papillon.
Shoulder height 4–6 in. Weight 1–6 lbs.

WALTER CHANDOHA

Monkey Terrier, the Affenpinscher, looks comically serious with simian face and bristling hair.

Affenpinscher

ONE LOOK AT HIM will tell you how the Affenpinscher came by his name, which means "monkey terrier" in German. His bushy brows, short muzzle, and protruding chin remind one of a monkey; his dark eyes flash a terrier's spirit.

Besides the nickname Monkey Face he could be called Fuzzywuzzy, for his coat looks like a double handful of bristles.

Sturdy in build, with cropped ears and docked tail, the Affenpinscher bears himself with amusing seriousness. Usually quiet, he can stir up a storm when danger threatens: fiery courage manifests itself against any aggressor.

This pluck made him well known as long ago as the 17th century in Europe, where he derived from small rat-catching dogs that abounded in Germany and the Low Countries. He is believed to be a progenitor of the Brussels Griffon. Certainly a strong family likeness exists, despite some differences: the Affenpinscher has a longer muzzle and sharper nose, his coat is longer and looser, and he is generally black against the Griffon's reddish brown.

The Griffon may have been crossed back into the Affenpinscher stock in the 19th century. The Miniature Pinscher may also have contributed to the present-day Affenpinscher, which no longer is a poor man's ratter, but a lady's pet.

Recognized in the United States only since 1936, the lively bundle of bristles might be more popular if he didn't so closely resemble the better known Griffon.

Smart and alert, he makes an excellent house dog and a devoted companion. Admirers confidently predict his star will rise. *Shoulder height about 10 in. Weight 8–12 lbs.*

WILLARD R. CULVER

Short muzzles and fringed beards give these sly Brussels Griffons an almost human expression.

Brussels Griffon

BEARDED AND GNOMELIKE, the Brussels Griffon can boast neither beauty nor blue-blooded ancestry. But his puckish charm has won him a place in the drawing rooms of society. No pampered pet despite his small size, the wiry redhead remains an unspoiled street urchin, jaunty and roguish and smart as a whip.

Ancestors of this canine Horatio Alger were Belgian street dogs—rough and shaggy but intelligent and alert. In days when cabs depended on real horsepower these little ruffians killed stable rats for their keep and were named *griffons d'écurie* (stable griffons) because their looks suggested the fabled monster that was half lion and half eagle.

Crosses with the Affenpinscher supposedly increased their rat-catching prowess. Crosses with the English Toy Spaniel and the Pug also helped reduce the street dogs in size and shorten their muzzles and coats. By 1880 the Brussels Griffon had become well enough established to make his mark at a Brussels dog show. Since then he has climbed slowly in esteem in the United States and Britain.

His reddish-brown coat is the same coarse texture as the Irish Terrier's. A smooth-coated variety, the Brabançon, is rare.

The Griffon's amusing expression is elfin, quizzical, almost human. Admirers claim he likes to imitate them by walking on his hind legs and using his paws as hands. Humorously called a "dowager's delight," he doesn't wait to be picked up but bounds up on a chair so his mistress does not have to stoop. Owners say he reads their thoughts.

He is often as ill at ease as a shy child in front of strangers, but is obedient and easily managed. He makes a sturdy comrade. *Shoulder height 6–8 in. Weight 8–10 lbs.*

Miniature Pinscher

ELEGANT, VIGOROUS, AND ALERT, the Miniature Pinscher is a relative newcomer to the American show ring, but lost little time capturing Best of Group awards.

Contributing to his success is the fact that he has the excellent proportions of a much larger dog. His wedge-shaped body is muscular, sturdy, and compact. Nothing is dwarfish about him, except his size.

The Minpin, as friends call him, originated in Germany several centuries ago. He was known as the *Reh Pinscher* (Roe Terrier) because he looked similar to a nimble and graceful tiny deer found in the forests. He probably descended from a larger black and tan terrier, possibly the Manchester, which he resembles except that his ears and tail are usually cropped.

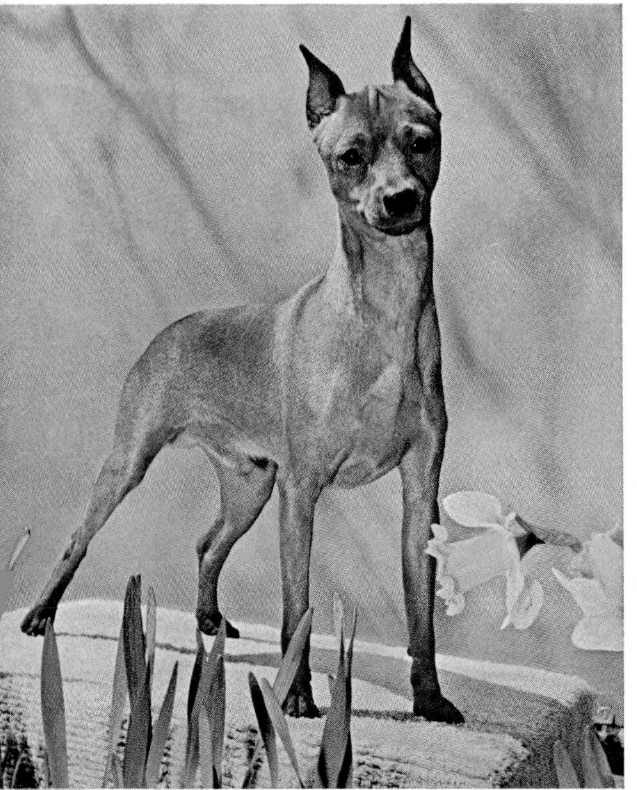

MARY ELEANOR BROWNING, PHOTO TRENDS

Native of Germany, the Miniature Pinscher is an alert watchdog. Lustrous coat needs scant care.

His real development began in 1895 with the formation of Germany's *Pinscher Klub.* The improved breed gained in favor in the early 1900's, and again after the setback of World War I. A few Miniature Pinschers appeared at American shows before 1928, but the formation of the Miniature Pinscher Club of America the following year gave real impetus to the Minpin's advance. His popularity has since risen steadily.

His lustrous coat is smooth, short, and straight. With almost no attention it looks neat. It has three color patterns: solid red or stag red; black with sharply defined tan or rust-red markings; solid brown or chocolate with rust or yellow markings.

This Doberman Pinscher in miniature makes a fine watchdog, surpassing many breeds in keenness of hearing. Like the Doberman, this little fellow shows a natural desire to guard home and property, and will not hesitate to grab a trouser leg of an intruder in his household.

A born showman, with style, intelligence, and pep, the Minpin loves to act. Not only will he eagerly do tricks that have been taught him, he may invent some of his own for his family's amusement. Some of these charming show-offs even try to talk, uttering wordlike sounds distinctly different from ordinary barking.

Professional entertainers have long recognized the Minpin's talents; watch the dog act in a circus or on television and you'll often find that the troupe's smaller members are Miniature Pinschers.

The pet Minpin enjoys playing with children, but he may resent being roughed up. He usually attaches himself to one person in the family and becomes a one-man dog. To that person he gives more than a toy-sized measure of devotion.

Shoulder height 10½–12 in. Weight 7–11 lbs.

Toy Manchester Terrier

A GLISTENING JET BLACK COAT, softened by markings of rich mahogany tan, gives the Toy Manchester a polished look. Sparkling dark eyes add to his lustrous appeal. He is named for Manchester, England, where he was bred in mid-Victorian times. But he was active in many parts of England long before.

First known as the Black and Tan Terrier, he is described in all essentials in the celebrated survey of English dogs by Dr. Johannes Caius in 1570, although the coat then was rougher and the legs shorter.

Two centuries later the Manchester was described as "a short-legged, crooked-legged dog." This has led to speculation that the Manchester might be related to the Dachshund. It is remotely possible that invading Saxons might have brought the Dachshund's ancestors to Britain in the fourth century A.D.

Before 1800, the black and tan terriers may have received an infusion of Greyhound or Whippet blood. But the Toy Manchester's main development appears to have occurred through selective breeding from unusually small offspring of standard-sized parents. The Toy looks like the larger variety of the breed except in natural ear carriage: erect in the Toy, folded in the Standard.

As early as 1840 the demand for tiny Manchester Terriers led to the development of sizes as little as 2½ pounds. This robbed the dogs of their stamina and discouraged their popularity. In 1938 the American Kennel Club modified the standard to allow a class of dogs up to 12 pounds and this has helped the breed.

The standardized black and tan markings of the short coat form clear lines of color division. Any white is a serious fault. *Shoulder height 6–9 in. Weight to 12 lbs.*

"Rip, the Ratter" takes a parlor stance, displaying the Toy Manchester's sleek black and tan coat.

WILLARD R. CULVER

Italian Greyhound

OLD ROMAN VILLAS bear the Latin warning *cave canem*—Beware of the dog. Instead of referring to the huge chained Mastiff that guarded the gates, one historian suggests, it might well refer to the Italian Greyhound. Roman matrons feared less that visitors might get hurt than that their tiny pets might be trampled underfoot!

The elegant Italian Greyhound adored by ladies 2,000 years ago was doubtless bred down by selection from the coursing Greyhound. His popularity spread throughout the Mediterranean world, and in the Renaissance reached countries to the north.

Frederick the Great, King of Prussia, took his Italian Greyhound with him wherever he went. The story goes that during the Seven Years' War the tide of battle once turned so quickly Frederick had to hide under a bridge. The little dog nestled in his arms while enemy troops thundered overhead. Had the dog barked, Frederick's fate would have been sealed. When his pet died, the king buried him with his own hands on the palace grounds in Berlin.

The Italian Greyhound entered English history early in the 17th century, finding favor with the wives of James I and James II. But the breed did not come into great vogue until Queen Victoria's day, when Britain's breeders perfected the whippetlike dog. Known in America since the late 19th century, he has remained uncommon.

His thin, glossy coat may be fawn, red, mouse, blue, cream, or white. Gracefully arched neck flows into long, sloping shoulders. His large eyes are full of expression.
Shoulder height 9–11 in. Weight about 8 lbs.

Yorkshire Terrier

THE SUPERB COAT of the Yorkshire makes him so valuable that one owner insured her pet for $25,000—$5,000 a pound. But if you asked the dog, he'd probably say his coat is nothing but bother.

He has to wear a ribbon to keep his forelock out of his eyes, and booties so that he won't ruin his precious coat when scratching. At meals he sometimes dons a mask to keep long whiskers out of his plate. He can't enjoy romping in the woods because of burs and dirt. He can't even lie down on straw or shavings but has to have a pillow.

Life for him is one combing and brushing after another, and the indignity of having his hair put up in curlers. To keep him neat almost requires a valet on 24-hour duty—not that he minds all the attention!

But he was not always so fancy. In the 19th century the Yorkie caught rats for millworkers in Yorkshire, England. He had just emerged from crosses between the Skye and other terriers. Selective breeding reduced him in size and lengthened his coat (one dog grew hair 24 inches long!).

He made his first appearance at a bench show in 1861 and climbed rapidly in public esteem—from workingman's ratter to aristocratic lady's pet—during Victorian times. About 1880 he came to the United States, where he has become extremely popular in recent years in fashionable circles. He has made a special hit with Hollywood stars.

Black at birth, the Yorkshire at maturity is bright golden tan with steel-blue hair extending from back of head to root of tail. Under this gleaming mantle his body is compact and well-proportioned. He has vigor and spirit, too, and only his master's alertness keeps him from rollicking about as larger terriers do.
Shoulder height 6–8 in. Weight 5–8 lbs.

MARY ELEANOR BROWNING, PHOTO TRENDS, AND (BELOW) WILLARD R. CULVER

Delicacy and impeccable manners long have made the Italian Greyhound a royal favorite.

A mantle of silk masks a vigorous body. As a mouser, the Yorkshire gives cats competition.

Other Canine Friends

MOST OF THE SPLENDID BREEDS so far surveyed were once little known to Americans. Hundreds more, long favorites in their native lands, would capture our fancy if we knew them better, as in the following chapter we may. But of all our favorites, one—call him mongrel, mutt, or just plain "dawg"—holds unchallenged sway. He plays hero and hellion, is faithful and flighty, submissive and stubborn, perpetually underfoot yet never can be found. Cops and robbers, or cowboys and Indians—he misses no fray.

Long months spent with this book's pedigreed canines have not dimmed staffman Howard E. Paine's affection for the mongrel, and he tells us why. Then we're off to Fredericksburg, Virginia, with National Geographic editor Frederick G. Vosburgh for the annual parade of patriot and pooch on historic Dog Mart day.

CHAPTER TEN

Favorite Dogs of Many Lands

THE BOY FOUGHT BACK hot tears. "I won't!" he said firmly, "I won't let you put my dog to sleep!" The distraught parents exchanged helpless glances. They had tried to explain to the lad that it would be merciful to have the softly whimpering dog, struck by a car, put out of his pain.

The boy looked at his trembling pet, lying with hindquarters strangely limp. He heard the tail thump feebly. "He'll get well, I know he will," the boy burst out. "He's got to get well."

And as the weeks went by, get well he did. Under a veterinarian's expert care bones began to knit, tendons to heal. Finally the bandages came off and the dog took his first steps. He would always limp. But this didn't matter, as long as boy and dog could be together.

The boy's love for his pet simply mirrors the love man has felt for his dog through the ages, whether costly purebred or lowly mongrel. Breed, shape of head, color of coat are secondary. You love him because he's a dog.

Each year the purebred population swells as increasing thousands buy registered dogs. Does this mean our mixed breed, mongrel, or mutt—call him what you will—is fading into obscurity? Most certainly not! He still outnumbers his pedigreed cousins roughly three to one, and he'll be with us as long as man offers food, shelter, and affection to the dog at his feet.

ond between boy and hound pups knows no bounds of pedigree.

ALTER CHANDOHA

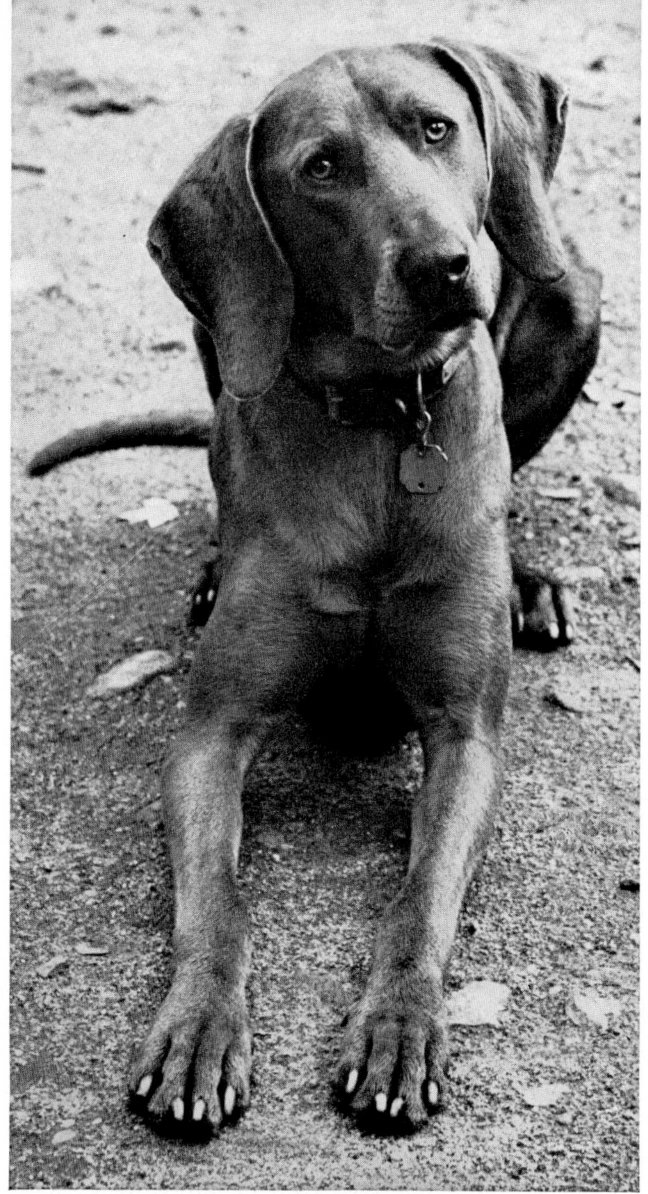

Redbone Hound, backwoods scion of Bloodhound and Foxhound stock, is a coon hunter's favorite. He's not to be found at a Westminster Show, but in the Ozark Mountains you'll hear his deep bawling voice.

Since before the Civil War this rough and ready hound has been tracking bear and wildcat as well as raccoon. Southerners long called him Saddleback for the black markings he once carried. But in the early years of this century breeders standardized the Redbone to his present rich red color. His shoulder height runs 21 to 26 inches.

With us, too, will be many breeds not yet among those recognized by the American Kennel Club. One authority estimates as many as 800 different breeds and varieties share man's love throughout the world.

The Portuguese Water Dog, or Cão d'Água, long retrieved tackle and nets for fishermen masters. His leonine mane and clipped hindquarters are startling reminders of how far our Poodles have strayed from their early water-dog days.

Few countries cannot claim at least one sheep or cattle dog as native to their lands as the language, customs, and dress: in Sweden, the Vallhund; in Italy, the Bergamasco; in Spain, the Catalan; in France, the Beauceron. The Aftcharka, a Russian sheepdog, grows such a long white coat it is shorn and spun into shepherd's clothing. Nootka Indians in British Columbia also have long valued the wool of the sheepdog that carries their name.

The world knows many hunting breeds, too, each as eager for the chase as your own hound or setter that, seeing you prepare for a day in the field, bounds merrily to the door. Hunting rabbits in Portugal's hills you'd likely follow the foxlike Podengo; in the Balearics, the fast, lean Ibizan Hound. In France the Vendeen Hound, like the rough-coated Welsh Hound, is the rabbit dog. In Japan it's the little Shiba.

Bird hunting, you might shoot over Germany's Münsterländer or Vorstehund, France's ancient Braque de Bourbonnais, or England's Arkwright Pointer.

Uganda tribes in Africa beat the brush for elephant and buffalo with packs of Baganda Hunting Dogs. India's rangy Poligar and Rampur resemble the Kangaroo Hound of Australia's outback. Canadian Indians hunt grizzly with the scrappy Tahltan Bear Dog. And so the list goes—Tosa, Banjara, Segugio, Akita —musical names echoing man's deep affection for his closest animal friend.

WHAT CONSTITUTES a dog breed? You might turn, in your old biology text, to the paragraph on "binomial nomenclature." In the 1700's, you will remember, it occurred to the card-index mind of Carolus Linnaeus to assign every living thing a two-part name. The first part represents the genus, or

Australian Kelpie "does the work of six men" on grazing land so sparse each sheep needs up to ten acres. Scottish for "little helper," the 30-pound Kelpie derived in the 1870's from smooth-haired Collie crosses with the native dingo. He stands 17 to 20 inches; colors of his flat coat include black and tan, blue, red, brown. Heavier, all-black strain is the Barb.

EDWARD HERBERT MINER AND (OPPOSITE) WALTER CHANDOHA

Plott Hound, hardy bear hunter of the Great Smoky Mountains, was brought to America from Heidelberg, Germany, by Jonathan Plott in 1750. The Plott family still breeds the black-saddled, brindle hounds. Hunting in packs, they show unmatched grit and stamina in tracking and baying big game. Besides bear, they hunt wild boar, wolves, and mountain lions. The United Kennel Club has registered them since 1946.

Border Collie, helpmate of shepherds through the centuries, stands guard over his woolly flock. Agile, fast, and keenly intelligent, this dog works well alone or with his master. Originally from Britain, his value as a livestock worker has made him increasingly popular on farms and ranches around the world. His coat varies widely in color and texture. A dog's height averages about 18 inches at the shoulder; he weighs from 30 to 45 pounds.

Ibizan Hound, also called Eivissenc or Podenco Ibicenco, takes his names from the Mediterranean island of Ibiza and his speed from greyhound-type forebears. U.S. fanciers have organized a club, but the breed is rare outside the Balearic Islands and the Spanish mainland, where it hunts rabbits and birds. The short-coated, chestnut and white or lion-colored dog stands about 25 inches high, weighs 40 to 50 pounds.

EVELYN M. SHAFER AND (CENTER) JAMES L. STANFIELD, NATIONAL GEOGRAPHIC PHOTOGRAPHER

general group; the second pinpoints its species, or special type.

Thus all members of the dog family share the genus name *Canis*. The wolf is *Canis lupus*; coyote, *Canis latrans*; jackal, *Canis aurens*; and every one of the domestic dogs, purebred and mongrel, *Canis familiaris*.

You may wonder how such varied dogs as the Chihuahua and St. Bernard can be given the same name. It's because genetically they're the same dog. A breed, Webster says, is a group of domestic animals whose development is governed by "human intervention." Only superficially do the breeds come into being, and each holds but a frail grip on its own identity.

As man discovered the dog's many talents, he bred it for special tasks: he put weight and brawn into working dogs and refined his hunting breeds; he made little dogs smaller and fast dogs speedier. Genetically among the most plastic of animals, the dog may be shaped almost at whim. The breeder can stretch it, dwarf it, lengthen its nose, flatten its face. He can bow its legs, alter its coat, experiment with its colors, reinforce or weaken its instinctive abilities, often in a matter of a few decades.

J. PIKE

Staffordshire Bull Terrier, bred for dog fights of the last century, owes his quickness, courage, and tenacity to the Bulldog and the Old English Terrier. Brought to the U.S. soon after the Civil War, he is valued now as an amiable companion for children.

Some years ago a man in South Africa revealed plans to "manufacture" the world's largest breed. Estimated to take 20 years in the making, the Colossus would weigh 250 pounds. Today's Great Dane reaches 150, the St. Bernard 175.

Two main techniques enable man to mold the dog he wants. In selective breeding he chooses from a litter only dogs that display desired characteristics and mates them with others similarly endowed. In cross-breeding, he brings together unlike breeds to combine desired traits from each. How many breeds have had their "sniffers" improved by a Bloodhound cross a few generations back!

The ease with which we can manufacture new breeds and modify old ones makes it clear why recognition goes only to those which reproduce true to type through several generations, have an organized group of fanciers, and are bred in sufficient numbers to warrant record-keeping and separate show classifications;

VICTOR BALDWIN

Spitz, long favored by many U.S. families, gets United Kennel Club recognition as the American Eskimo. With his heavy whitish coat, plume tail, and fancy ruff he looks like a Samoyed in miniature. He weighs but 18 pounds. Slow to accept strangers, he makes a good watchdog. He bears the name of the classic ancestor of many northern breeds, grouped as "spitz type."

© HULTON PRESS

Finnish Spitz, once used by Lapps for tracking bear and elk, now hunts capercaillie, the large European grouse. Barking at the treed birds has earned him the name Barking Bird Dog of Finland. An efficient watchdog, the breed is better known in England than in the United States. Color ranges from rich red to cream; height is 17 to 19 inches, weight is about 35 pounds.

WIDE WORLD

Tibetan Spaniel lacks a few "feathers" when he is four months old. Mature, he'll look much like the Japanese Spaniel or a short-haired, long-legged Peke. This amateur geographer seems to be hoping he'll capture America's fancy as he did India's, where he has long been recognized. His silky coat is black, black and tan, red, or fawn; weight 5 to 15 pounds.

Bluetick, Walker, and Trigg Hounds, like the Redbone and Plott, are favorites with southern hunters. Bred for field, not show, these local, "family" breeds earn highest praise from the fox and coon hunting fraternity. Bluetick, named for its color, is a sturdy, 80-pound coon dog. Walker and Trigg Hounds are lean, long-legged strains of the American Foxhound that have won fame for their speed and endurance.

© HULTON PRESS

Tibetan Mastiff, brawny shepherd and fierce guard dog of the Himalayas, is seldom encountered outside Tibet. Imagine the shock when a burly pair was received by an American who had ordered two little Tibetan Terriers! Closely resembling the ancestral mastiff type, he sports a heavy coat, usually black, sometimes with tan or red. He weighs 130 to 150 pounds.

ROBERT DOISNEAU, RAPHO-GUILLUMETTE

Truffle Dog sniffs out buried table delicacies. Dogs don't naturally hunt truffles, so Poodle crossbreds and other dogs are trained to hunt them. Truffle-garnished food teaches them the scent. Italy boasts a special school. Here a *truffleur* works with wooden-shoed master in France. Truffle dogs are so single-minded in their work they are even allowed on game preserves.

Australian Cattle Dog, also known as the Queensland Silent Blue Heeler, is a herder of almost legendary renown among stockmen of his native land. New to the United States, he is winning admirers among ranchers for his no-nonsense manner and inborn ability to work with cattle. He stands 18 to 20 inches high at the shoulder; weighs about 35 pounds.

Husky, Spitz, and Laika, are terms frequently applied to general types within the great family of arctic dogs. Americans often call all sled dogs Huskies; English group sled dogs and certain herd dogs as Spitz; in Russia many working breeds are classed as Laika. From the Aleutians to Greenland, from Scandinavia through Siberia, the family shows regional differences through inbreeding, but all are good workers.

JAMES L. STANFIELD, NATIONAL GEOGRAPHIC PHOTOGRAPHER

it may take years for an imported breed, like the recently recognized Australian Terrier, to be adopted as a member of America's family of dogs.

Commerce and conquest, travel and exploration have brought to light many breeds. Dutch traders in the 17th century probably first introduced the Pug to Europe from the Orient. British troops in 1860 brought home from China's Imperial Summer Palace the royal "lion dog"—the Pekingese. Nineteenth century travelers in Siberia discovered the beautiful Samoyed, later used by Fridtjof Nansen and other polar explorers. Time will tell what new foreign dog brought back by some American serviceman will catch public fancy.

The American Kennel Club has a "Miscellaneous" class in which unregistered breeds may be shown. Besides the Australian Cattle Dog, Australian Kelpie, Bearded Collie, and Border Collie, these include the Cavalier King Charles Spaniel, Ibizan Hound, Miniature Bull Terrier, Spinoni Italiani, and Staffordshire Bull Terrier. While breeders hope the class will lead to full recognition, the American Kennel Club makes no promises.

MARY ELEANOR BROWNING

SIMPLY MATING DOGS of two different types does not create a new breed, though it may produce a crossbred of considerable merit. Some people like German Shepherd-Collie crosses, for instance, claiming a steadier dog than the sometimes over-sensitive show breeds.

Police in Israel and Australia have recently begun to use a cross between a Bloodhound and a German Shepherd, whose combination of scenting power, strength, and agility makes him nemesis to the fugitive and savior to the lost.

Some mixed breeds have achieved fame. Bravo, a Malamute-Husky cross, shared man's first long, dark winter at the South Pole. Tschingel, another mixed breed, scaled 15,782-foot Mont Blanc; and the mongrel

Boykin Spaniel, best known in the southeastern United States, flushes wild turkey and excels in water work. A man named Boykin is said to have developed the mahogany- or liver-colored breed from a highly intelligent spaniel of unknown origin that had wandered into church in Spartanburg, South Carolina. Looking like a small American Water Spaniel, the Boykin stands 15 to 17 inches high, weighs about 35 pounds.

Mascot Bravo shared the lonely darkness of man's first winter at the South Pole.

Born at McMurdo Sound, Antarctica, this Malamute-Husky cross never knew the Arctic for which his Alaskan and Siberian parents were named.

Nor did he ever feel the bite of a sled harness on his shoulders. Clowning and roughhousing his way into the hearts of the 18 men who braved the 1957 winter at the South Pole Station, he became the most spoiled dog on the continent. Polar wits said he kept burglars away!

Leaving vapor trails in the crisp air, Bravo frisked "around the world" many times. But even he couldn't long stand the intense cold. To get all four paws off the ice, he perched on a scrap of cardboard like a circus lion balancing on a ball.

At right, Bravo sprawls at the feet of Lt. (jg) John Tuck, Jr., bearded military commander at the Pole, who bottle-raised him from birth.

Above, Lieutenant Tuck and Dr. Paul A. Siple, scientific leader at the Pole, show Bravo his honorable discharge before a National Geographic Society audience in Washington.

Instead of selling Bravo as surplus property, the Navy, at Dr. Siple's behest, proclaimed him a VID (Very Important Dog), gave him an honorable discharge, and put him under orders of his old friend Lieutenant Tuck.

THOMAS J. ABERCROMBIE AND (ABOVE) JOHN E. FLETCHER, NATIONAL GEOGRAPHIC STAFF

Drill sergeant barks orders to young recruits. This all-American mutt combines Collie, Golden Retriever, perhaps Chow Chow; the youngsters are Vermonters. The scene: Thetford Center.

Laika soared to even greater heights as the world's first space dog. Nipper, a black-and-white mongrel mostly of Smooth Fox Terrier stock, scaled peaks of another sort. A portrait brought him fame as RCA-Victor's world-famous trademark.

Distinction also came to Owney, the adventurous pet of an Albany, New York, postal clerk. Owney enjoyed riding mail trucks and trains, and traveled to every state, to Canada, and Mexico. But that was just a warm-up. Carrying kit bag and letter of introduction, he once girdled the globe in 132 days.

Only through continued, methodical breeding does the crossbred dog achieve purebred status. In the United States, only a few dogs, like the Boston Terrier, the Chesapeake Bay Retriever, the American Foxhound, and the American Water Spaniel, enjoy natural citizenship in the roster of AKC recognized breeds.

All other dogs, true to American tradition, have come to these shores as immigrants, to win their own place in the New World. Some in time have come to be accepted as distinctive new breeds. But most have simply joined that great American melting pot as the ubiquitous mongrel, favorite of them all, resembling this breed or that, but forever hopelessly, unidentifiably conglomerate.

For all his scenting power, his nose might better be chiseled of walnut. A cottontail or coon he may be more disposed to adopt than to pursue. Loosed amid a flock of sheep, he'd probably scatter them to every compass point. Homely, raffish, and appealing—this is the accident that is our mongrel, whose intelligence and loyal companionship earn the abiding love of unnumbered families everywhere.

"He was a ghastly mongrel," wrote novelist Hugh Walpole of his cherished Jacob. "I tremble to think of the many different breeds of dogs that have gone to his making—but he had Character, he had Heart, he had an unconquerable zest for life."

Sparse is the day's news that carries no story of some heroic mongrel dog that sniffed gas or smoke in the night; that warned noisily of intruder or close danger,

Mongrel mascots wouldn't trade places with any pedigreed pooch. Spot's probable ancestry includes terrier and spaniel; Hobo's mostly Black and Tan Coonhound, with some Fox Terrier.

J. BAYLOR ROBERTS, HOWELL WALKER, AND (OPPOSITE) B. ANTHONY STEWART, NATIONAL GEOGRAPHIC STAFF

Lifelong companionship asks no pedigree. Adventures of youth and memories of age are shared by purebred and mongrel alike. A sort-of-spaniel seadog (left) shoves off for distant shores; crossbred collie-setter (above) enjoys quiet sunset years with his Blue Ridge Mountain family.

DAVID W. CORSON, A. DEVANEY

ANNE REVIS GROSVENOR

pulled a youngster from a busy street, barked for help at the lake's edge, led the men to the lost child; or that, with indomitable spirit, fought his way through accident and injury to limping health, or found his way across many miles to his master's doorstep.

In many-colored coat and multitude of shapes and sizes stands the beloved mixed-breed, his place long assured as the world's favorite dog. But mongrel he is and mongrel he must remain. The more diversified his ancestry, the dimmer his chance of standardizing into an eventual breed, for he has a built-in barrier, one sadly known by all whose nondescript Prince or Tippy has lived out his span:

Where in the world would you find another exactly like him?

AUCTION
"Champ"
BLANKENBECK

CHAPTER ELEVEN

Dog Mart Day in Fredericksburg

"We are going to the dogs," said big-lettered signs in Fredericksburg, Virginia. It sounded grim, but all it meant was that the historic city on the Rappahannock was holding its annual Dog Mart, older than the Nation itself.

"Come, bring all the family and all the dogs. Spend the day," concluded the announcement.

Four of us from the National Geographic accepted. On a bright October day punctuated with barks, bays, and the sonorous notes of hunters' horns, we saw a unique intermingling of historic sites and hounds, of puppies and patriot shrines.

Traffic on U.S. Highway No. 1 halted as hundreds of dogs and their masters paraded streets paved with history. Virginians vied in foxhorn blowing, country fiddling, and hog calling, and put on a pageant, "Patriot's Dream." Pamunkey Indians danced. Dogs demonstrated their education in obedience trials and show. A derby-hatted auctioneer boomed forth in trombone tones. Enough dog to delight any small boy could be bought for as little as a dollar.

By the end of the day, everybody's puppies were dog-tired.

Many a Virginian leading a dog was about the age George Washington was when he lived as a lad at Ferry Farm across the river and, according to some

"Hold still, Washington! Don't you want to win the blue ribbon at Fredericksburg today?"

sources, went to school in Fredericksburg. Even after young George's family moved to Mount Vernon, he was wont to return.

Once two local damsels were arrested for "robbing the cloathes" of 19-year-old George while he was bathing in the nearby Rappahannock. Whether the clothes themselves or only the valuables they contained were stolen, Spotsylvania County court records do not state. They do show that Ann Carroll was acquitted and that in the case of Mary McDaniel the court ordered "that the sheriff carry her to the whipping post and inflict fifteen lashes on her bare back."

The future Father of His Country had no hand in the punishment decreed for luckless Mary, having sailed for the West Indies.

Fredericksburg's dog-going custom antedates even this painful incident. In fact, Fredericksburgers say, it is 29 years older than the city's name.

"In 1698 a truce was declared between settlers and Indians of eastern Virginia," explained the general chairman of the Mart. "This cease-fire afforded opportunity of trading the white men's superior hunting dogs for the red men's furs, gold, and handicraft articles at the Leaseland settlement, later named for

Photographs by B. Anthony Stewart, J. Baylor Rober

Precious pets all preened, youngsters are primed for the parade that opens Dog Mart day.

nd John E. Fletcher, National Geographic Photographers

Traffic stops when dogs are on the march. From miles around owners come to parade their prides. City scents bewilder the lean, business-like hounds, which predominate.

Suited up and ready to go, a couple of clowns—a girl and her Toy Poodle—head for the parade.

Frederick, father of King George III."

Thus was born the Fredericksburg Dog Mart, today a 270-year-old tradition.

AS IN INDIAN DAYS, this is still hunting country, and the hounds, setters, and pointers rank as the elite of the show. Old-timers in hunting caps looked a bit worried the previous year when a much barbered powder-blue

B. ANTHONY STEWART AND (OPPOSITE) WILLIAM ALBERT ALLARD, NATIONAL GEOGRAPHIC PHOTOGRAPHERS

Miniature "French" Poodle, owned by a woman, emerged as a strong contender for Best in Show. They relaxed when the beribboned essence of canine elegance was beaten out for the blue ribbon by a big competent-looking Bluetick Hound bitch named Tidewater.

Hunters hereabouts follow their foxhounds with automobiles. "We head them off with cars, then get as close as we can on foot," explained the mayor. "Too many barbed wire fences for horses."

Careening over country roads, the autos do about everything but take fences. They enable these latter-day hunters to keep at least within hearing distance of the melodious chase.

Every dog has his day; even the Ugliest Mutt wins a prize when all Fredericksburg goes to th logs. Hunt-minded Virginians crowd close as judges, intent as bird dogs, pick Best Hunting Dog.

"Over, Stormy!" A champion Weimaraner takes the hurdle at his mistress's command; spectators line the show grounds to watch. The dog holds three obedience trial "degrees"; C.D., C.D.X., and U.D., which stand for Companion Dog, Companion Dog Excellent, and Utility Dog.

The day's events include hog calling, Indian dances, a pageant, even fiddling contests. Everything is free on this occasion but the hot dogs.

Hark to the horn! Each hound pack knows its master's call. He uses the haunting, resonant notes to guide his dogs to game or call them in when the hunt is over. One year a six-year-old girl who "can outblow her maw" boldly took her place in the line, but a six-foot male whooped off with the prize.

Drum majorettes put on the dog for the big parade. These baton-swinging girls attend James Monroe High School, named for the Fredericksburg resident who became fifth U.S. president.

These Virginia hunters are great yarn spinners. "Once I had a bird dog that was jumpin' a fence when he caught the scent of a wild turkey," said a hunter from the Wilderness. "He came down astraddle the fence and hung there, pointin' that turkey."

In the obedience trials some of the feats rivaled even such tall tales. Outstanding star was Stormy, a talented Weimaraner from Richmond. When paper money was spread on the grass and he was told to pick out the note that would buy him the most meat, he unerringly chose a $20 bill, disdaining the ones.

It wasn't the dollars; it was the scents. His nose knew the bill his mistress had touched.

More people than Fredericksburg's whole population (which numbers 15,000) usually turn out for this canine convention, held annually when autumn paints Virginia's woods and coverts. Outsiders are drawn both by the dogs and by the city's historic sites, including the old homes of Washington's mother and sister; the law office of James Monroe; the house where John Paul Jones once lived with his brother, a Fredericksburg tailor; and scenes of some of the bloodiest battles between the Blue and the Gray.

The Dog Mart was 88 years old when James Monroe hung out his shingle in 1786. One big day each year Fredericksburg is a mixture of hounds and history, pooches and patriotic shrines.

Who can resist a Beagle puppy's mournful eye? If the kids are along, you're lost. Cowboy play is forgotten as boys search for a dog as pet; girls are smitten with puppy love. All kinds of dogs, mongrels as well as pedigreed, go on the auction block at Dog Mart. Some pups can be had for a song.

Dog-tired near the end of the big day, pals slumber in a baby buggy. Jostling crowds, yapping dogs, and clarion-voiced announcer failed to disturb silky-haired Joanne and her Cocker pup Silver. Perhaps next year, when both are older, they will see the end of the gala day.

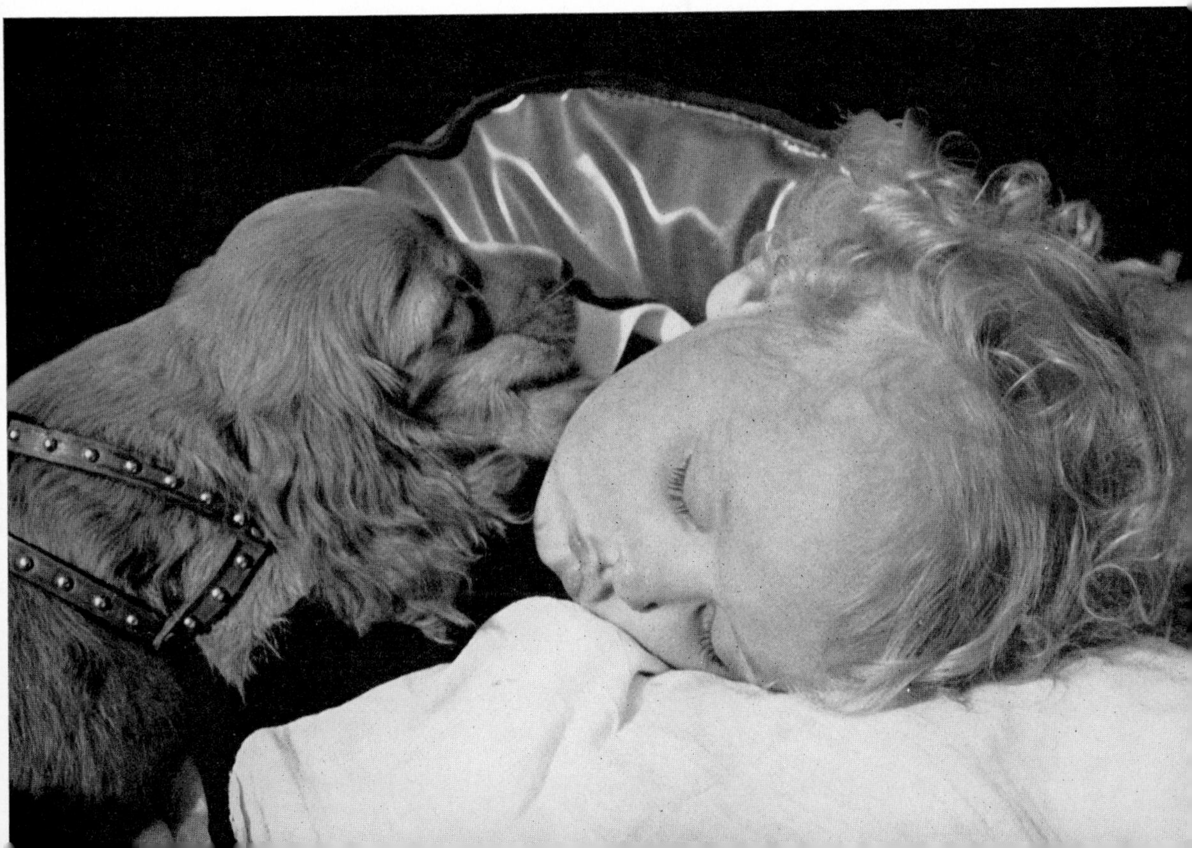

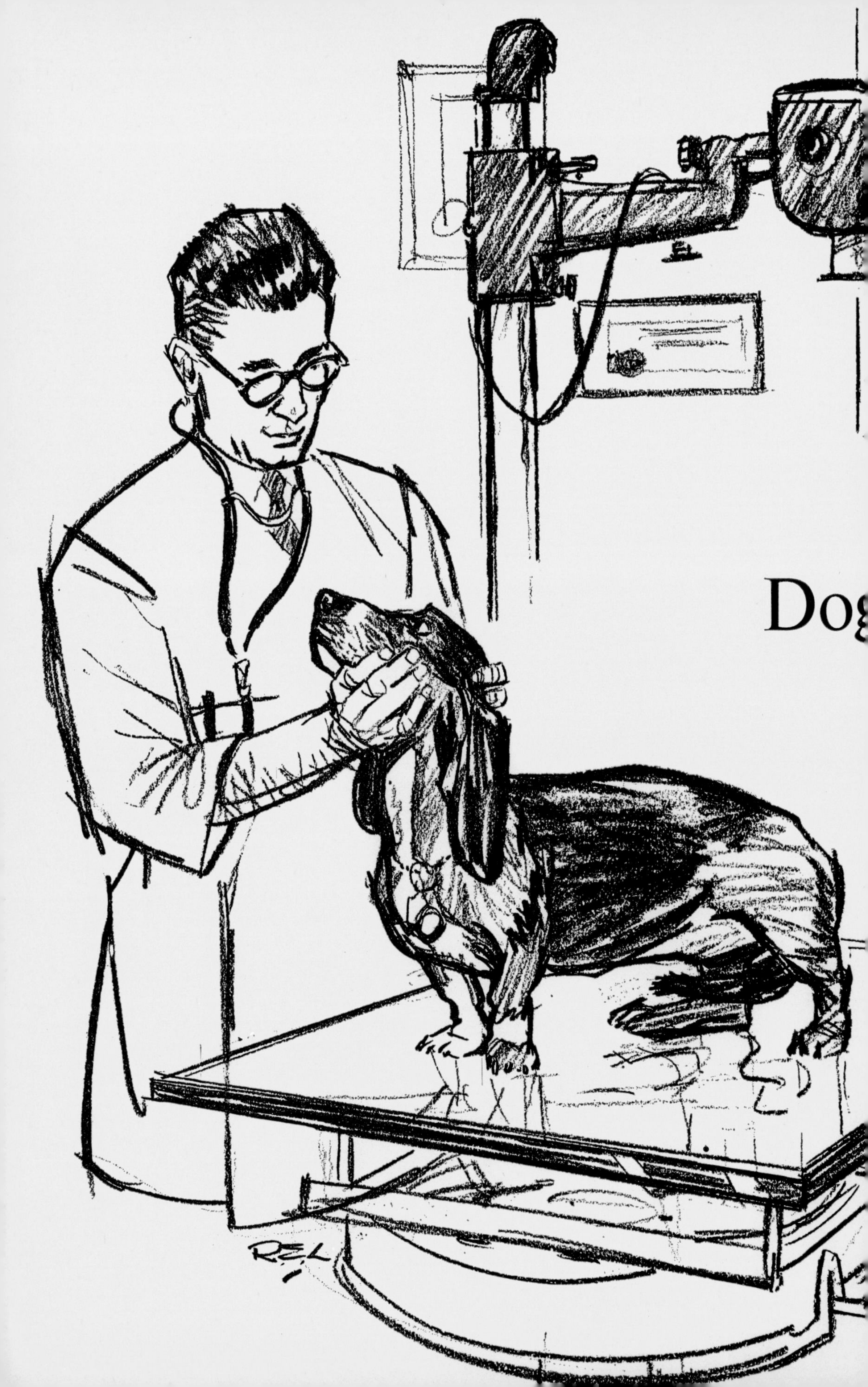

Dog

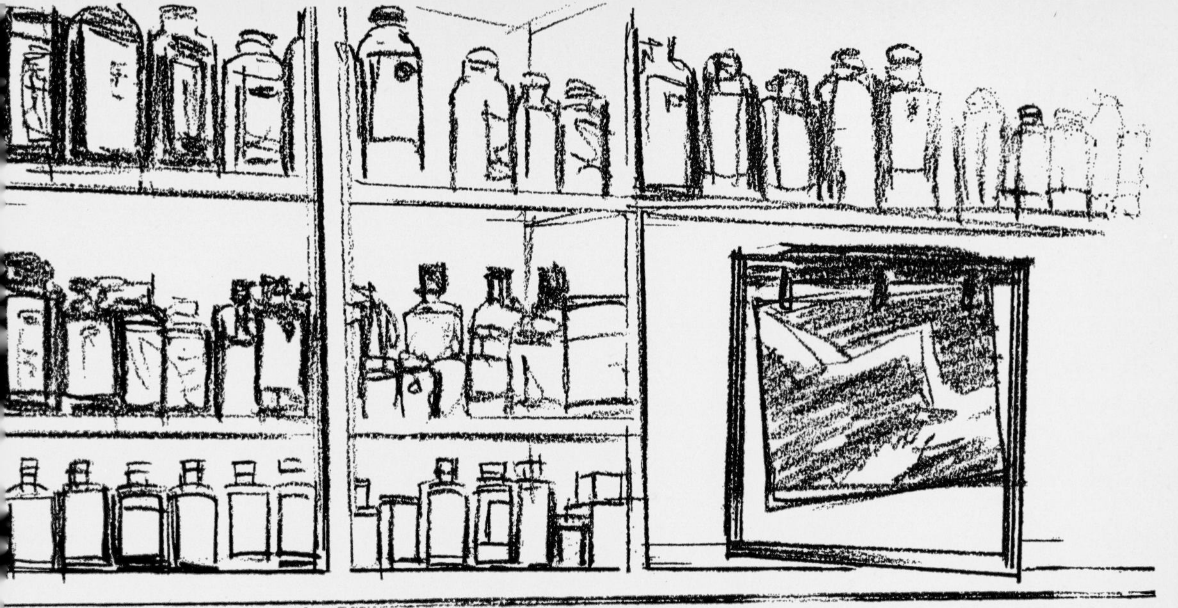

Care and Training

MEDICAL SCIENCE is making heartening progress in canine health. Like their masters, dogs may now eat balanced meals. Tranquilizers soothe their nerves, wonder drugs cure their ills. These longer-lived dogs even get hearing aids. But basic to happy days ahead for pet and owner are these fundamentals: thoughtful choice of a dog, loving care, and sound training.

Many times in Arthur Frederick Jones's long years with the American Kennel Club, people brought him their problems in raising pets. Some sought his advice on what breed would be best and how to find the right pup. Others wanted pointers on feeding, housebreaking, and teaching their dogs good manners.

Now in this final chapter he offers practical suggestions and answers to questions you may have about the dog in your life.

How to

Slurping happily from his favorite dish, fast-growing Boxer pup General enjoys the daily meal set out by his young master Willson Offutt (following pages).

Photographs by J. Baylor Robert.

ARTHUR FREDERICK JONES

CHAPTER TWELVE

Choose, Care for, and Train Your Dog

ONE FINE SATURDAY MORNING you may find yourself driving out into the countryside, the family in the car, children excited and noisy. You're off to buy a puppy. Everyone's excited at the prospect. Yes, even you are, although admittedly you did take a bit of persuading. But as the tires hit the gravel driveway leading past whitewashed apple trees to the trim, green and white kennel buildings, sudden doubts cross your mind.

"Is this the right breed for me and my family? How will I know which puppy to pick? What about housebreaking, feeding, shots, and all the things I'll have to know once the pup is home?"

Like choosing a sweetheart, choosing a dog is an emotional thing, all wrapped up in personalities—your background, tastes, interests, way of life. For any number of reasons you may choose a tiny Chihuahua, a floppy-eared Cocker Spaniel, or even an impressive Irish Wolfhound. I once met a frail, 90-pound woman whose constant companion was not a toy breed but a huge Great Dane. This seemingly mismatched dog-owner combination got on beautifully.

You may want a pet to grow up with your children, to help them learn about care and responsibility. Perhaps you want a hunting dog as a companion in open field and briery swamp. Or, if you live in a compact city apartment, it may be a little terrier or a toy breed that's on your list. Home owner or parent,

National Geographic Photographer

the protecting watchfulness strong in so many breeds will be important to you.

Reading about the various breeds in this book and discussing them with your family will help you a long way toward making a thoughtful choice, and a happy one.

WHATEVER YOU DO, don't rely on the "friendly tip," a risky practice, for there's a bull market on misinformation. At my office at the American Kennel Club one day I had a phone call from a man who wanted to know where to buy a dog. Unfortunately, he couldn't resist showing off his "knowledge" of dogs.

"I'm looking for a big watchdog," he informed me, "but not a Doberman Pinscher because they'll turn on their own masters. And I don't want a German Shepherd; they're part wolf, aren't they? I like a Chow's looks but I hear they're treacherous."

This came out almost in a single blast. As patiently as possible, I said to my caller, "Let's take it one breed at a time.

"Certainly there are bad-tempered Dobermans," I told him, "just as there are too-sharp specimens in any breed, but an overwhelming number of them are wonderfully loyal companions, good watchdogs, and lovable pets. Furthermore, they have intelligence enough to know *when* to be tough."

I explained to him that the tale about close-up "savage" wolf blood in the German Shepherd was a myth, and that it wouldn't make a great deal of difference anyway, since most authorities believe dogs originally descended from a wolflike ancestor. "A lot of sled dogs are part wolf," I told him. "There's a great deal of stamina in wolf blood, and intelligence too."

The Chow Chow was one of the most popular breeds in the 1920's. It became too popular, in fact, for reputable breeders to supply the demand. Operators of "puppy mills" took over to provide cheap pups for those who wanted to climb on the bandwagon. As a result, many "Chows" bore only faint resemblance to the fine old Chinese breed. Many were sold without registration certificates or were given forged pedigrees. Obviously, the unscrupulous breeders paid no attention to the breed's temperament. The result was a wave of unfortunate incidents in which unsuspecting children and adults were bitten by these misfit dogs.

The need for a watchdog is one big reason why people buy pets, but there is much misunderstanding as to what constitutes a watchdog, including the whiskered contention: "If you want your pet to be a vicious watchdog, feed him gunpowder."

There is no need for a vicious watchdog in civilized communities. The ordinary house pet will do an adequate job without making himself a neighborhood nuisance and a liability to his owner. *In no instance should a private citizen maintain a guard dog trained to attack*, because such an animal is as dangerous as a cocked pistol. He needs specialized handling by people trained

Willson keeps a short leash on General when teaching him

for the job, as in police departments or the armed services. Nor is it a matter of size alone. The city resident, for example, need not keep a large watchdog. Housebreakers will steer clear of any place they know has a dog. Almost any dog will give an alarm; in fact, tiny toys are the most alert. Where police protection is scant, some householders like to have a toy or small dog inside the house and a big dog outside.

The isolated country home owner will naturally want a larger dog, one that ranges in size from upper medium to giant. He has many breeds from which to choose, including the German Shepherd, Doberman Pinscher, Rottweiler, Belgian Sheepdog, Giant or Standard Schnauzer, Boxer, Airedale Terrier, Collie, Great Dane, Newfoundland, Dalmatian, Poodle, Akita, and Chow.

One of the finest watchdogs I've ever known was my son's Cocker Spaniel. If he barked at night, I knew someone was near who didn't belong there. To encourage his good work, I always went downstairs, told him he was a good boy, and let him see me try the doors and windows. You should always give praise and a bit of fondling for any good deed. It means much more than tidbits.

GENERALITIES are dangerous, especially when applied to the characteristics of the 120 recognized breeds. But in the main, you will find quieter temperaments among the gun dogs, most of the hounds, and the larger working dogs than you will in the three other groups. Terri-

heel outside his home in Chevy Chase, Maryland.

Passing in review, wee Boxers tumble over each other in eagerness to display their personalities. Seeing a litter together helps you pick an active, alert, self-possessed pup.

ers, with few exceptions, have an extremely alert nature that is not in tune with people who like to relax. The same is true of most toys and half of the non-sporting dogs. There are, however, many exceptions to this rule. Here's one I remember well.

I had gone to Pennsylvania to see a kennel of prize-winning Pekingese. I expected to find glass-enclosed cages in a big sunny room where weather was something just talked about. Instead, these Pekes were kept in a kennel scarcely different from that for big sporting dogs. Puzzled, I asked the owner why.

"We don't believe in coddling them," she explained with a smile. "They're just as rugged as . . . well, as my husband's English Setters."

At my look of doubt, she went on. "When I first thought of breeding and showing Pekingese, my husband fairly snorted. He didn't want any part of it. Well, despite his protests, I bought some Pekes. At first he'd hardly look at them. Then one day I missed one of my top specimens. I was frantic. We looked everywhere. No Peke!

"Then, just at dusk, I saw one of my husband's setters loping across the field. Behind him I made out a second figure, almost indistinguishable, doing his best to keep up. Yes, it was my beloved little prize winner, working his tiny legs like pistons. What made it especially difficult for him was that he carried a quail in his mouth.

"Never again did my husband object to my having Pekingese. He was convinced they were all dog."

To help you choose a breed, the American Kennel Club offers information from its New York headquarters. It does not recommend one breed over another, but will furnish the names of some reputable breeders of the one or two breeds you inquire about. And in the AKC library, open to the public, you will find dog books dating back to the 16th century and periodicals from all over the world.

Once you have decided which breed suits you best, you've taken a major step in selecting your dog. The next important step is the choice of the right individual. No two dogs, even within the same litter, are exactly alike, either in looks or in temperament. While dog breeders within the past century have done much to standardize breeds—to make the "brand name" mean something—they can go only so far.

Today when a breeder mates two Airedales, for instance, he knows that in 63 days, if all goes well, he'll have a litter of puppies that look and act like their parents. The same is true of the other recognized breeds because the basic qualities have been established. But no breeder can say that the pup you buy will make a perfect pet for you.

Ask the kennel owner to show you an entire litter together, or a group of unrelated puppies in the same pen. A puppy's temperament is more apparent when he is with others than when alone. The mentally and physically sound pup will hold his own in any puppy game. You can note if the pup is too quick to take offense, or too shy to mingle. Eliminating the shy and the bad-tempered ones, you now have to choose from among several pups that seem equally well-geared to life. Perhaps you will like the color or markings of one better than the others.

Perhaps it may be a matter of sex. Since the average pet owner doesn't want to be bothered with unexpected litters, male pups are most in demand and many female pets are spayed. (This operation, in which the reproductive organs are removed, should be performed at seven to ten months. Some veterinarians suggest an alternate operation—tying off the Fallopian tubes—that likewise eliminates the possibility of puppies.)

One objection to spaying is that it may produce obesity. But excessive weight gain can be prevented in the spayed animal, just as in a female that has not been spayed, by adequate exercise and proper control of the diet. Some people also believe that spaying changes the animal's personality.

Some pet owners think that unless mated a dog will fall prey to all sorts of illnesses. This is untrue. There may well have been cases where a pet might have lived a longer, healthier, and happier life had he or she been bred, but my own observation of family dogs is that it makes little difference whether or not they have a love life, and veterinarian opinion largely supports this view.

When you have decided whether you want a male or female pet and have settled on the pup which appeals to you, it's a good idea to see if you appeal to the pup. Have the kennel owner separate your choice, then kneel or crouch so the pup will not be frightened by your size; speak to him and extend your hand. Don't wave at the little fellow, just hold your hand steady so he'll know instinctively it is a friendly gesture. If your offer of friendship is accepted, that's the puppy for you.

When he comes close to be petted look for signs that indicate general health. Discharge of mucous matter from eyes or nose can mean anything from a slight infection to early stages of distemper, and you'd better ask the kennel owner to take the puppy's temperature. (Normal for a dog is around 101° to 102°.) If the kennel owner is sincere the dog's welfare will concern him, and he should be happy you've noticed something amiss. If he objects, forget about buying a pup there.

Other danger signs are patches in his coat; they can mean mange, ringworm, or eczema. If the legs are crooked and joints enlarged, you can guess that the breeder has not given enough cod-liver oil (principal source of vitamin D) to prevent rickets. Insides of ears should be pink, smooth, and free from inflammation. Teeth should be white, and gums pink and firm; discolored teeth usually mean some serious sickness, such as distemper.

Roll the pup over on his back. If his tummy is greatly distended, ask the kennel owner if he has just been fed. The distention could indicate worms. At the same time notice if he has any swelling on his underside, particularly around the navel. If so, it is probably hernia, and you'd better consider another

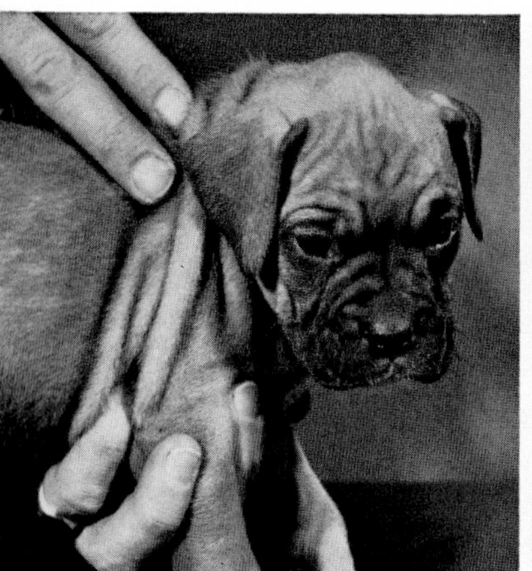

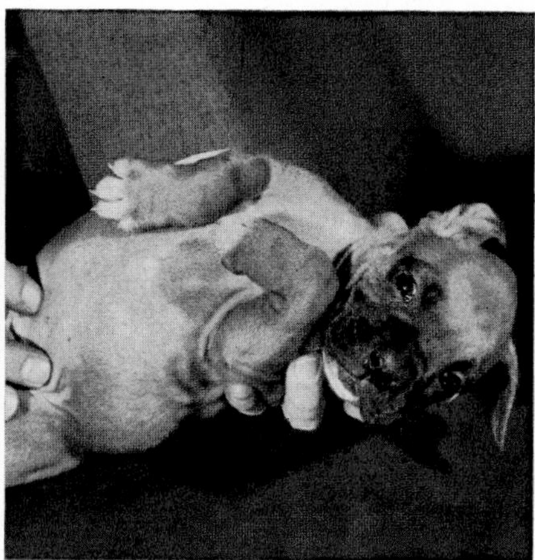

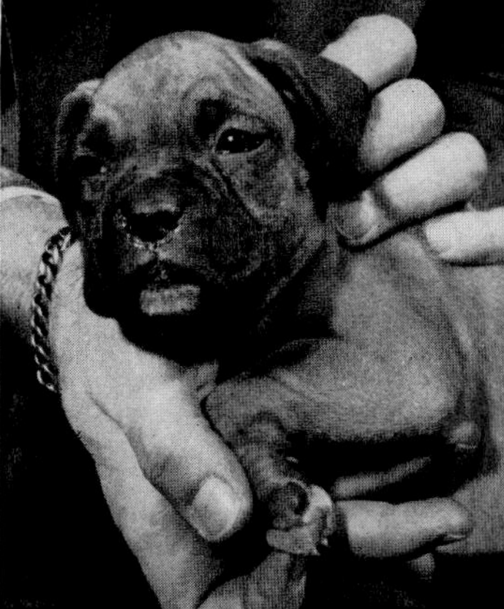

Look the pup over carefully against patchy coat, distended abdomen, crooked or swollen joints

pup. There's also congenital deafness. You can test for this by getting behind the puppy and snapping your fingers to see if it attracts his attention.

AFTER YOU HAVE SATISFIED yourself that your pick of the puppies has no apparent physical handicaps or mental quirks, the next question is price. This can vary a great deal, so much so that no single rule covers every aspect of today's pricing. The housewife who a few years ago added nicely to her pin money by selling puppies for $50 to $75 apiece simply cannot compete in today's market, even if she offers them at $100 or $125. Her price tag may be justified by the rising cost of everything that goes into the care and raising of a puppy, but now there is new competition.

When AKC registrations approached the million-a-year level a few years ago, professional merchandisers became attracted to the pet field. By arranging to buy their stock at exceptionally low wholesale prices they are able to undersell most private competition at retail level. Although the great majority of chains and large stores that sell this way are doing an honest business, some dealers are causing the AKC such concern about the purity of pedigrees that it now employs full-time investigators to monitor the activities of producers and brokers of purebred dogs for the pet market.

Breed popularity or scarcity, rather than size, determines the price of a dog. A pure white Miniature Schnauzer, for example, recently was advertised at $495 and an all-white German Shepherd at $300—stiff prices for pets that are barred from the show ring. The rare Akita sells for $200 and up; the number-one breed, Poodle, for $125; a Labrador Retriever for $85; Bernese Mountain Dog, $250; that hearty eater, the Irish Wolfhound, $400; Lhasa Apso, $190. And these are prices for pets, not dogs of show quality.

Much too frequently in recent years it has been said that raising purebred dogs is as lucrative as striking oil or finding uranium. One young enthusiast,

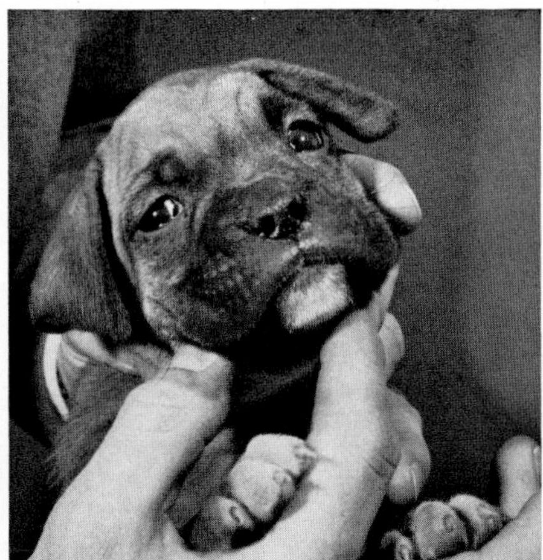

anger signs of poor health. Ears should be pink, eyes clear of mucus, teeth white, gums firm.

fired up by a magazine article, asked an old-timer "Is it really true that there's big money in purebred dogs?"

The oldster nodded his head slowly and drawled, "There should be, I've put an awful lot of it in myself."

The amateur sportsmen who breed show specimens seldom break even on their kennels. They breed dogs because they love dogs, because they are striving always for the perfect specimen, and because they enjoy being part of a competitive hobby. They usually sell puppies only because they must reduce the number of mouths to feed and help defray their expenses. Breeders of the best type often are more concerned with the kind of home a puppy will have and the character of his purchaser than in the price he brings. Some breeders won't sell a puppy until they have visited the puppy's prospective home.

While you wouldn't be normal if you weren't looking for a bargain, any asking price far below your area's average could prove costly. Your pet's purchase price is only a fraction of what you will spend on him over the years, so invest in a sound pup. Otherwise you may suffer the emotional shock of falling in love with him only to find that he has little hope of survival to a happy, healthy adulthood.

Above all, avoid the mistake of one young lady who came to me to find out how she could make money on her female Miniature Poodle.

CHOOSING A DOG? KEEP THESE POINTS IN MIND

- **A big dog requires more food, exercise, living space than a little dog. Can you give him all these?**
- **A long-hair needs frequent grooming; shedding can be a housekeeping problem.**
- **A peppy, affectionate dog makes a fine playmate for the whole family. A quiet, reserved personality is easier to relax with and is more likely to be a one-man dog.**
- **A female will have to be spayed or kept in check when in heat if you wish to avoid a pack of dogs around and the care and expense of whelping and raising pups.**
- **A puppy will need long training; a grown dog will require less time and effort, but may already be attached to his previous owner.**
- **Go to a dog show to see the breeds in action.**
- **Write to the American Kennel Club, Breeder Information Service, 51 Madison Ave., New York, N.Y. 10010, for information on breeders of selected breeds.**
- **At the kennels check the condition of the dog's eyes, ears, teeth, legs, joints, paws, coat, skin, abdomen, also temperature.**
- **From the breeder get a round-the-clock diet, advice on grooming and care, evidence that the pup has been wormed, record of immunizations, signed application for registration.**
- **Don't shop for bargains. You get what you pay for. Always "look a gift dog in the mouth." Initial cost is a minute part of what you will spend on a dog in his lifetime.**

"Mimi is a perfect darling," she told me, "but I think we paid too much for her. If we could raise some puppies, we could at least get back what we paid."

Her thought was not a new one. I could have tried to dissuade her with a few words but instead began asking questions. Did her pet come of show stock? She didn't know. Did she have a copy of the pedigree with her? No, nor was she sure what a pedigree signified.

I explained that it would show if there were any recent champions in her Poodle's ancestry. This would establish the value of Mimi's puppies. Unless there were some champions her pet might have to be entered in shows and make her own reputation—if she were good enough.

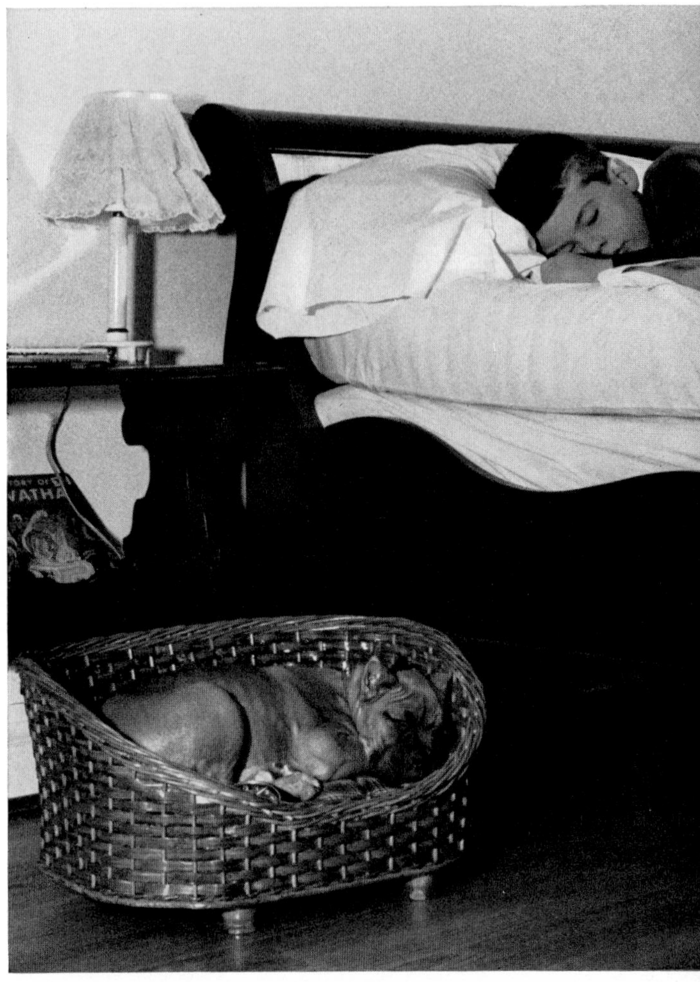

Pals bunk together, pup off the floor, out of drafts. Hot water bottle and ticking clock comfort General, just separated from litter.

The young lady didn't know what showing a dog entailed, so I explained how dogs were evaluated in the ring, how they earned points toward championship ranking, and how much it might cost to make Mimi a champion. (Traveling expenses, food, lodging, entry fees, professional handlers' fees, and so forth, are estimated to average close to $5,000 per title in a highly competitive breed.) Costs are high because a popular breed has little chance of gaining points at every show entered, particularly at the "majors," which offer three or more points each. A dog becomes a champion when he has 15 points, but the total must include two majors under two different judges.

This discouraged the young lady, but she brightened quickly and asked why think in terms of champions. I told her that only puppies of show potential command big prices. Pet prices hardly warrant the expense of breeding, and I went through the items she would have to pay out, starting with a fee for the stud dog, veterinarian's charges for prenatal care, whelping, shots for distemper and hepatitis, and worming. There would also be nutritional supplements while Mimi was expecting, and so on. I wish I could say the young lady's urge to become a dog breeder had been dampened. It had not.

A couple of days later she bought Mimi to the house for me to appraise. I did, but perhaps I should have been brutally frank instead of diplomatic. I suggested that the Poodle's back could have been a little shorter. Actually, she was much too long to win at a show. I mentioned that Mimi's muzzle might have had a little more depth. The truth was she was definitely too snipy, and rather than saying that her forelegs should have been a little straighter, I should have come right out and stated that she had a "fiddle front." Mimi's owner went right ahead with plans for her to have pups to sell.

Months later I heard that Mimi had died at whelping time, and all the puppies were stillborn. Of course, this had nothing to do with the Poodle's quality. Rather it was evidence of improper care due to the urge to cut expense and make money.

Big event in General's day is mealtime. Diet should include meat, eggs, milk, green vegetables, bone meal, no starchy foods.

THE PUPPY you choose will, of course, have all the earmarks of a healthy specimen, but it would still be wise to take him immediately to a veterinarian. He'll give him shots for distemper, leptospirosis, infectious canine hepatitis, and rabies. It may be repeating what has already been done, but it will do the puppy no harm.

Let's assume that the puppy passes the veterinarian's exam with flying colors. He'll be at least three months old, for a reputable breeder would not have sold you a pup any younger. On your application for AKC registration fill in three alternate names.

Three names are required because your first choice may already be registered. No more than one Beagle, Chihuahua, Dachshund, Boxer, or so on can be registered by the same name. Because multiple-word names have a better chance of being accepted some dogs sport quite fancy appellations. It simplifies matters if part of the name can serve as a call name. Take Water Tower Deacon's Mike. Water Tower is the name of the kennel that bred him; Deacon the name of his sire; and the prosaic Mike what you say when you want him front and center.

It'll be Mike from now on, and you should start using this call name as soon as possible. Talk to him, using the name, on the way home. Get him used to associating it with things that concern him—food, for instance. Let's assume the kennel owner was thoughtful enough not to feed the puppy before turning him over to you; if he had, the pup might have been carsick on the way home. So the pup is hungry when he gets to his new home. While he is looking over the premises, identifying all the new smells, set out his meal. Then call him by name to eat it.

Your puppy at three months will be started on solid food and a four-times-a-day feeding schedule (except toys, which are fed five times—breakfast, lunch, supper, with an afternoon and late-evening snack). Quantities will vary, of course, with the size of the breed, but all pups require basically the same foods: milk formula (1 tablespoon lime water, 1 tablespoon lactose to the pint of milk), slightly heated egg, chopped raw beef, chopped cooked vegetables, toast, and the all-important cod-liver oil or other suitable vitamins.

Recommended vegetables are spinach, carrots, onions, string beans, fresh carrot or beet greens, and kohlrabi. Not advised are the more starchy corn, peas, lima beans, parsnips, and potatoes.

Ask the kennel owner to write out a menu for the particular breed you buy, so you can follow his food requirements exactly.

By the sixth month a puppy is off formula and on whole, evaporated, or powdered milk. The cod-liver oil increases until at 11 months it is double the amount

Feeding strengthens the bond of friendship but isn't the only way to win a dog's affection.

given at three months; it is usually discontinued at the end of the puppy's first year. The number of meals is cut down as he gets older, and the meat content is increased. When he is full-grown (18 months or older) one meal a day should suffice. Feed him at the same hour each day, sometime between noon and 6 p.m. A grown toy will need about one-half pound of food a day; a small breed, one pound; a large breed, two pounds; a giant, five pounds.

Millions of dog owners find prepared dog foods, canned or dry, adequate for their pets. To maintain peak health, however, a dog needs fresh meat and vegetables too. You might vary his diet by giving him kibble or dog meal mixed with fresh raw beef, lamb, or horse meat some days, canned dog food mixed with vegetables on others, and occasionally some kidney, heart, or other organic meat. Cottage cheese is another good source of protein, especially for overweight dogs. Some large families can feed a dog at practically no extra expense on well-balanced leftovers.

Never give chicken, fish, pork, or lamb bones to your pet; they may splinter and lodge in his throat or intestines.

HOUSEBREAKING A PUPPY EARLY is a matter of knowing that nature moves a very short time after a meal is eaten. If you accustom the puppy to going outside for relief immediately after eating he will soon become housebroken. Some pups can be trained in two weeks. Others take much longer.

Housebreaking calls for instant punishment or praise. Take pup out or put on papers right after meals for early success. A yard and good weather make paper training unnecessary.

NEAL P. DAVIS

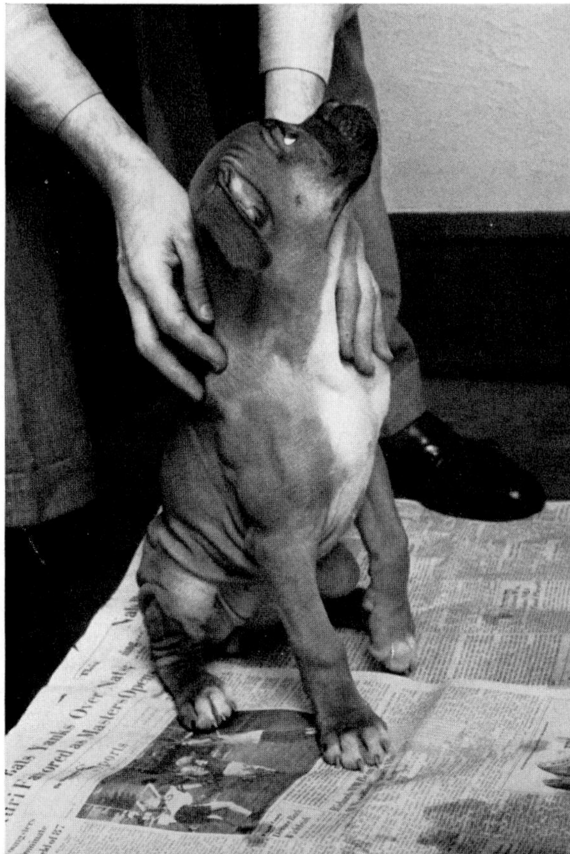

This is a handy time to accustom him to a leash, which may be completely new to him. You'll be using it in much of his training. Give a light tug on the leash, but also say "Come, Mike." If in the city, take him to the curb or to some spot that won't offend the neighbors. After he has relieved himself, say "Good boy, Mike."

This one-step training is by far best, but if you live in an upper-floor apartment, you may find the pup messing up the elevator before he is able to reach street level. You must then resort to an intermediate step—training him to paper.

After feeding, watch to see when the puppy shows signs of wanting to relieve himself. Then carry him quickly to newspapers spread out on the floor. Unless your pup is an apt pupil, it will probably take a couple of weeks before he gets the idea and goes to the papers at the proper time.

Housebreaking is probably the hardest part of owning a dog, and the older the puppy the harder it becomes. It calls for persistence on your part. Puppies instinctively do not like to mess up their beds, so your objective is to transfer this repugnance to include all parts of the house except the newspapers.

As for a proper bed for the new puppy, all he really needs is a spot that is out of drafts, raised a few inches off the floor. It should have sides high enough so that he can curl up snugly, and a cushion with a cover easily removable for periodic cleaning.

"How often do I bathe my puppy?" is one of the first questions a new owner asks. He rarely if ever needs a bath if you give proper daily care. Brushing regularly will keep him clean and free of doggy odor and fleas. To bring up the gloss on his coat, wipe him off with a slightly damp cloth. When you do bathe him, dry him thoroughly so he won't catch cold.

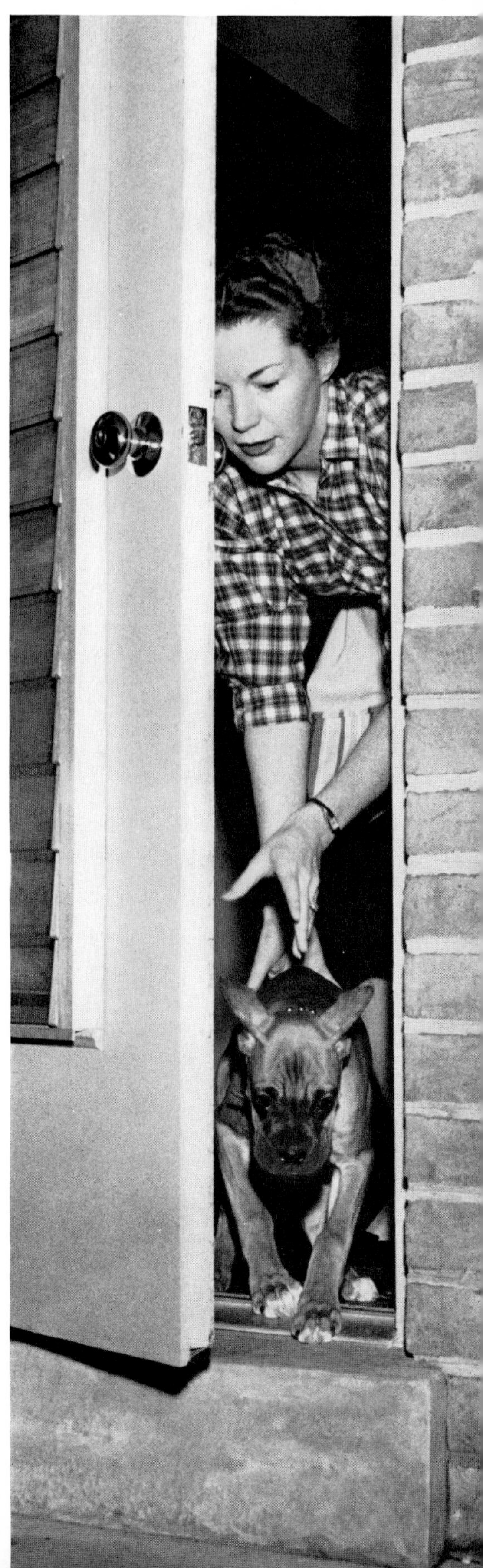

Housebroken, General always goes out after meals.

As your puppy gets older his toenails will grow so long they click when he walks. You can clip the nails yourself, but it is advisable to watch the veterinarian do it a few times before you attempt it. It is easy to cut off too much and cause the dog pain and bleeding. Another job for an experienced hand is cleaning tartar from a dog's teeth. Watch how it's done before you try it.

Most breeds have little eye trouble, but some like the Cocker are prone to conjunctivitis, an inflammation of the mucous membrane of the eyelid. There is a considerable discharge. Treat the condition by bathing the eyes with a two per cent solution of boric acid. Use of any other drug in the eyes of your dog should be on the advice of a veterinarian.

Probably the pet owner's most frequent concern is keeping the dog's bowel movements balanced somewhere between constipation and diarrhea. Either condition is usually a matter of diet. In the case of constipation, simply give a dose of milk of magnesia (ranging from 1/4 teaspoon for the tiniest dog to a full

FEEDING AND CARING FOR YOUR DOG

- **Follow menu and instructions the breeder gives you for feeding your new puppy.**
- **Give cod-liver oil or suitable vitamins regularly during the pup's first year.**
- **Include in pup's diet meat, eggs, milk, bone meal, green vegetables, and fats—food elements essential to health and growth.**
- **Don't feed starchy, fried, ice-cold, or highly seasoned foods, hard-boiled eggs, pork, cheese (except cottage cheese), pastry, candy.**
- **Don't give chicken, fish, or chop bones.**
- **Don't overfeed.**
- **Feed with same bowl, in same place, at same time each day.**
- **If he refuses to eat his dinner, put it away; don't leave it on the floor.**
- **Don't worry if he doesn't chew his food. His teeth tear it; gastric juices do the rest.**
- **Bed down your pup away from drafts in a place that is reserved for him.**
- **Brush his coat often. Bathe only when necessary, never let him get chilled.**
- **For fleas or lice, dust with flea powder daily during severe infestations; work it in against grain of coat.**
- **For ticks, use aerosol sprays, liquids, powders, and creams. In time, ticks develop resistance to once-lethal chemicals, so new ones are constantly being developed. Ask your veterinarian which ones are the most effective for your dog.**
- **For worms, often indicated by sluggishness or loss of appetite, take dog to veterinarian for diagnosis and treatment.**
- **Consult veterinarian about shots for rabies, distemper, infectious hepatitis, leptospirosis.**
- **Make companionship, understanding, and TLC (tender, loving care) the rule.**

tablespoon for a giant). For diarrhea, dose him with kaolin and pectin. This trouble may be caused by nothing more than too much water taken in his food or immediately after eating. But it could be a symptom of something more serious, calling for examination by the veterinarian. Diarrhea may indicate worms.

Round worms are most common with puppies. They are white, several inches long, and can be seen with the naked eye in the stool or when vomited. If you suspect worms, take your pet to the veterinarian immediately. There are excellent vermifuges, but since all contain poison you shouldn't try to do the job yourself. Unless you examine the dog's stool with a microscope you can't tell what you'll eliminate, and certainly you don't want it to be the puppy.

Parasites such as fleas, ticks, and lice pose another problem. Once they make your pet their home they can cause you both a lot of trouble. The best insurance is daily grooming. If fleas or lice do latch on to him, you can get rid of them with a number of good commercial powders, most of which have a pyrethrum base. Stand your pet on newspapers, start back of his ears, and dust him all over carefully. Then brush him down thoroughly and wipe him with a damp cloth. Lice are more persistent than

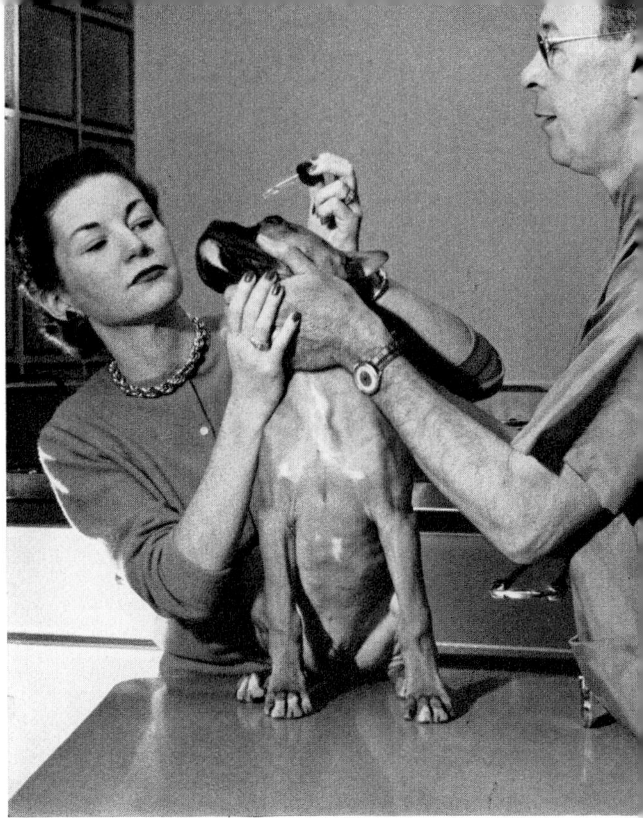

Medical care is best handled by the veterinarian, who should give shots for distemper, leptospirosis, infectious hepatitis, rabies. Here General gets boric acid for an eye infection.

Noseprint identifies a dog as a fingerprint does his master. The novel technique is required when buying canine insurance. This Cocker Spaniel has just signed on the dotted line.

fleas, so go over him also with a fine-toothed comb. The tick, scourge of dog owners in some areas, is an even closer-clinging parasite.

For generations owners have sponged their dogs with different solutions to rid them of ticks. One was simply two teaspoons of creolin to a gallon of water; another, a tablespoon of kerosene to a quart of milk. These did the trick but irritated the dog's skin and necessitated a bath after the treatment.

Now an aerosol spray is available that eliminates both ticks and fleas. Certain powders are often effective with long-coated dogs, and a cream applied on the ears and between the toes blocks the main entryways for ticks. When tick infestations are particularly severe, it is wise to spray those areas of the house which the dog frequents. Consult your veterinarian for the latest methods and drugs developed for the elimination of external parasites.

The care of a puppy is very similar to the care of a young child. At pre-talking age your own youngster may suddenly start crying. He's unable to tell you what's wrong, so it's up to you to find out. A hand on the forehead tells you quickly if fever is indicated. If it is, you check with a thermometer. In the case of a dog, his nostrils may be excessively dry and warm; he may have a discharge from them, and his eyes may be dull. Use a rectal thermometer.

If his temperature is around 101° there's nothing serious to worry about, but if it goes over 102° better consult your veterinarian. New dog owners should not try to treat by themselves anything that involves fever. But most of the time your puppy's problems will be minor matters of health and first aid.

Because they have a lot of time on their hands, most dogs are inclined to be hypochondriacs. You should be thankful they are, because here's a wonderful opportunity to become a real buddy. His cuts and scratches, his

Symbol of authority, a rolled-up newspaper lets the hand remain a symbol of friendship. Discipline is vital if you want your pup to be a well-mannered dog. General quickly learns that misbehavior brings prompt correction.

stepped-on toes, his bumps on the head, and the pebbles he picks up between his toes are options on the purchase of gilt-edged love, loyalty, and obedience. You can exercise these options simply by giving your full attention to treating the "injury."

Many believe that the feeding pan is the way to a dog's heart. It helps, of course, but you'll get much closer to your pet by taking his "ailments" seriously, for he loves to be pampered.

Dogs like to hear the human voice. Most people who work around animals talk to them continually. I picked up the habit on a stock farm where I spent the first twenty summers of my life. I learned that a dog feels much closer to you, and obeys you better, if you treat him as an equal. Some animals will even respond to the tones of your voice.

Once our Airedale Danny was eavesdropping by the kitchen table during a midnight snack and heard me say: "There's nobody quite like this fellow, but as a watchdog I'm afraid he's a washout."

His eyes flicked open. I shouldn't have said that, and for two reasons. First, although he had challenged no one, we hadn't been bothered by prowlers since we bought him. Second, Danny had a dry sense of humor.

Loving the attention, General is brushed daily to keep him free of ticks, lice, and fleas. Bathing a pup can result in a chill, so the best rule is to groom him frequently.

A couple of hours later I was sound asleep when furious barking made my feet hit the floor in a hurry. Without pausing for robe or slippers, I dashed downstairs. Danny was pawing at the back door, growling. Certain there was a prowler around, I opened the door and let Danny out. He took his time to circle the house and enjoy the crisp winter air, while I shivered. Back to bed I went and under the warm covers. It seemed hardly a minute later (it was actually two hours) when the same uproar tumbled me out of bed again. When I got downstairs Danny had stopped barking. This time he greeted me with wagging tail and a mischievous glint in his eye.

"Okay, big boy," I said to him with a smile, "you win your point. I'm sorry

I disparaged you as a watchdog." He looked really happy then! I could almost believe it was because now he could meaningfully stow away "disparage" in that retentive brain of his.

You have it in your power to make any puppy into an ideal companion. I know from experience that your pet will respond to love, companionship, and understanding. If you want him to give you full measure, you'll have to give him the same. And once you form a perfect team with your dog, practically no goal is beyond reach.

THE DAY YOU BOUGHT YOUR PUP and made your first tentative advances of friendship you started to train him in your ways. When you fed and cared for him you advanced another step. Now at five or six months, depending on the puppy and upon your success in getting close to him, you should have the groundwork well laid. Your pet is housebroken, will answer to his name, and will follow you without question. Now you can teach him to go up and down stairs.

Most puppies are afraid of stairs, but if he loves you he will follow. Don't start with the open cellar steps; if he fell it might take months to undo the harm. Leave him on one floor and go up to the next. He may take a few minutes but

Basic English of canine etiquette, DOWN, LIE DOWN, SIT, HEEL, are taught on leash, held short fo

he'll seek you out. Carpeted stairs make it easier. Then leave him upstairs and go down. Again, he'll come to you. Later, when he has gained confidence, he will be ready for open cellar steps.

Perhaps the most useful commands for your pet to learn are "Sit" and "Lie Down." Either one will keep him from racing to the door when the bell rings or from jumping up on visitors. Both should be taught when he is on leash. When training, hold the leash short or close to the collar for maximum control of the dog.

To get across the idea of "Sit," give the command and at the same time raise the leash sharply so that he is thrown off balance and sits of necessity. Repeat this until he realizes that he must sit or you will jerk his leash. When he does it on command only, praise him, and stroke him on the head.

To put over what "Lie Down" means, keep the leash tight, and from a position directly in front of him, pull it quickly to the floor while giving the command. You can use your foot to force the leash down, while holding up the free end. You may have to repeat the lesson many times. For quicker results use a chain slip collar which tightens when the leash is pulled.

A dog, particularly a large one, can make a nuisance of himself by jumping up on you or your guests. When breaking him of this habit, you may find

control. Consistency and repetition are training's keys. Hand gives signal but doesn't spank.

NEAL P. DAVIS

TRAINING YOUR DOG

- **Start housebreaking at about three months. Take pup out right after eating or put him on newspapers.**
- **Teach pup to come, sit, lie down, and heel on command. Train on leash, held short for maximum control.**
- **Give him praise and a pat each time he performs well. Don't make food a reward.**
- **Teach him to stay alone quietly. Slam the door so he thinks you've gone out; when he howls, surprise him and scold him sharply, then leave and ignore him.**
- **Train not to jump on people, climb on furniture, beg or steal food. Tempt, watch, instantly correct him.**
- **Train him to exercise teeth and jaws on a hard rubber toy instead of furniture, books, or clothing.**
- **Break him early from chasing vehicles. Douse him with a water pistol from a moving car, or with a long leash jerk him up short when he begins to chase.**
- **Scold immediately after misbehavior so he'll associate punishment with crime.**
- **Consistently use one tone of voice and set of words to praise him, another to scold.**
- **Don't call your dog to you to be punished; he may learn never to come when called.**
- **Never punish with your hand; use a rolled newspaper. Your hand should mean only kindness.**
- **Be consistent, affectionate, patient. Remember repetition is the basis of learning.**

Spellbound audience displays superb canine

yourself wrestling with him if you push him down with your hands. Instead, bring your knee gently but firmly up against his ribs.

The only other command important to the average pet owner is "Heel"—the command to walk quietly at your left side without straining on the leash. Take your dog out, holding the leash short for maximum control. If he lunges ahead, give a tug on the leash and say "Heel."

Don't use your bare hand to tap him. Use something like a rolled-up newspaper that will not really hurt him. In training, always remember that consistency and repetition are the keys to success. Don't bribe him with food;

LEO COHEN, GILLOON

Discipline in an Oakland, California, obedience class. Well-trained dogs will "stay" until called.

rewards should never be more than a word of praise or an affectionate pat.

Once you have started working with your puppy, you will find it a fascinating pastime. Your success in teaching him to follow simple commands may encourage you to go on to more advanced obedience training. You will find that you can train your dog to do almost anything within the range of his physical capabilities, provided you first show him what you want him to do.

You needn't take your dog to an obedience class, but you may find it will speed his training and you may enjoy meeting other dog owners.

When outside, it's a good idea to keep your dog on leash to safeguard him

ILLUMINATION (PAINTED C. 1440) FROM GASTON DE FOIX'S "LE LIVRE DE CHASSE" (WRITTEN 1387-91), MANUSCRIPT IN BIBLIOTHEQUE NATIONALE, PARIS

WOODCUTS FROM JACQUES DU FOUILLOUX'S "LA VENERIE" (1561), ADAPTED FROM THE FRENCH AS "THE ARTE OF VENERIE" (1576) BY GEORGE TURBERVILLE.

from dogfights and from being struck by automobiles. If another dog attacks, you can swing your pet out of danger with the leash. Holding your dog close, use the free end of the leash as a whip to ward off the other dog.

If your dog slips outdoors unnoticed and you find him in a fight, do you wade right into the melee and grab your pet? Not if you're smart, for either dog may bite you by mistake. One of the best ways to break up a dogfight is to douse the dogs with a pail of water or a garden hose.

What causes dogs to fight? Nobody knows for sure. My Airedale was never pugnacious, but when he was a pup a neighbor's crossbred Bulldog took delight in rushing at him with teeth bared. Danny was frightened at first, but after several such incidents I said to him "Look, this guy is just a bluff. He knows you're on leash." Next time out I used a length of rope instead of a leash. When the troublemaker came near I let out the rope and said "Go boy, go!" Danny took off after him and the dog scampered, tail between his legs. I stopped Danny, of course, when the rope was completely paid out. After that the bully never took a chance walking on our side of the street.

It was different with my son's Cocker Spaniel. He was friendly with most dogs, but once when he was young an Irish Setter, off leash, made a pass at him. After that our Cocker couldn't stomach the breed; no matter how much bigger

When wonder drugs were witches' brews and hounds served knighthood's sport, a canine clinic looked like this. Robed kennelmen at upper left administer a pill or potion. Others examine the foot of a St. Hubert Hound, doctor a spaniel's ear, bandage a Greyhound's leg.

Pups whelped by the contented hound below are bedded down in "a Barrell or a Pype well dryed" with "strawe therein." Equip your kennel with skirted scent posts and "a little chanell of good fountayne water," advises an Elizabethan gentleman, who also prescribes decoctions to "put down your dogges throate to drinke." For worms, "boyle the huskes of Walnuts in a pot with a quart of Vynegar"; add "Aloe cupaticque, a Hartes horne burned, and Rosyne, as much of the one as of the other." Hardest to cure are "seven sundrie sorts of madnesse," the worst of which is "ye burning hote madnesse, or the desparat madnesse."

LIBRARY OF CONGRESS

UNITED PRESS INTERNATIONAL

"He's this big, and the handsomest doggy in the world. Please, mister, have you seen him?"

they were, he'd scare them away. Most times he was on leash, but one summer at the beach he chased an Irish Setter right up the steps and into the setter's home. Our Cocker politely stopped just outside the open door.

Any pet dog may become jealous if his owner pays too much attention to a strange dog. An owner who fondles someone else's dog in the presence of his own is as indiscreet as the man who kisses another woman in front of his wife. Jealousy, of course, is the root of much evil, whether in human or canine circles.

Jealousy in your dog will generally stem from the appearance of unfairness.

Some years ago a tragic instance of a dog's jealousy hit the front pages. The breed is unimportant; it could have been any breed. For several years this dog was the sole, pampered pet of a young childless couple who went overboard with affection for their pet. Then a baby was born. Immediately, the dog was relegated to a minor role in the household. He took this stoically for a time, but the obsession grew that the baby was the cause of his demotion. One day, left alone with the infant, he attacked it fatally.

But countless babies arrive in dog-dominated households and are quickly accepted. There is a great temptation to lavish all the attention on a newborn baby, but the smart dog owner not only continues to pet his dog but encourages him to become the infant's guardian. It marks increased rather than decreased importance for him.

Dogs like such responsibility. A kennel owner told me that one of her champion Great Danes was a real worrywart about the children. The big dog slept in the room with them, and if their breathing was the least bit irregular the canine nurse would summon the mother. The children's mother wisely made a point to praise the Dane each time for her watchfulness.

BURT GLINN, MAGNUM

IN DOG-SHOW CIRCLES the most frequent winners are happy dogs. The owner of several dogs can't give them much individual attention, so he encourages his handler to make a pet of the outstanding one. I remember one Poodle that was a big winner at shows right across the continent. During this tour Curly was never out of sight of his handler. Hotel clerks took one glance at the quiet, dignified dog and decided that he could share the room. However, one clerk had other ideas.

"Tender, loving care" reaches peak when a canine pal is hurt. Boy carries injured buddy to the SPCA.

The handler asked if the hotel took dogs.

"Yes," said the clerk. Then, after the money was on the counter, he added, "but not in your room."

"In that case," the handler said politely, "I can't stay here."

"You've paid," snapped the clerk, "I can't give your money back now."

The handler said nothing, pointed to the bills still on the counter, and ordered, "Curly, fetch!" In one bound the Poodle made the retrieve. The clerk stood gaping as man and dog walked quietly out of the hotel.

The dogs that make the best integrated members of family and community are those that have the TLC treatment—tender, loving care. They are so in tune they seem to forget they are dogs; to all intents and purposes they are four-footed people. The most striking demonstration of this is America's "Cinderella dog," the buff-colored Cocker Spaniel that rose from obscurity to become 1957 National Field Champion Prince Tom III, U.D., through his love for Tom Clute, his owner, trainer, and handler.

Tom Clute did not even pick Prince Tom; the pup was a surprise birthday gift. And though he had a pedigree, his branch of the family had strayed far from the standard of perfection by which show specimens are judged. But time was to prove he had a full endowment of his breed's qualities.

Clute knew nothing about raising puppies. He raised the little Cocker by trial and error, a very unorganized effort. But he sincerely tried to do his best for the little fellow, and after each mistake he'd seek advice. Despite the fumbling, a oneness developed between tyro owner and scrawny pup.

I noticed this when I first met the pair at the American Spaniel Club show shortly after Prince Tom had won the national championship. (This coveted title always before had gone to English Cockers, generally bigger and better qualified to retrieve pheasants.)

I saw the closeness of dog and master again when Prince Tom was spotlighted

MARC RIBOUD, MAGNUM

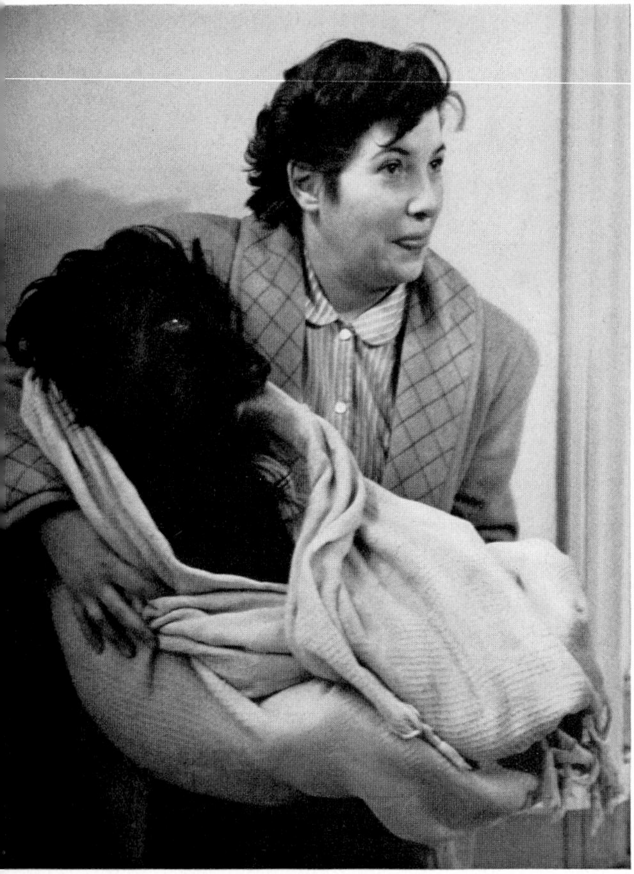

An injured pet is rushed to a veterinarian's care in Paris. Anguish over a hurt dog approaches that universally felt for a hurt child. Quick action here helped to insure full recovery.

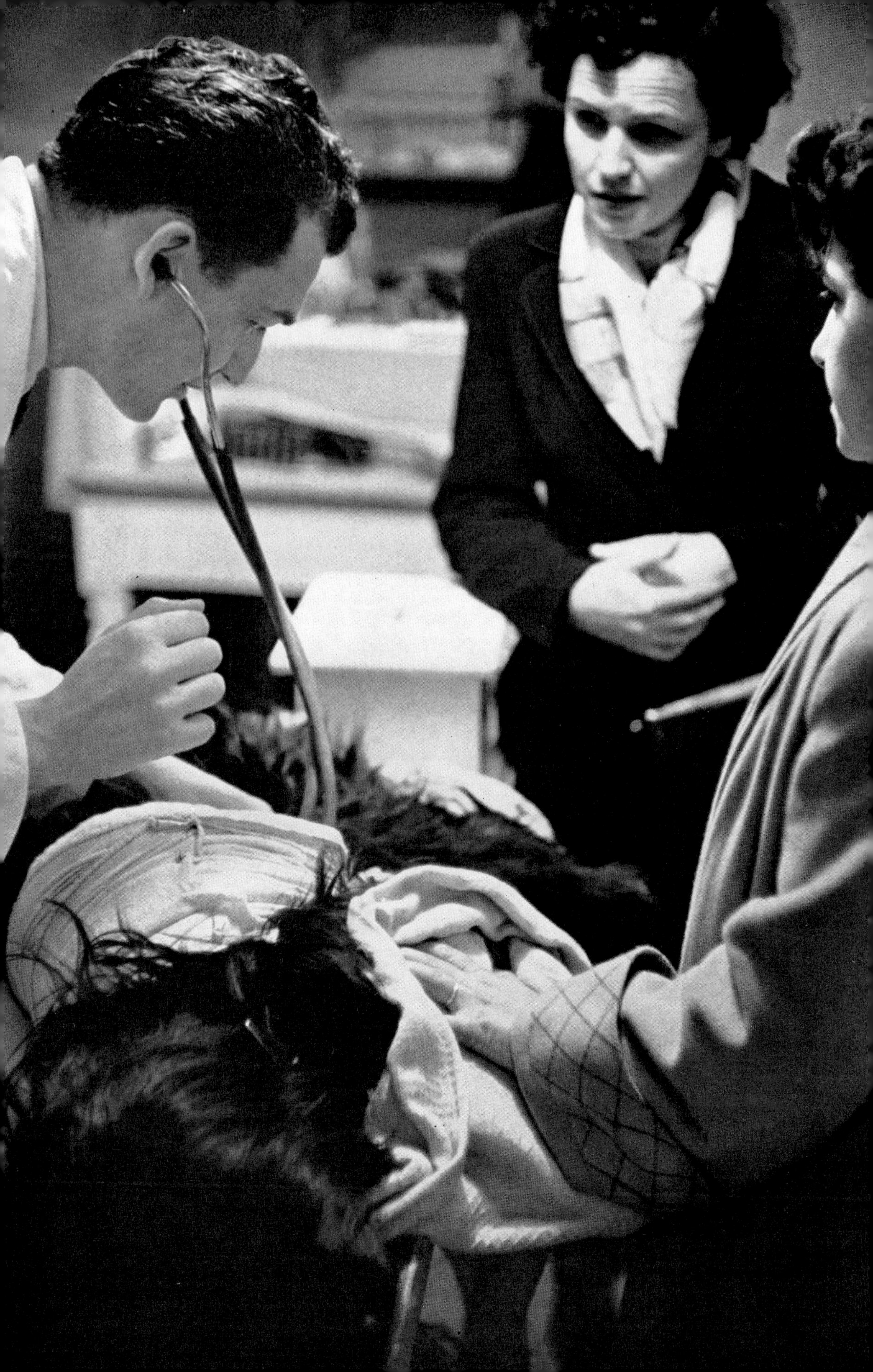

WHEN YOU TRAVEL

If you leave your dog behind

- **Accustom him to the kennels before you go by leaving him there for short intervals. He'll adjust easily if he knows you'll return.**
- **Have a friend visit him occasionally if you are to be gone long.**
- **If you leave him with a neighbor, provide his caretaker with his own equipment and food. Leave veterinarian's phone number.**

If you take your dog in a car

- **Take food and water pans, his brand of dog food, sleeping rug, grooming equipment, sedatives in case of illness or accident, long leash and collar with identification.**
- **Ask veterinarian for health certificate and record of distemper and rabies shots, required in many states, Canada, and Mexico.**
- **Before departure feed him only lightly. When traveling, feed less than usual.**
- **Exercise him morning and afternoon, and allow for three or four rest stops during the day.**
- **Don't let your dog put his head out the window. The wind may irritate his eyes or ears, and dust could injure his eyes.**
- **Stay in a motel if possible, so the dog can go outside easily. Don't leave him alone in strange quarters; he may scratch and chew furnishings or slip out and get lost.**

If you take your dog on train or plane

- **Put him in a large, strong, well-ventilated crate, or attach strong leash and muzzle.**
- **Send along his own food and pans; attach feeding instructions for the attendant.**

If you take your dog by ship

- **Check your travel agent on quarantine laws for dogs entering foreign countries. Britain, for example, requires a six-month quarantine; France, none.**
- **Ask about kenneling provisions aboard ship, or if dog can be kept in stateroom.**
- **Take a health certificate and record of rabies and distemper shots.**

in the Westminster exhibition, "Gun Dogs in Action." The little dog stopped the show through his obvious eagerness to do all that Clute asked, instantly.

Some time later my phone rang. It was Tom Clute, visiting a friend in town. "What about that great little dog of yours," I asked. "Where is he?"

Tom was surprised at my question. "He's right here. I never go any place without him."

Those few words told the story. The two Toms had been together constantly, day and night, since the day they met. Neither was happy without the other.

Remember about the Toms. If you're ready and willing to make a steady companion and confidant of the pup you buy he will develop into a dog with great personality. Taking him places with you and telling him things will make him easier to train. And don't act as if you were doing him a favor. He'll sense it if you do. You must want to have the pup with you, as Clute did. It was months before Clute tried formal training, but by then the Cocker had picked up a number of tricks he'd do with obvious enjoyment.

Chic Miniature Poodle turns a Doberman's head, but prefers human company.

A PROSPECTIVE PET OWNER should think of a dog as a responsive creature. Buying one should not be confused with buying a washing machine or a television set. Your dog will become a member of the family. He'll ask for—and deserve—care, love, confidence, and constant companionship. He'll respect you for the training and discipline you give him, too. It won't take you long to realize that only by pouring into him these essential ingredients will he become a great dog.

Dogs live a short time—ten or fifteen years at most—but they manage to crowd a lot of living into their span. They're well worth knowing!

GAINES DOG RESEARCH CENTER

INDEX

Illustrated breed biographies are indicated in **bold face,** other illustrations in *italics,* and text references in roman.

INDEX

FOR ADDITIONAL REFERENCE

Readers of MAN'S BEST FRIEND will find stimulating, informative reading in other books published by the National Geographic Society. These volumes are obtainable only from the Society's headquarters, Washington, D. C. 20036, plus postage. Write for publications catalog.

WILD ANIMALS OF NORTH AMERICA A close-up of your animal neighbors. Action photographs, dramatic paintings, vivid narratives by leading naturalists reveal the lives of 138 species. 400 pages, 407 illustrations. $7.75

SONG AND GARDEN BIRDS OF NORTH AMERICA See—and *hear*—America's sweetest singers. This 400-page book presents life histories of 327 species; 508 color pictures. Six bird-song records included! $11.95

WATER, PREY, AND GAME BIRDS OF NORTH AMERICA Winged denizens of the wilds come to life in 329 illustrated biographies. 464 pages, 600 color pictures. Six records capture the sounds of 97 species. $11.95

Song and Garden Birds and *Water, Prey, and Game Birds,* two-volume set in deluxe slipcase. $20.95

WONDROUS WORLD OF FISHES New enlarged edition unveils the life secrets of 375 species. The 374 entertaining pages, enriched by 420 color pictures, will lure you to North America's rivers, lakes, and seacoasts. $9.95

A man's best friend is . . .

PAUL J. SHANE, LA CROSSE TRIBUNE, WISCONSIN

. . . his dog.

NATIONAL GEOGRAPHIC SOCIETY

WASHINGTON, D. C.

Organized "for the increase and diffusion of geographic knowledge"

GILBERT HOVEY GROSVENOR
Editor, 1899-1954; President, 1920-1954
Chairman of the Board, 1954-1966

THE NATIONAL GEOGRAPHIC SOCIETY is chartered in Washington, D. C., in accordance with the laws of the United States, as a nonprofit scientific and educational organization for increasing and diffusing geographic knowledge and promoting research and exploration. Since 1890 the Society has supported 1,042 explorations and research projects, adding immeasurably to man's knowledge of earth, sea, and sky. It diffuses this knowledge through its monthly journal, NATIONAL GEOGRAPHIC; more than 50 million maps distributed each year; its books, globes, atlases, and filmstrips; 30 School Bulletins a year in color; information services to press, radio, and television; technical reports; exhibits from around the world in Explorers Hall; and a nationwide series of programs on television.

NATIONAL GEOGRAPHIC MAGAZINE

MELVILLE BELL GROSVENOR Editor-in-Chief and Board Chairman
MELVIN M. PAYNE President of the Society
GILBERT M. GROSVENOR Editor
FRANC SHOR, JOHN SCOFIELD Associate Editors

Senior Assistant Editors
Robert L. Breeden, James Cerruti, W. E. Garrett, Kenneth MacLeish
Jules B. Billard, Allan C. Fisher, Jr., Carolyn Bennett Patterson

Assistant Editors: Andrew H. Brown, William Graves, Robert P. Jordan, Joseph Judge, Edward J. Linehan, Samuel W. Matthews, Bart McDowell, Howell Walker, Kenneth F. Weaver

Senior Editorial Staff: Thomas Y. Canby, William S. Ellis, Rowe Findley, Bryan Hodgson, Elizabeth A. Moize, John J. Putman, Merle E. Severy, Gordon Young; Senior Scientist: Paul A. Zahl

Foreign Editorial Staff: Luis Marden (Chief); Thomas J. Abercrombie, David S. Boyer, Howard La Fay, Volkmar Wentzel, Peter T. White

Editorial Staff: Harvey Arden, Kent Britt, Mike W. Edwards, Noel Grove, Alice J. Hall, Werner Janney, Michael E. Long, John L. McIntosh, Ethel A. Starbird, George E. Stuart (Archeology)

Art Director: Howard E. Paine; Charles C. Uhl (Assistant)

Research: Margaret G. Bledsoe (Chief); Ann K. Wendt (Associate Chief); Newton V. Blakeslee (Assistant Chief for Geographic Information); Carolyn H. Anderson, Susan L. Anderson, Judith Brown, Marcia M. Butler, Susan Day Fuller, Bette Joan Goss, Jan Holderness, Lesley B. Lane, Levenia Loder, Jean B. McConville, Carol M. McNamara, Frances H. Parker, Frances W. Shaffer. *Correspondence:* Carolyn F. Clewell, Clifford R. DuBois

Library: Virginia Carter Hills (Librarian); Patricia Murphy Smith (Assistant Librarian), Louise A. Robinson

Editorial Administration: Joyce W. McKean, Assistant to the Editor; Virginia H. Finnegan, Winifred M. Myers, Shirley Neff, M. Jean Vile (Editorial Assistants); Dorothy M. Corson (Indexes); Evelyn Fox, Dolores Kennedy (Travel); Jeanne S. Duiker, Lorie Wendling, Mary Anne McMillen (Records)

ILLUSTRATIONS STAFF: ***Illustrations Editor:*** Herbert S. Wilburn, Jr. *Associate Illustrations Editor:* Thomas R. Smith. *Art Editor:* Andrew Poggenpohl. *Assistant Illustrations Editors:* David L. Arnold, O. Louis Mazzatenta, Charlene Murphy, Robert S. Patton, Elie S. Rogers, W. Allan Royce, Jon Schneeberger, Mary Griswold Smith. *Layout and Production:* H. Edward Kim (Chief). *Picture Editor:* Bruce A. McElfresh. *Research:* Paula C. Simmons. Barbara A. Shattuck (Asst.). *Librarian:* L. Fern Dame. *Assistant Librarian:* Carolyn J. Harrison

Geographic Art: William N. Palmstrom (Chief). *Artists:* Lisa Biganzoli, William H. Bond, John W. Lothers, Robert C. Magis, Ned M. Seidler. *Cartographic Artists:* Victor J. Kelley, Snejinka Stefanoff. *Research:* Walter Q. Crowe (Supervisor), Virginia L. Baza, John D. Garst, Dorothy A. Nicholson. *Production:* Isaac Ortiz

Engraving and Printing: Dee J. Andella (Chief); John R. Metcalfe, William W. Smith, James R. Whitney

PHOTOGRAPHIC STAFF: ***Director of Photography:*** Robert E. Gilka. *Assistant Directors:* Dean Conger, Joseph J. Scherschel. *Photographers:* James L. Amos, James P. Blair, Victor R. Boswell, Jr., Bruce Dale, Dick Durrance II, Gordon W. Gahan, Otis Imboden, Emory Kristof, Bates Littlehales, Robert W. Madden, George F. Mobley, Robert S. Oakes, Winfield Parks, Robert F. Sisson (Natural Science), James L. Stanfield. Lilian Davidson (Administration). *Film Review:* Guy W. Starling (Chief). *Photographic Equipment:* John E. Fletcher (Chief), Donald McBain

Photographic Services: Carl M. Shrader (Chief); Milton A. Ford (Associate Chief); Jon R. Adams, Herbert Altemus, Jr., David H. Chisman, Lawrence F. Ludwig (Assistant Chief, Phototypography), Claude E. Petrone, J. Frank Pyles, Jr., Donald E. Stemper; Joan S. Simms (Asst.)

RELATED EDUCATIONAL SERVICES OF THE SOCIETY

Cartography: William T. Peele (Chief); David W. Cook (Associate Chief). *Cartographic Staff:* Margery K. Barkdull, Charles F. Case, Ted Dachtera, Richard J. Darley, John F. Dorr, Russel G. Fritz, Richard R. Furno, Charles W. Gotthardt, Jr., Catherine M. Hart, Donald A. Jaeger, Harry D. Kauhane, Manuela G. Kogutowicz, Charles L. Miller, Robert W. Northrop, Richard K. Rogers, John F. Shupe, Charles L. Stern, Douglas A. Strobel, Tibor G. Toth, Thomas A. Wall, Thomas A. Walsh

Books: Jules B. Billard (Chief); Seymour L. Fishbein (Assistant Chief); Thomas B. Allen, Ross Bennett, Charles O. Hyman, Anne Dirkes Kobor, David F. Robinson, Wilhelm R. Saake, Verla Lee Smith

Special Publications and Educational Filmstrips: Robert L. Breeden (Chief); Donald J. Crump (Associate Chief); Philip B. Silcott (Assistant Chief); William L. Allen, Josephine B. Bolt, David R. Bridge, Linda Bridge, James B. Caffrey, Margery G. Dunn, Ronald Fisher, William R. Gray, Mary Ann Harrell, Jerry Kline, Margaret McKelway Johnson, Geraldine Linder, Robert Messer, H. Robert Morrison, George Peterson, Cynthia Ramsay, Tee Loftin Snell, Joseph A. Taney, George V. White, Merrill Windsor

Recording Division: John M. Lavery (Chief)

School Service: Ralph Gray (Chief and Editor of National Geographic School Bulletin); Charles H. Sloan (Assistant Chief); Joseph B. Goodwin, Ellen Joan Hurst, Anne H. Oman, Patricia F. Robbins, Veronica Smith, Janis Knudsen Wheat

News Service: Windsor P. Booth (Chief); Paul Sampson (Assistant Chief); Donald J. Frederick, William J. O'Neill, Robert C. Radcliffe; Isabel Clarke

Television and Educational Films: Dennis B. Kane (Chief); Sidney Platt (Supervisor, Educational Projects); David Cooper, Carl W. Harmon, Jr., Patricia F. Northrop; Marjorie M. Moomey (Chief of Research)

Lectures: Joanne M. Hess (Chief); Robert G. Fleegal, Mary W. McKinney, Gerald L. Wiley, Carl E. Ziebe

Explorers Hall: T. Keilor Bentley (Curator-Director)

EUROPEAN OFFICE: W. Edward Roscher (Associate Secretary and Director), Jennifer Moseley (Assistant), 4 Curzon Place, Mayfair, London, W1Y 8EN

ADVERTISING: *Director:* William A. Boeger, Jr. *Assistant Director:* James L. Till. *National Advertising Manager:* William Turgeon, 1251 Ave. of the Americas, New York, N.Y. 10020. *Regional managers—Eastern:* George W. Kellner, New York. *Midwestern:* Robert R. Henn, Chicago. *Pacific:* Thomas Martz, San Francisco. *Los Angeles:* Jack Wallace. *Canada:* Robert W. Horan, New York. *Automotive:* John F. Grant, New York. *Travel:* Gerald A. Van Splinter, New York. *European Director:* Richard V. Macy, 21 rue Jean-Mermoz, Paris 8e, France. *Production:* E. M. Pusey, Jr.